RETHINKING ROLAND BARTHES
THROUGH PERFORMANCE

Thinking Through Theatre seeks to advance theatre and performance studies by exploring the questions performance itself is uniquely capable of asking, and by interrogating the ways in which it asks them. The series seeks to problematize the distinction between 'making' and 'thinking' by stressing their interrelation and by identifying in theatre and performance practices aesthetic and political forms of thought and action.

The ***Thinking Through Theatre*** series aims to examine theatre and performance practices as material forms of thought, and to articulate the knowledge embedded within them. The series examines the ways in which theatre is continually rethinking the possibilities of movement, space, action, image, voice, and so on, exploring the logics of creative invention and critical investigation that enable performance to operate as a mode of thought *sui generis*.

Series Editors
Maaike Bleeker (Utrecht University, Netherlands), Adrian Kear (Wimbledon College of Arts, University of the Arts London, UK), Joe Kelleher (University of Roehampton, London, UK) and Heike Roms (University of Exeter, UK)

Published Titles
Thinking Through Theatre and Performance
edited by Maaike Bleeker, Adrian Kear, Joe Kelleher and Heike Roms
Nomadic Theatre: Mobilizing Theory and Practice on the European Stage
by Liesbeth Groot Nibbelink

Forthcoming Titles
In Solitude: The Philosophy of Digital Performance Encounters
by Eirini Nedelkopoulou
Performance Criticism as Political Event: Nonconforming Practices and Covert Poetics
by Diana Damian Martin
Theatres of Powerlessness: Acts of Knowledge and the Performance of the Many
edited by Edit Kaldor and Joe Kelleher

RETHINKING ROLAND BARTHES THROUGH PERFORMANCE

A Desire for Neutral Dramaturgy

Edited by
Harry Robert Wilson and Will Daddario

LONDON • NEW YORK • OXFORD • NEW DELHI • SYDNEY

METHUEN DRAMA
Bloomsbury Publishing Plc
50 Bedford Square, London, WC1B 3DP, UK
1385 Broadway, New York, NY 10018, USA
29 Earlsfort Terrace, Dublin 2, Ireland

BLOOMSBURY, METHUEN DRAMA and the Methuen Drama logo are trademarks of Bloomsbury Publishing Plc

First published in Great Britain 2023
Paperback edition published 2024

Copyright © Harry Robert Wilson, Will Daddario and contributors, 2023, 2025

Harry Robert Wilson, Will Daddario and contributors have asserted their right under the Copyright, Designs and Patents Act, 1988, to be identified as the authors of this work.

For legal purposes the Acknowledgements on p. xvi constitute an extension of this copyright page.

Cover image: Portrait of Roland Barthes, circa 1980.
(Photo © Louis MONIER / Gamma-Rapho / Getty Images)

All rights reserved. No part of this publication may be reproduced or transmitted in any form or by any means, electronic or mechanical, including photocopying, recording, or any information storage or retrieval system, without prior permission in writing from the publishers.

Bloomsbury Publishing Plc does not have any control over, or responsibility for, any third-party websites referred to or in this book. All internet addresses given in this book were correct at the time of going to press. The author and publisher regret any inconvenience caused if addresses have changed or sites have ceased to exist, but can accept no responsibility for any such changes.

A catalogue record for this book is available from the British Library.

A catalog record for this book is available from the Library of Congress.

ISBN: HB: 978-1-3503-3084-9
PB: 978-1-3503-3088-7
ePDF: 978-1-3503-3086-3
eBook: 978-1-3503-3085-6

Series: Thinking Through Theatre

Typeset by Newgen KnowledgeWorks Pvt. Ltd., Chennai, India

To find out more about our authors and books visit www.bloomsbury.com and sign up for our newsletters.

To Tashi, Ezra and Poppy and the memory of my mum, Jo (HW)

CONTENTS

List of Figures   x
Notes on Contributors   xi
Acknowledgements   xvi

INTRODUCTION: CONTEMPORARY PERFORMANCE AFTER
ROLAND BARTHES   1
   Harry Robert Wilson

Part I
A DICTIONARY OF TWINKLINGS

Chapter 1
FIVE THESES FOR A DRAMATURGY OF PERFORMANCE   35
   Lin Hixson and Matthew Goulish

Chapter 2
CEASELESSLY POSITING AND EVAPORATING MEANING: A
PERFORMANCE SCORE   45
   Pablo Pakula

Chapter 3
LOOKING THROUGH OLD PHOTOGRAPHS   51
   Andy Field and Deborah Pearson

Chapter 4
RECIPES/ADDENDUMS/SOUVENIRS   65
   greenandowens (Katheryn Owens and Chris Green)

Chapter 5
WAYS TO SUBMIT   77
   Ira Brand

Chapter 6
ALL THE SENSE OF REAL: A WORLD OF WRESTLING 85
   Simon Bayly

Chapter 7
PRACTISING NEUTRAL DRAMATURGY(IES) 99
   Will Daddario and Harry Robert Wilson

Part II
RETHINKING ROLAND BARTHES, THEATRE, PERFORMANCE

Chapter 8
WE'VE NEVER MET BUT WE MAY HAVE FOUGHT 111
   Simon Bayly and Ira Brand

Chapter 9
FOR THE LOVE(RS) OF DRAMATURGY: ON ROLAND BARTHES'S AMATEUR 117
   Swen Steinhäuser

Chapter 10
THE DISTURBANCE OF ONE SYSTEM BY ANOTHER 137
   Claudia Kappenberg

Chapter 11
BAFFLING DRAMATURGY: BETWEEN THE OBVIOUS AND THE OBTUSE 157
   Mischa Twitchin

Chapter 12
CHOREOGRAPHY, CAPTURING AND BARTHES'S NOTION OF THE PUNCTUM 171
   Sandra Parker

Chapter 13
BODY AND MASK: DRAMATURGIES OF THE FACE IN ROLAND BARTHES 185
   Michael Bachmann

Chapter 14
TRACING BARTHES'S EASTERN THEATRES: *EMPIRE OF SIGNS* AND THE STAGING OF INDIVIDUAL CULTURAL INTERPRETATION 207
   Pamela Genova

Chapter 15
UNRAVELLING TEXTUAL SOUNDSCAPES: READING BARTHES'S 'THE GRAIN OF THE VOICE' THROUGH SÖDERBERG'S *ENTANGLED PHRASES* AND LINEHAN'S *BODY OF WORK* 225
   Rosa Lambert

Index 243

FIGURES

2.1	Spatial arrangement for 'The Death of the Author' score	46
7.1	*After Camera Lucida*, 2017. Citizens Theatre, Glasgow. Harry Robert Wilson	102
7.2	*Cock and Bull*, 2015. Laura Bradshaw and Nic Green	104
7.3	*Kairos*, 2016. Buzzcut Festival, Pearce Institute, Govan. Harry Robert Wilson	106
9.1	Perhaps the student's sanatorium at Sainte-Hilaire-du-Touvet in the Isère in the Alps between Grenoble and Chambery or the university sanatorium at Leysin above Aigle in Switzerland	118
9.2	Illustration of a rikka work from the *Rikka-no-Shidai Kyūjūsanpei-ari (Ikenobō Senkō Rikka-zu)*, by Ikenobō Senkō II. Between 1628 and 1635	133
10.1	*Flush, or the possibility of moving towards an impossible goal.* Kappenberg, 2004	141
10.2	Image with performer in black dress in counterbalance: *Swan Canal*. Kappenberg and Seror, 2011	149
10.3	Image with police wrestling with the performer: *Swan Canal*. Kappenberg and Seror, 2011	152
12.1	*The View from Here*, 2005–7	179

NOTES ON CONTRIBUTORS

Michael Bachmann is Senior Lecturer in Theatre Studies at the School of Culture and Creative Arts, University of Glasgow. His research focuses on performance and media history from a comparative perspective, looking at theatre in relation to other art forms and institutions (including radio, film, literature, museums/archives, legal discourse and digital media).

Simon Bayly is a London-based writer, theatre-maker and educator. He worked for 20 years in the Department of Drama, Theatre and Performance at the University of Roehampton, across the fields of performance and the practices of organization and collectivity. He directed the London-based live arts company PUR, active between 1992 and 2008 and is currently researching a philosophy of meeting, gathering and assembling, as well as working in the community-led housing sector. Publications include the book *A Pathognomy of Performance* (2011) and essays on the philosophical concept of 'thing', meeting as a social genre, the project as the unit of contemporary work, the anxieties of dramaturgy, the value of waste and the forces of vibration.

Ira Brand is an artist, writer, performance-maker and curator. She graduated from Dartington College of Arts in 2007, and in 2019 completed the DAS Theatre Masters in Amsterdam. She makes live, interdisciplinary performance: solo stage shows, one-to-one pieces, duets or participatory work. She has worked extensively across the UK, and internationally, including at Festival Theaterformen, Braunschweig; Theaterszene Europa, Köln; Frascati, Amsterdam; TREMA! Festival, Recife; Malavoadora, Porto; Matadero, Madrid; Kanagawa Arts Theatre, Yokohama; Monty Kultuurfaktorij, Antwerp; wpZimmer, Antwerp; The Basement, Auckland; and Abrons Arts Centre, New York. She is also one of the co-directors of the award-winning artist collective Forest Fringe.

Will Daddario is a founding member of Performance Philosophy and editor of the *Performance Philosophy* journal and book series. He is the author, with Matthew Goulish, of *Pitch and Revelation: Reconfigurations of Reading, Poetry, and Philosophy through the Work of Jay Wright*, and project editor for a three-volume series dedicated to Wright's selected plays. Together with his wife, Joanne Zerdy, Will founded Inviting Abundance in Asheville, North Carolina, where he undertakes grief work and educational consulting. Learn more at invitingabundance.net

Andy Field creates projects that invite people to consider their relationship to the places they live in and the people they live with. Over the past decade this has manifested itself across a range of forms and disciplines, including street games, event scores, installations, studio theatre shows and one-to-one performances. A key strand of Andy's practice involves making work in collaboration with young people with the aim of enabling them to play a meaningful part in the civic discourse of the cities and towns in which they live. www.andytfield.co.uk

Pamela Genova is David Ross Boyd Professor of French and Presidential Professor at the University of Oklahoma. Her research spans nineteenth, twentieth, and twenty-first centuries' French literature and culture. She has published numerous articles and essays, along with three books: *André Gide dans le labyrinthe de la mythotextualité* (1995), *Symbolist Journals: A Culture of Correspondence* (2003) and *Writing 'Japonisme': Aesthetic Translation in 19th-Century French Prose* (2016). Notable recent work includes her essay on Félix Fénéon and *La Revue Blanche* for the catalogue accompanying a 2019–20 travelling exhibit (at the New York MOMA and the Paris Musée d'Orsay and Musée Quai Branly).

Matthew Goulish co-founded *Every house has a door* in 2008 with Lin Hixson. He is dramaturg, writer and sometimes performer for the company. His books include *39 Microlectures: In Proximity of Performance* (2001) and *The Brightest Thing in the World: 3 Lectures from the Institute of Failure* (2012). His essays have appeared most recently in *Richard Rezac Address* (2018) and *Propositions in the Making: Experiments in a Whiteheadian Laboratory* (2020). He teaches in the Writing Program of the School of the Art Institute of Chicago.

Lin Hixson co-founded *Every house has a door* in 2008, the Chicago-based performance company that she directs. She was director of the performance group Goat Island (1987–2009). She was awarded the United States Artists Ziporyn Fellowship in 2009, and a Foundation for Contemporary Arts fellowship in 2014, and received an honorary doctorate from Dartington College of Arts, University of Plymouth, in 2007 (awards shared with collaborator Matthew Goulish). She has received fellowships from the National Endowment for the Arts, the Illinois Arts Council and the Chicago Dancemakers' Forum. Her writing has been published in the journals *Poetry*, *Performance Research* and *Parallax*, as well as the anthologies *Imagined Theatres: Writing for a Theoretical Stage* (2017) and *The Creative Critic: Writing as/about Practice* (2018). She is Professor of Performance at The School of the Art Institute of Chicago.

Claudia Kappenberg is a performance and media artist and Subject Lead Fine Art at the University of Brighton, UK. Her work has been shown internationally and takes the form of live performance, participatory events and screen-based work. At the heart of her practice is an interrogation into that which makes us human. Recent writing has been published in *MIRAJ* (2021), *Performing Process: Sharing Dance and Choreographic Practice* (2018), *Syncope in Performing and Visual Arts* (2017) and *The Oxford Handbook of Screendance Studies* (2016). In 2020 she co-curated the online Screendance season *grounded* with Fiontán Moran, Curator Tate Modern.

Rosa Lambert holds an MA degree in Theatre and Film Studies from the University of Antwerp, where she graduated in 2017. Rosa is currently working at the UAntwerp Research Centre for Visual Poetics on her PhD project 'Moving With(in) Language: Kinetic Textuality in Contemporary Performing Arts', funded by the Research Foundation Flanders (FWO). Her research interests include the corporeality and spatiality of language, the status of text in contemporary theatre, the affinity between poetry and dance, the theatricality of writing, language philosophy, (post-)phenomenology and performance philosophy. Her work has been published in *Documenta*, *Critical Stages/Scènes Critiques* and *European Journal of Theatre and Performance*.

Katheryn Owens and Chris Green (greenandowens) are two artist academics currently undertaking a fully collaborative, co-authored, practice research PhD in Performance Studies at the University of Plymouth. Their research is focused on the performance of millennial precarity, drawing on their everyday experiences (of labour, housing, money). This is explored through their practice of performance writing, which often takes the form of zines, craft, sound recordings and DIY artworks. Barthes's writings on the writerly inform their methodological approach. They are interested in the significance and potentiality of friendship in order to carry out relations of care.

Pablo Pakula is a performance-maker, live artist and practice-based scholar. In 2006, he co-founded Accidental Collective (www.accidentalcollective.co.uk), a performance company that frequently focused on interactivity and site-specificity. He has been making solo live art work since 2014 (www.pablopakula.com), presenting work at venues like Camden People's Theatre, festivals like Buzzcut and Tempting Failure, and live art club nights like Deep Trash. He has been teaching in Higher Education since 2006, as an Associate Lecturer at the University of Kent, and as a visiting lecturer/practitioner at Central School of Speech and Drama, and Canterbury Christ Church University. He has been a permanent Teaching Fellow at the University of Birmingham since 2017.

Sandra Parker is a Lecturer in Dance at the University of Melbourne, Faculty of Fine Arts and Music, Victorian College of the Arts, Melbourne, Australia. As a practicing choreographer and interdisciplinary artist, Parker has received numerous grants and awards, including the Australia Council for the Arts Fellowship and a residency at the Cité internationale des arts, Paris, in late 2019. She was the recipient of the University of Melbourne Early Career Researcher Grants Scheme 2017.

Deborah Pearson is an artist/writer/curator and founder and co-director of Forest Fringe. Her work has been staged at some of the most prestigious festivals and venues throughout Europe, North America, South America, the Middle East and Asia, and translated into over six languages. She was among the first cohort of resident artists at Somerset House Studios in London and is currently both Senior Lecturer of Dramaturgy at University of the Arts London and an Associate Research Fellow at Birkbeck. She holds a practice-based PhD from Royal Holloway where she was a Reid Scholar. Together with her Forest Fringe co-directors Andy Field and Ira Brand, she was named in the Stage 100 most influential people in UK theatre in 2009 and 2016 and has won several awards for her solo artistic practice and for Forest Fringe.

Swen Steinhäuser is an artist, curator, dramaturg, writer and landscape gardener based in Manchester, UK. He studied Theatre at Dartington College of Arts, and Cultural Studies at the University of Leeds. Swen has worked extensively as a theatre practitioner, as well as an Associate Lecturer in post-dramatic and movement-based forms of devising in a variety of institutional contexts.

Mischa Twitchin is a lecturer in the Theatre and Performance Department, at Goldsmiths, University of London. He was a British Academy Postdoctoral Fellow (2014–17) and has contributed chapters to several collected volumes, as well as articles in journals such as *Performance Research* (an issue of which, 'On Animism', he also co-edited). His book, *The Theatre of Death: The Uncanny in Mimesis: Tadeusz Kantor, Aby Warburg and an Iconology of the Actor* is published by Palgrave Macmillan in their Performance Philosophy series, and examples of his own performance – and essay-films – can be seen on Vimeo: http://vimeo.com/user13124826/videos.

Harry Robert Wilson is an artist-academic based at the University of Bristol, UK. Harry has a PhD from the University of Glasgow; his research focusses on interdisciplinary explorations of live art and performance, photography, documentation, digital art and new media through critical theory and artistic research. He has published in *Performance Philosophy*, *Performance Research*, *IJPADM* and *Contemporary Theatre Review* and was Digital Thinker in Residence at the National Theatre of Scotland, UK (2018–19). Recently Harry has been exploring intersections between immersive technologies and intimate performance and examining the increasing use of digital and internet technologies in performance work during Covid-19.

ACKNOWLEDGEMENTS

This book would not have been possible without Harry's doctoral project that precedes it. Harry would like to thank his supervisory team for that project: Dee Heddon and Carl Lavery at the University of Glasgow and Pernille Spence at Duncan of Jordanstone College of Art and Design, Dundee. Thank you, Dee, for also providing valuable mentorship, support and advice (in general, but) specifically at the proposal stage of this book's development.

Harry would also like to thank Katie Gough for suggesting that Will might know someone suitable to collaborate with on editing the book. He did, and it has been an extremely rich and creative collaboration.

Will would like to acknowledge the profound importance of Roland Barthes's grieving practice on his own life, as well as the ongoing support of Joanne Zerdy and the artful baffling of all paradigms made possible by Finlay, Phalen and Ren.

We would both like to thank the Thinking Through Theatre series editors Maaike Bleeker, Adrian Kear, Joe Kelleher and Heike Roms for having faith in the book and for their generous feedback and encouragement at crucial stages along the way. Thanks to Anna Brewer, Aanchal Vij, Ella Wilson and all the staff at Bloomsbury/Methuen for their support and guidance in assembling the collection.

Harry would like to thank Chris Hall, Jess Thorpe and Rachel O'Neill for their friendship and advice and John and Karen Wilson, Shona and Julian Gore for making many things possible. Finally, thanks to Tashi Gore, partner and unofficial producer, for her continual support, in work and in life.

INTRODUCTION: CONTEMPORARY PERFORMANCE AFTER ROLAND BARTHES

Harry Robert Wilson

Barthes the secret reference

Marianne Alphant: Your choreography's secret reference is the work of Roland Barthes. How do you account for its importance?
Jérôme Bel: Reading Roland Barthes has been decisive for most of my pieces. It is not an exaggeration to say that without his work my work would not have been what it is ... what I have read of Barthes' writings has always been with me and ... consoled me. When I no longer knew what to do, I only had to open one of his books to be stimulated and glimpse solutions to my problems. My technique was to replace the word 'literature' or 'language' with 'theatre' or 'show' ... to get masses of ideas straight away and to see spectacular possibilities arising. (Bel 2002)

The interview above appeared in the catalogue for the 2002 Centre Pompidou exhibition *R/B* on the life and works of literary theorist and cultural critic Roland Barthes. Documentation of French choreographer Jèrôme Bel's 1997 dance performance *Shirtology* – which took direct influence from Barthes's 1967 book *The Fashion System* – was also screened as part of the exhibition. While Bel's interest in Barthes has been well documented (Corrieri 2011; Lepecki 2006; Siegmund 2017), Alphant's suggestion that Barthes is a kind of secret influence on Bel's work is interesting when considering the various, and often peripheral, ways in which Barthes has acted as an important interlocutor in the developments of contemporary performance practices since the 1980s. Bel's own influence on theatre and performance practice is a useful example of this – where work that was initially responding directly to Barthes's writing becomes a key reference point for performance companies such as Forced Entertainment, Goat Island and post-dance choreographers across Europe (while often losing the direct connection with Barthes).[1]

As Sunil Manghani has recently observed, the Pompidou exhibition marked the beginning of a 'revival' and a 're-positioning' of critical interest in Barthes (2020: 3). This is echoed in a renewed interest in Barthes in theatre and performance theory and practice. Scholarly works in theatre studies from the past fifteen years have revisited Barthes's later writing on pleasure, desire and affective meaning in order to theorize theatrical reception and examine moments of performance that resist semiotic analysis (Bleeker 2008; Bottoms and Goulish 2007; Duggan 2012; Kartsaki 2017). Moreover, the performance works discussed in this book such as Deborah Pearson's *History History History* (2016), the work of *Every house has a door* and artists working between performance, visual art and writing directly and indirectly evidence the continuing influence of Barthes's work on the thinking and practicing of performance makers.

Despite these examples there has been little sustained attention to the enduring ways in which Barthes's thought is put to use by performance practitioners and scholars. This book draws out the secret references and peripheral influences of Barthes on contemporary performance practice. Barthes is a central, and often-cited, figure in the development of semiological tools to analyse meaning-making, and in the move from structuralism to post-structuralism, but also the 'afterlives' of Roland Barthes (Badmington 2016), his posthumous influence, invite a return to the ways his thought may endure in and through performance. Considering a wide range of Barthes's texts, from his early writing on myths and meaning, to personal reflections on love, loss and desire and the more recently available lecture courses at the Collège de France, this

---

1. Evidence of this influence can be found in Tim Etchells's programme note for Bel's *Shirtology* (1997) (Etchells 1999: 212–13) and in Matthew Goulish's description of viewing Bel's *The Last Performance* (1998) (Bottoms and Goulish 2007).

book asks what we can learn about Barthes and about performance by thinking them through together.

In the sections that follow in this introductory chapter, I provide a justification for a return to Barthes in relation to performance in the twenty-first century and offer a contingent history of the impact of his thought in theatre and performance theory and practice. Specifically, I re-examine why it might be useful to bring Barthes in closer proximity to live performance, what his own practices of writing and (lecture) performance might offer performance scholars and makers methodologically and position this book in relation to the renewed interest in Barthes. I then trace Barthes's influence on Theatre Studies disciplines by loosely following his move from myth and structuralism in the 1950s, through a post-structuralist fascination with the proliferation and deferral of meaning in the 1960s and 1970s and finally towards the kind of desire-led obsession with what lies beyond meaning in his final works and his lectures at the Collège de France (between 1977 and 1980). I am wary that this may appear initially as a neat chronology. I would like to assure readers of this book that the more complex temporalities of influence are also embraced here in the untimely and deferred impact of Barthes's work on contemporary performance. The structure of the chapters that follow, across two parts, each approaching the bringing together of 'Barthes' and 'performance' differently, also resists any such chronological arrangement: the contributors to this book have responded to a range of positions from across Barthes's work – from the essays of *Mythologies* right through to his last lecture course on *The Preparation of the Novel*. The essays here do not, therefore, see Barthes's final period as the *culmination* of his thought but instead examine specific *incidents* of thought, and their intersections with performance, from across his entire oevre.[2]

Returning to Barthes and performance

In his early work, Roland Barthes wrote prolifically about theatre. In particular, between 1953 and 1960, Barthes enthusiastically celebrated

2. In the introduction to the posthumously published collection of Barthes's essays *Incidents* (2010), publisher François Wahl describes the incident in Barthes as an attempt 'to grasp the immediate' in writing, an encounter between reader and writer and their 'desire to write' (Barthes 2010: vii).

the experiments of Jean Vilar at the Théâtre National Populaire (TNP) and the touring productions of Bertolt Brecht's Berliner Ensemble. And then he stopped. In *Performance Degree Zero* (2006), Timothy Scheie argues that one reason for Barthes's abrupt end to theatre criticism in 1960 was a result of the failure of written language and structural analysis to account for the stubborn materiality of live bodies. Scheie writes of performance as a 'theoretical impasse' (19) for Barthes, one that 'illuminates' the 'pervasive reluctance' for performance theory to resolve the problem of the performer's presence (5).[3]

Scheie's work can be seen as an invitation to reconcile Barthes's thought with theatre and performance – to see beyond his fascination with Brechtian theatre practice and to consider Barthes's continuing relevance to studies of contemporary live performance of all forms. In *Postdramatic Theatre* (2006), Hans-Thies Lehmann argues that Barthes's attraction to Brecht brought about a 'peculiar blindness' and a 'perceptual block' to experimental theatre forms after epic theatre. Lehmann writes that:

> Barthes could not 'see' the whole line of new theatre that led from Artaud and Grotowski to The Living Theatre and Robert Wilson, despite the fact that his semiotic reflections ... about the image, the *sens obtus* (obtuse sense), the voice, etc., are of great value for the description of precisely this new theatre. (2006: 30)

This collection aims to 'join up' Barthes's thought with the experimental forms and practices of performance that have emerged in the wake of his writing in the 1970s and 1980s and have continued to develop into the twenty-first century: to guide Barthes through the impasse created by his writing at a particular historical moment. What would Barthes have made of various forms of what Lehmann has termed postdramatic theatre – or the expanded field of performance modes and textual strategies found in live art, postmodern dance or collaboratively devised work, for instance? How do his ideas continue to influence practitioners and scholars in these disciplines? How might more recent theoretical developments in theatre and performance studies invite us to reconsider Barthes's significance?

---

3. See, for example, Scheie's discussion of the 'evacuation' of the live body from Phelan and Auslander (2006: 9–10).

While the scope of Scheie's book is meticulous and detailed, it too suffers from a reluctance to discuss concrete examples of live performance events. This is the gap that this book addresses directly: by inviting performance makers and scholars to consider Barthes, and to directly discuss instances of practice, this volume attempts the tricky task of attending to what Laura Cull Ó Maoilearca terms 'the resistant materiality of performance's thinking' (2012: 25). By thinking theatre and performance through Barthes, and rethinking Barthes through theatre and performance, we can examine the ways that writing about performance might put the body back into his theory, contributing to existing work on the ways that performance writing and theatre scholarship can write the live, and begin to account for, or at least directly address, the stubborn substance of live performing bodies.

A(n un)timely look at Barthes through *The Neutral*

But why return to Barthes now, when his ideas may seem unfashionable or even outdated in Theatre and Performance Studies?[4] The deferred publication of Barthes's three lecture courses at the Collège de France (which were originally delivered between 1977 and 1980) provide an interesting illumination of this apparently anachronistic approach. Barthes's lecture notes have arrived posthumously, with a delay of nearly thirty years (in their English translation).[5] These posthumous publications have led, in Anglophone contexts, to an examination of the 'afterlives' of Barthes or the 'new Barthes' – a renewed interest in 'Late Barthes' across fields of literary studies and visual culture. Invoking Derrida's elegy for Barthes in *The Work of Mourning* (2001), Sunil Manghani has argued that the emergence of Barthes's posthumous

---

4. This was a question I returned to frequently during my practice-as-research PhD project 'Affective Intentionalities: Practising Performance with Roland Barthes's *Camera Lucida*'. This book is a continuation of that work in some senses, but also an attempt to widen the scope of that project by opening up this question to other theatre and performance makers and academics. A full text of the complementary writing for my doctoral project can be accessed online (see Wilson 2018).

5. Sunil Manghani notes that this was a result of Barthes's editor at Edition de Seuil, and then literary executor, François Wahl, refusing to publish the lectures (see Manghani 2020: 5).

works 'is as much a reminder to *read* Barthes again; or rather a reminder of our (unwitting) postponed reading of him' (2020: 25).

The late lectures invite a re-reading of Barthes's thought: Patrick ffrench has argued that instead of these posthumous works giving us a more complete sense of 'the whole Barthes', they serve to 'scatter Barthes further, to intensify an effect of dissemination already at work in the publications of his lifetime' (2018: 149). One example of this can be found in the way that the Barthes we see in the lecture courses appears to owe more to a Deleuzian mode of thought where affect, process and becoming are favoured over either the early structuralist Barthes or the Derridean-inflected deconstruction of 'The Death of the Author', *Empire of Signs* and *Roland Barthes by Roland Barthes*.[6] In his lecture course on The Neutral, for example, instead of creating a system of meaning to decode the Neutral, Barthes explores what he terms, a 'dictionary ... of twinklings' or an 'inventory of shimmers' (2005: 10, 77): a mode of analysis that is led by the incremental plus/minus of intense relations (instead of the binary yes/no of structuralism). Explicitly linking Barthes to the Spinozan/Deleuzian line of affect theory, Melissa Gregg and Gregory Seigworth read Barthes's proposition in *The Neutral* as a call for a form of analysis that takes into account 'the progressive accentuation ... of intensities, their incremental shimmer: the stretching of process underway, not position taken' (2010: 11).

A result of the late arrival of these lectures on *How to Live Together* (Barthes 2013), *The Neutral*, and *The Preparation of the Novel* (Barthes 2011) is that they are virtually unremarked upon in theatre and performance disciplines, where Barthes is often positioned as a high structuralist semiologist or an exponent of the post-structuralist deferral of meaning found at the edges of signification.[7] And yet, Barthes's observations in these courses, on the lecture as a mode of performance, on time and space, on neutrality as an active deferral, on affect, composition, praxis and rhythm have clear implications for thinking and practicing in and through theatre and performance. Barthes's lectures practice a kind of time-based unfolding of thought:

---

6. Although Badmington (2020) still sees a specifically Derridean form of deconstruction in *The Neutral*. See also Scheie (2006) on the influence of Derrida on Barthes.

7. See notable exceptions in Lagaay (2016), Barker and Goulish (2017) and Willis (2018).

for two hours every Saturday, over a number of weeks, Barthes explored methods of theory which marry thinking and doing, a certain kind of openness of thought that suits the episodic, performative format of a lecture series.

What do we find when we read Barthes again in this context? A politicized desire to embrace contingency, openness, the inconclusive. A certain desire for the pleasures of reading texts – for the always ongoing production of meaning and the joys of entering freely into a work of art or text. While it has become commonplace to read work about empowering and emancipating the spectator in theatrical situations, for example, do we ever hear about the role joy plays in this manoeuver? To affirm the spectator's always-ongoing production of meaning over and above the predetermined meaning of a performance arranged by playwrights and directors is to emphasize the liberating and pleasurable act of making meaning. We need Barthes today because we need more freedom and joy to engage with the theatricality and textuality of the world. As is expressed in this volume, artists are returning to Barthes and finding that his writing, and these lectures in particular, enable a certain kind of relation to theoretical thinking, a relationship to thought that keeps meaning free flowing, where thinking is a bit like performance.

These ideas are most clearly expressed in *The Neutral*, Barthes's penultimate lecture course at the Collège de France from 1978. In this course he describes his lectures as a search for Neutral forms across a range of practices and encounters. He defines the Neutral not as some potentially problematic ambivalent state but as an active non-choice, 'that which outplays the paradigm' of language (2005: 6). The Neutral suspends the conflict involved in choosing one meaning over another. For Barthes, The Neutral is 'the temptation to suspend, to thwart, to elude the paradigm, its menacing pressure, its arrogance → to exempt meaning', allowing a release of meaning's conflict 'its parrying, its suspension' (7). The Neutral is a form that frees meaning from the 'fascism of language' (189). In order to practice a form of the Neutral, Barthes employs his own dramaturgical device: inspired by the aleatory composition practices of John Cage, he uses a random structuring device to arrange his lectures around a series of thirty figures. In Barthes's own words, 'each figure is at the same time search for the Neutral and *performance* of the Neutral' (11, my emphasis).

Neutral dramaturgies, then, could be identified in 'thought and practice of the non-conflictual' (Barthes 2005: 44) – structures that suspend the violence of a binary choice, a radical kind of non-conflict which thwarts the paradigm.⁸ These suspensions take on even more potent resonances in the post-Trump, post-Brexit, post-Covid-19 increasingly divided 'Culture Wars' of Western political discourse. Could practices of the Neutral offer a kind of antidote to the deadlock of our current political moment – where politics, at least in Europe and the United States, are reduced to left and right, conservative and liberal, leave/remain, mask/anti-mask? To baffle or outplay that paradigm is to create a space adjacent to this dominant discourse riddled by binary opposition where it is possible to collaborate in the production of meaning without signifying an allegiance to any pre-given authority. What is this baffled paradigm for theatre and performance? The answer to that question will surely be discovered by pursuing a desire for the Neutral.

The reflections collected here both directly and indirectly explore a desire for neutral dramaturgies. They also tease out the peripheral influences of Barthes, the way he might be carried in our work, through hidden or unexplored traces. Ultimately, this book takes up Derrida's reminder to re-read Barthes, to think about his deferred influence on theatre and performance and to contribute to the rich cross-disciplinary work that is part of a renewed interest in Barthes in the wake of his posthumous publications.

Structure of the book and contributions

Rethinking Roland Barthes through Performance is arranged into two parts to explore a range of different methods for bringing Barthes into dialogue with performance practice. Part I, 'A DICTIONARY OF TWINKLINGS', gathers together practitioner reflections and performative texts made directly in response to Barthes's work. The 'twinklings' in this section exist in moments where neutral dramaturgies may be glanced shimmering at the edges of the writing. That is, Barthes is not, or not always, directly discussed in these contributions, but instead the authors put something of Barthes's methods into play in their performance of his ideas. Our editorial/curatorial approach to this section has been to resist the academic urge to make the links between Barthes and performance explicit in order to encourage a more active

---

8. Of course this has resonances with postdramatic theatre and performance forms that might seek to rethink theatre as drama based on conflict (see Lehmann 2006).

mode of readership. As Barthes writes 'everything about the Neutral is about sidestepping assertion' (2005: 44). We discuss this strategy in more detail in our chapter on 'PRACTISING NEUTRAL DRAMATURGY(IES)' (Chapter 7).

With this in mind, we start with Lin Hixson and Matthew Goulish's 'FIVE THESES FOR A DRAMATURGY OF PERFORMANCE' (Chapter 1), in which the writers approach Barthes indirectly through the work of Nathalie Léger (who compiled and annotated Barthes's last lecture notes *The Preparation of The Novel* as well as curating the Pompidou exhibition in 2002). Hixson and Goulish use Léger's writing as a jumping off point to explore five aspects of their dramaturgical approach in making performance with their company *Every house has a door*. In Chapter 2, Pablo Pakula documents his teaching of Barthes's seminal essay 'The Death of the Author' to performance students by presenting us with a performance score for an improvised exercise where meaning 'ceaselessly posits meaning ceaselessly to evaporate it' (Barthes 1977: 147). Andy Field and Deborah Pearson's dialogue in Chapter 3 approaches Barthes's notion of the *punctum* through some misremembered theory and Field's sometimes inaccurate impressions of Pearson's informal trilogy of works *Like You Were Before* (2010), *The Future Show* (2012) and *History History History* (2016). Like Barthes's own intensely personal writing in *Camera Lucida*, Field and Pearson's touching personal correspondence says as much about their friendship, disrupted in some ways by the early stages of the Covid-19 pandemic, as it does about Barthes. Also exploring friendship is greenandowens's contribution (Chapter 4), a series of recipes developed for their project exploring food, friendship and performance. Inspired by Barthes's notion of the writerly text, and the performative functions of cooking, sharing and writing about food, greenandowens's chapter implicitly invites us to consider recipes as readerly texts that, approached in a more playful way, might invite more writerly engagements. Chapter 5 is a text written by Ira Brand for Theaterformen festival in Hannover. Brand was due to perform her participatory wrestling performance *Ways To Submit* there in 2020 but was unable to due to the Covid-19 pandemic. Her written version powerfully evokes the textures and atmospheres of the performance, filtered through Brand's attempts to capture absent presences through documentation of the piece. Simon Bayly's companion piece to Brand's reflections (Chapter 6) attempts a 'writing towards the real' in the form of a prose poem that invokes Barthes indirectly through some of the tropes of his later work. Bayly works with a freely associative writing style to unpick his experience of wrestling with Brand when he participated in her show as an audience member in 2019. Finally, in Chapter 7, Will Daddario and I explore some of our thinking behind the editorial approach to this section through an examination of Barthes's approach in *The Neutral*. In this short essay, we refer to a series of performance examples that indirectly serve to illuminate the idea of neutral dramaturgy(ies).

In the spirit of explicating the relationships between 'Roland Barthes' and 'Performance' in more overt ways, Part II, 'RETHINKING ROLAND BARTHES, THEATRE, PERFORMANCE', takes a more conventional approach.[9] The contributions in this section of the book either read performance works *in relation* to the ideas developed in Barthes's writing or read Barthes's writing through the lens of theatre and performance studies. The section contains essays that apply Barthes's concepts to contemporary dance and experimental theatre as well as practice-research reflections from performance-makers wishing to trace the influence of Barthes on their practice.

Acting as a bridge between Parts I and II, we start with an email exchange between Bayly and Brand (Chapter 8) contextualizing their writing in Part I of the book and exploring the links between Barthes, Brand's performance and wrestling more explicitly. In Chapter 9, Swen Steinhäuser takes up Barthes's notion of the amateur and reads this through processes of devising and the contemporary performance pedagogies practiced during Steinhäuser's training at Dartington College of Arts. In a particularly Barthesian approach, the form of Steinhäuser's text aims to echo the ideas he is exploring through a dramaturgical structure of the constellation. In her essay 'THE DISTURBANCE OF ONE SYSTEM BY ANOTHER' (Chapter 10), artist Claudia Kappenberg returns to her outdoor performances *Flush* (2004) and *Swan Canal* (2011) to unpack Barthes's idea of 'silent expenditure' from *A Lover's Discourse* and 'non-action' from *The Neutral*. An engagement with Barthes helps to illuminate the political aspects of Kappenberg's site-specific interventions that aim to challenge ideas of productivity and usefulness in the context of global capitalism. In Chapter 11, Mischa Twitchin directly engages with ideas of the 'left-handed' expression and 'neutral dramaturgy' by (re)examining Barthes's writing on the abstract calligraphic paintings of Cy Twombly. Twitchin explores the

---

9. We didn't think we would have been able to get away with a whole book about Barthes that did not address Barthes directly, although we did consider it momentarily.

between-spaces of neutral dramaturgy as a baffling of the paradigmatic forms of contemporary drama. Sandra Parker (Chapter 12) and Rosa Lambert (Chapter 15) explore Barthes's terms punctum and *grain*, respectively, applying them to those slippery moments between meaning and affect in contemporary dance practices. Where Parker explores the punctum as the destabilizing of choreography's ability to capture the moving body in known forms, Lambert explores dance works that incorporate text and voice to explore their 'kinetic potential' and as sites of dance in themselves. In Chapter 13, Michael Bachmann examines competing concepts of the face across Barthes's writing – the face as legible mask and the face as stubborn affect – to tease out two models of signification in theatre/performance. Finally, Pamela Genova examines Barthes's *Empire of Signs* for instances of performance (Chapter 14). From tempura chefs, calligraphy and everyday performances of self to Japanese puppet theatre, Genova explores the ways that Barthes's Western encounter with Japan is a markedly performative one and how Japan allows Barthes to reexamine Western dramaturgies.

To provide a context for these two sections, the second half of this introductory chapter traces some of Barthes's key concepts and their influence on theatre and performance disciplines over the past forty years or so. This stages a move from Barthes's enthusiasm for semiology and his celebration of Brechtian theatre in the 1950s to his influential writing on textuality and the death of the author – which informs discussions of postmodern theatre and dance that emerged in the 1980s and 1990s – and more recent applications of concepts that attempt to tease out tricky affective responses to artworks (such as grain, *jouissance*, punctum). Finally, I return to Jèrôme Bel's practice to trace a series of neutral dramaturgies across his and Goat Island's work. While this introduction presents a chronology of sorts, it is hoped that in the following chapters, readers may dip in and out, read across and between and relish the opportunity to explore Barthes's scattered influence across a range of disciplines and practices. This book aims to build up a patchwork of the secret references of Barthes and explore just some of the 'infinite variation[s]' (ffrench 2018: 150) that arise when we consider Barthes through performance.

Decoding myths and disturbing bodies

A significant influence on approaches to performance analysis in theatre and performance disciplines is Barthes's collection of essays

Mythologies, originally published in French in 1957 and translated into English in 1972. Barthes's approach has informed the development of systems of politicized analysis of a range of media and cultural practices. As Mark Fortier has written, Barthes's importance in the theory of theatre was to go beyond Saussure and Peirce and apply semiotic analysis 'to specific cultural activities [and] nonverbal as well as verbal signification' (2002: 22). Similarly, Philip Auslander has argued that in his examination of signifying processes in a range of sociocultural habits and artefacts, 'Barthes anticipated some of the central concerns of performance studies' (2007: 49).[10]

The essays in *Mythologies* aim to decode the ideological myths that accompany a range of pop culture artefacts from wrestling, movie stars and photography to fashion magazines, 'Soap Powders and Detergents', as well as popular French foodstuffs such as 'Wine and Milk' or 'Steak and Chips'. Barthes describes his approach as one of *demystification* – an attempt to 'unmask' the process by which petit-bourgeois culture is transformed into something natural (1972b: 8).

Barthes was highly influenced by Swiss linguist Ferdinand de Saussure's methods of semiological analysis but combines this with a Brechtian Marxist approach to expose mass-culture's presentation of 'Nature itself as historical' (1972b: 122). As noted above, the influence of Brecht on Barthes's thought was significant and is present long after Barthes stops writing specifically about theatre. Barthes describes being 'dazzled' by Brecht's production of *Mother Courage* in Paris in 1954 (Barthes in Scheie 2006: 45) and Brecht's cultural-materialist dramaturgical strategies give political weight to Barthes's application of semiotics during the 1950s. After Barthes's abrupt end to theatre criticism in 1960, Brecht becomes the recurring reference point for his ideas on Japanese theatre, Eisenstein's cinema and photography.[11]

Scheie argues that in his celebration of Brechtian theatre, Barthes weaves together 'a materialist grasp of history, Sartre's humanism, and Saussure's synchronic and detached analysis of structure' (2006: 53).

---

10. Namely, Auslander references Barthes's application of performance terms to wider sociocultural fields and Barthes's interest in the performativity of writing. See also discussions of Barthes in some key theatre and performance studies textbooks: Counsell and Wolf (2001); Balme (2008); Aston and Savona (1991).

11. See discussions of Brechtian gestus in *Empire of Signs* (Barthes 1982) and 'The Third Meaning', 'Diderot, Brecht, Eisenstein' and 'Lesson in Writing' in *Image Music Text* (Barthes 1977).

In his conflation of these competing theoretical positions – and his borrowing and reworking of Brecht – Barthes assembled a kind of Utopian vision for theatre as 'an exemplary instance of committed semiosis' (ibid.). It is this Marxist-inflected Brechtian-Sartrean semiotics that is held in tension for Barthes for a brief time in the mid-1950s but eventually gives way to a full embrace of structural analysis in the 1960s when Barthes employs a more rigorous structuralist method to explore the specific communication modes of images, narratives and the fashion system.[12]

It was also during this period, in an interview with *Tel Quel* magazine from 1963, that Barthes discusses theatrical signification as a 'real informational polyphony ... a density of signs' (1972a: 261–2). As noted by Elaine Aston and George Savona in *Theatre as Sign-System*, Barthes identifies some provocative questions for the analysis of theatrical signs that were subsequently taken up by theatre semioticians such as Tadeusz Kowzan (1968) and Patrice Pavis (1985) (Aston and Savona 1991: 9). Barthes classifies theatre as a 'cybernetic machine' constantly emitting messages that are 'simultaneous and yet of different rhythm'. Barthes asks: 'what relations do these counterpointed signs ... have among themselves?'; 'do they combine in a single meaning?'; 'how is the theatrical signifier formed? What are its models?' (1972a: 261–2). The field of theatre semiotics has responded to these questions, and theatre's density, in attempts to map and analyse how theatre communicates meaning.[13]

Yet theatre semioticians such as Pavis (1997) and Keir Elam (1983) have been critical of the failure of semiotics to account for the pre-linguistic perceptions of theatre spectators. Both draw on Barthes's later term punctum (discussed below) to argue that semiotics misses out the passion, the feeling, the 'sensual materiality of the signifiers' (Lehmann in Pavis 1997: 215). Similarly, for Barthes, while Brecht's theatre offers the clearest model of the 'dense semantic act' of theatrical communication (1972a: 261), he is fascinated elsewhere by the sensuous theatricality of live bodies. In peripheral moments of his writing in the 1950s and 1960s, Barthes observes, but cannot account for, signs that are in excess of meaning, such as the actor's body.[14]

12. See 'The Rhetoric of the Image', 'Introduction to The Structural Analysis of Narratives' collected in *Image Music Text* (1977), *S/Z* (2002) and *The Fashion System* (1983).
13. See for example Fischer-Lichte 1992; Elam 2002.
14. See Scheie on the stubborn substance of the woman on a train or on the hysterical theatricality of drag performers (Scheie 2006: 73–7, 131–5).

While Theatre Studies has dealt more often with Barthes's definition of theatricality as a 'density of signs', Barthes, in his essay 'Baudelaire's Theatre' from 1954, shifts the emphasis to the duality between sensuality and signification. In a discussion of Baudelaire's unfinished plays, Barthes defines theatricality as 'a density of signs *and sensations*', the 'perception of sensuous artifice' (1972a: 26; my emphasis). Instead of identifying theatre's density in the polyphonic (but nevertheless intelligible) signs, theatre's density here can be located in the actor's 'disturbing corporeality', a double: 'at once a living body ... and an emphatic, formal body, frozen by its function as an artificial object' (1972a, 27–8). Theatricality for Barthes is the double nature of theatrical signs as both real and representation, a tension that troubles the clearly communicated messages of Brecht. Both theatre's density and the live body's corporeality challenge Barthes's structuralist approach in the 1950s and 1960s, and yet, Barthes's inability to account for theatre's disturbing bodies captures a tension at the heart of theatricality, what Gerald Siegmund has referred to as the tension between materiality and signification (2017: 64–5).

For Barthes in the 1950s and 1960s, anything in excess of signification is unhealthy, disturbing.[15] However, as Barthes's work moves away from structuralism in the late 1960s, towards more deconstructive concepts and modes, he employs a range of critical terms for that which lies outside of signification: grain, jouissance, the punctum. Rather than expelling the materiality of the signifier, as in his writing about Brecht, these later works explore a fascination with, and an attempt to theorize, the affective qualities of artworks beyond meaning. Before examining these terms and their more recent influence on theatre and performance, it is important to chart the move from structuralism to post-structuralism in Barthes's work through the shift from work to text (see below) and in his proclamation of the death of the author in 1968. These moments in Barthes's writing have had a profound and lasting impact on the theorizing of theatre practices in the 1980s and 1990s that similarly attempted to explore the free play of meaning through deconstructive methods.

Death of the Author / Textuality

In an often-quoted section from his 1968 essay, 'The Death of the Author', Barthes defines text not as the single message of an 'Author-God' but as

---

15. On theatrical costume as an unhealthy sign that prevents readability, see Barthes's essay from 1955 'The Diseases of Costume' (Barthes 1972a).

a 'multi-dimensional space', a 'tissue of quotations' in which a number of writings rub up against each other (1977: 146). With this argument Barthes concludes that it is the reader, rather than the author of a text, who constructs meaning. Barthes's essay marks a shift in his work from methods of structuralist decoding to a post-structuralist emphasis on the 'infinitely deferred ... exemption of meaning' (147). Barthes's essay is published the year after Derrida's *Of Grammatology*, and while Barthes does not directly reference Derrida in his work from this period it is clear that they share an interest in the deferral of meaning, open texts and a shift from examining signified meaning to considering the pluralities of the signifier.[16]

In a slightly later essay from 1971, Barthes distinguished between the *work*, as an object with a closed meaning to be decoded, and the *text*, a space between the object and the reader made up of 'an explosion, a dissemination' of meaning (1977: 159). For Barthes, text is not limited to works of literature but is a process of endless play found across media: 'the stereographic plurality of its weave of signifiers' (159).

In *S/Z*, Barthes's book-length study of Balzac's *Sarrasine* (originally published in 1973), he develops these ideas to make a further distinction between the *readerly* and the *writerly* text. The readerly is a classic text that imposes a meaning on the reader and therefore makes them idle – they can only ever be a 'consumer' of texts and their only choice is the 'referendum' between accepting the text's meaning or rejecting it (2002: 4). By contrast, the writerly text turns the reader into a 'producer' and constructor of meaning – it is not an object like a book but a set of relations between signifiers and those who read them: 'the writerly text is a perpetual present ... ourselves writing, before the infinite play of the world ... is traversed, intersected, stopped, plasticized by some singular system' (5).

Gerald Rabkin (1983 and 1985) and Elinor Fuchs (1996) have been important figures in applying post-structuralist theories of text to theatre and performance disciplines. In *The Death of Character* (1996), Fuchs locates in francophone critical theory a 'vocabulary and grammar' to account for the new kinds of theatre she was watching in New York in the 1980s. She saw (and subsequently made strong arguments for) affinities between avant-garde theatre practices of The Wooster Group,

16. On Derrida's influence on Barthes see Rabaté 1997, Burgin in Batchen 2011 and Badmington 2016 and 2020. Timothy Scheie argues that, in addition to Derrida's influence, Barthes holds certain rival influences in Jacques Lacan, Phillipe Sollers and Julia Kristeva (Scheie 2006: 100–1).

Robert Wilson, Suzan-Lori Parks and the 'crisis of representation' that plays out in much post-structuralist theory in the 1960s and 1970s. Fuchs cites the theories of text in Foucault, Derrida and Barthes; the postmodernism of Baudrillard and Lyotard and the feminist readings of psychoanalysis in Cixous, Irigaray and Kristeva as key reference points in her and her contemporaries' 'mental swoon' towards postmodernism in the 1980s (1996: 1–2).

Rabkin's part in this turn is explored in an essay in *Performing Arts Journal* from 1983, 'The Play of Misreading: Text/Theatre/Deconstruction'. In a discussion of the critical outcry that surrounded Richard Foreman and Lee Breuer's radical stagings of classic texts at New York's Public Theatre in the early 1980s, Rabkin calls for theatre criticism to embrace the 'continental speculation' of new critical theory that had such an influence in other arts, philosophy and social sciences in the 1970s (47). In particular, Rabkin discusses Derrida's deconstructive approaches, Barthes's and Kristeva's theories of textuality as well as the work emerging from the 'American deconstructors' at Yale, to call for alternative methodological approaches to theatre analysis – one that frees the text from closure and instead embraces the 'free play of signifiers' (49). Rabkin calls for a return to theory, through the work of these deconstructionists, to provide a language for the radical approaches to text that were being explored by the avant-garde theatre artists such as Foreman, Breuer, The Wooster Group and Mabou Mines. Rabkin suggests that 'deconstruction provides a model whereby these radical and disruptive strategies may ... be comprehended' to restore the 'symbiotic relationship between new art and new theory' (59–60).

The practice of the experimental New York theatre company The Wooster Group is exemplary of the way that theatre of the 1980s and 1990s explored the possibilities of post-structuralist theories of text. Works such as *L.S.D. (...Just the High Points...)* (1984), *Brace Up!* (1990) and *House/Lights* (1999) are notable for their juxtaposition of a range of cultural texts in their collagistic dramaturgies. *L.S.D.*, which literally placed a series of texts on stage – from the random readings from books by Timothy Leary, William Burroughs, Aldous Huxley, Allen Ginsberg and Jack Kerouac in Part I, to the sped-up and rewritten version of Arthur Miller's *The Crucible* in Part II – presented an embodiment of Barthes's configuration of the text as a 'tissue of quotations ... that blend and clash' (1977: 146). As Bonnie Marranca has written, The Wooster Group produce 'anthology-like scripts ... always in search of an author' (2003: 2). Barthes's influential claim that meaning is located in the reader of texts has been taken up by scholars seeking to contextualize The Wooster Group's practice within critical theory. In Rabkin's later essay, 'Is there a Text on This Stage' (1985), he draws on Barthes to unpack the Group's use of *The Crucible*, which led to legal challenges and finally a 'cease and desist' order from Arthur Miller. Rabkin identifies in their work a conscious rejection of authorial intent 'in order to force its audiences' active participation' (1985: 145).

Other writing on The Wooster Group from this time, while not directly referencing Barthes, clearly borrowed from the vocabularies of post-structuralist theory. In 1985, David Savran observed that The Wooster Group's process of making a piece 'does not begin with a theme or message to be communicated' but that 'ideas and themes that emerge from pieces do so only in retrospect, as a residue of the textualizing process' (1985: 108). Furthermore, he explicitly locates the construction of meaning in the audience's reception of the work and writes that 'each spectator will be assured a different chain of associations and way of making sense of the action ... rendering a single meaning impossible' (ibid.).

Similarly, while The Wooster Group did not claim to be primarily exploring textual concepts from French critical theory, they did describe their approach in ways that echo across Barthes's discussions of textuality. Director of The Wooster Group, Elizabeth LeCompte, spoke of her method as one in which she 'allows as many interpretations as possible to co-exist in the same time and same space' (in Savran 1985: 108). In the same interview, co-founder of and performer with the group, Ron Vawter, directly echoed Barthes's language in 'The Death of the Author' when he stated that, 'an event which can be interpreted only one way inhibits and limits the possibility', preferring to see the Group's work as 'an opportunity for a meaning, rather than an expression of a single meaning' (in ibid.).[17] While The Wooster Group's process may not consciously attempt to translate theories of text to performance practices, Barthes's ideas and those of other post-structuralist writers had disseminated beyond the academy by the mid-1980s, influencing cultural practitioners as well as theorists. Euridice Arratia observed in The Wooster Group's process of making *Brace Up!* that LeCompte would read from Barthes's book *Empire of Signs* during rehearsals ' "to

---

17. Compare with Barthes's 'To give a text an Author is to impose a limit on that text, to furnish it with a final signified, to close the writing' (1977: 147).

clarify herself," to articulate something that she has been thinking of but has had trouble "defining verbally"' (Arratia 1992: 138).[18]

In the related practices of postmodern dance, Susan Leigh Foster's 1986 work, *Reading Dancing*, was influential in its application of post-structuralist theories of text to dance performance. Foster's work is heavily informed by Barthes's distinction between readerly and writerly texts to distinguish between the unified symbols and references of Martha Graham to Merce Cunningham's focus on the dancer's body and the invitation for the viewer to complete meaning. Foster argues that Graham's dance is readerly; it 'suffocates the reader with its single, intended message' (1986: 240 n. 26); whereas, in Cunningham and the Judson choreographers she sees versions of Barthes's death of the author and the writerly through an 'emphasis on choreographic conventions and the viewer's active role in interpreting them' (242 n. 43). Foster draws on semiology and post-structuralism to trace the signifying strategies of contemporary American dance, creating a dance history that follows Barthes's movement from work to text.

As explored above, Barthes's direct influence on practice has been well documented in the conceptual 'post-dance' of Jérôme Bel. Bel credits the work of Barthes, Gilles Deleuze, Michel Foucault, Louis Althusser and Julia Kristeva as having a clear impact on his approach to performance, sometimes describing a direct translation of theoretical concepts to theatrical and choreographic practice (Bel 2004). In particular, Bel credits Barthes's concepts of the zero degree of writing (discussed below) and the death of the author as shaping his thinking about how to 'activate the spectator' in his first three performances *Nom donné par l'auteur* (Name Given by the Author 1994), *Jérôme Bel* (1995) and *Le dernier spectacle* (The Last Performance 1998) (Bel 2005).

So the impact of Barthes and his contemporaries during this time are evident in the moments where both performance theorists and practitioners find new ways to articulate practice – deliberately

---

18. More implicit influences of Barthes's death of the author can be seen in the performance writing practices of contemporary devising companies. In *Certain Fragments*, Tim Etchells, the director of UK-based Forced Entertainment, discusses his difficulty coming to terms with his students referring to the concept of an authentic 'voice' to describe their writing style, instead favouring writing made from 'a collection of texts, quotations, strategic and accidental speakings – not a coherent thing, much less the single-minded author of some text' (1999: 101–2).

attempting to move away from the closed meanings of a playwright-led theatre, or modern dance, toward the endless play of signifiers in the here and now of performance reception. In the practices discussed, we see a playing out of Barthes's ideas through the stuff of live performance: What better place is there to test out the performative and open textualities than in live performance's theatricality, the density of signs and sensations, the resisting of fixed meaning and the embracing of production as an activity? The hallmarks of these influences may now be more implicit, but they form a key backdrop to more recent contemporary performance practices – especially given that a number of university theatre departments (in the UK at least) have continued to teach the works of The Wooster Group, Jérôme Bel, Robert Wilson (and others) and the contextualizing theory that informs readings of their work.[19]

In the following section, I outline an even more delayed application of Barthes in theatre and performance disciplines through his concepts of the obtuse meaning, grain, jouissance and the punctum.

Obtuse meaning / Grain / Jouissance / Punctum

If the concept of the death of the author opened up texts to the variety of meanings available to the reader, much of Barthes's writing in the 1970s went even further to examine encounters with artworks that suspend, lie beyond or are in excess of meaning. Barthes develops a number of terms to describe his experience of these moments, culminating in his theory of the photograph's punctum: the accidental, non-intentional detail that affectively bruises the viewer. Derek Attridge has situated Barthes's last book, *Camera Lucida*, as the culmination of a career-long obsession with theorizing what takes place at the edges of signification. He cites jouissance, the haiku and *satori*, *signifiance*, the obtuse meaning and, of course, the punctum as a long list of terms that 'attempt to capture a moment of breakdown in the codes of signification' (Attridge 1997: 78).

---

19. Rather than achieving Barthes's and Bel's desire for an absence of style in the zero degree of performance, however, this has led in many cases to the adoption of what Heddon and Milling have termed a 'postmodern style' in devising practices (see Heddon and Milling 2006: 215–17).

Remarkably, these moments of breakdown often involve encounters with performing bodies (even if they are sometimes mediated by film, recorded music, photography or writing). In Barthes's 'The Third Meaning' from 1970, he identifies something 'erratic' and 'obstinate' in a film still of two courtiers showering gold coins over the czar from Sergei Eisenstein's *Ivan the Terrible* (1944). This third meaning, beyond the informational or symbolic code, 'seems to extend outside culture, knowledge, information; analytically, it has something derisory about it: opening out into the infinity of language' (1977: 55). Or in 'The Grain of the Voice' from 1972, Barthes discusses the sonic materiality of a singer's voice through Julia Kristeva's distinction between pheno-text and geno-text. Transposed to singing, Barthes terms the pheno-song as 'everything in the performance which is in the service of communication, representation, expression'; whereas, the geno-song is the voluminous energy of the voice, 'the space where significations germinate "from within language and in its very materiality"' (182). The grainy corporeality of the singing voice foregrounds the 'voluptuousness of [the] sound-signifiers' producing, for Barthes, a radical pleasure: jouissance (182–3).

Barthes elaborates on the concept of jouissance in his 1973 book *The Pleasure of the Text*, where he explores the concepts of pleasure and jouissance as they relate to his experience as a reader (and writer) of texts. In Barthes's taxonomy, the pleasure of the text is an enjoyment based on a confirmation of the subject's (reader's) identity and in relation to their cultural values, a 'homogenising movement of the ego' (Heath in Barthes 1977: 9). In contrast to this (although importantly not simply in opposition), Barthes explores the text of jouissance which produces a 'radically violent pleasure' that 'shatters – dissipates, loses' the subject's identity (ibid.).[20] Barthes notes that the text of pleasure is 'the text that contents, fills, grants euphoria; the text that comes from culture and does not break with it, is linked to a comfortable practice of reading' whereas the text of jouissance is 'the text that imposes a state of loss, the text that discomforts … unsettles the reader's historical, cultural, psychological assumptions, the consistency of his [sic] tastes, values, memories, brings to a crisis his relation with language' (1975: 14).

20. Of course Barthes was not the only theorist working with ideas of radical pleasure. Barthes's terms are derived from Lacanian Psychoanalysis and Lacan's definition of jouissance as 'beyond the pleasure principle' (Lacan 1998: 184). Feminist critical theorists Julia Kristeva, Luce Irigaray and Hélène Cixous further developed their own concepts of feminine jouissance across their work on *écriture féminine* (see Cixous 1976; Irigaray 1991; Kristeva 1984).

While Elaine Aston and George Savona's *Theatre as a Sign-System* focusses on a semiotic approach to reading theatre and performance, they do explore the possibilities of theatrical analysis beyond the limits of signification. Referring directly to *The Pleasure of the Text*, they discuss plays that 'disrupt textual expectations and discomfort or unsettle the reader' (1991: 33). They cite Kenneth Tynan's comments on the first production of *Waiting for Godot* (1955), which, according to Tynan, forced a re-examination of the rules of drama. Aston and Savona identify in this example 'a process of engagement whereby what is known becomes "unknown", i.e. the disruptive pleasure of *jouissance*, and which, in consequence, invites a rethinking of the world as it exists' (1991: 33).

Much more recently, Eirini Kartsaki (2017) has worked closely with Barthes's *The Pleasure of the Text* in her examination of repetition in performance. Kartsaki's approach is to 'refigure' the texts of a series of writers (from Lacan and Barthes to Henri Bergson) through her embodied encounter with them. Kartsaki pursues connections between the work of these writers and various moments of repetition in theatre and performance, tracing methods from Samuel Beckett and Gertrude Stein through Yvonne Rainer and Trisha Brown and the influence of these key artists on contemporary performance practices. In one chapter, Kartsaki configures repetition as an experience of jouissance through the 'forceful promise of pleasure' in Pina Bausch's *Bluebeard* (1977) (2017: 17). Kartsaki argues that repetition, like that which she experiences in Bausch's work, can function like Barthes's version of the writerly text, inviting the viewer to actively engage with the construction of meaning. Kartsaki writes that certain types of repetitive movement and structure encourage her not only to observe repetition but also to perform it: similar to Barthes's reader, 'I am not merely watching, I am doing much more; I am part of the work, performing from the inside' (50). Kartaski suggests that this active engagement with repetition can be 'difficult, strenuous, but also ecstatic, fervent' echoing some of the difficult pleasures of Barthes's jouissance (49).

In the comfortable/uncomfortable, cultural/non-cultural structure of pleasure/jouissance we can recognize some of the characteristics of Barthes's later terminology of *studium*/punctum. Barthes develops his dual concept of studium/punctum in his final book, *Camera Lucida: Reflections on Photography* (1993). For Barthes, the studium describes the coded 'field' of the photograph as it relates to cultural and political knowledge: a 'classical body of information' that provokes 'a kind of general interest' in the photograph (25-6). The studium is an education in signs and their meanings, the knowledge and activation of culture in the viewing of photographs (26–8). The punctum, on the other hand, exists outside of the rational, cultured system of codes that make up the studium. The punctum is a detail in the photograph that 'will break or punctuate' the coded field of the studium and 'wound' or 'prick' the viewer (26). Barthes locates this 'off-centre detail' in a number of photographs: from a woman's shoes in James Van Der Zee's *Family Portrait* (1926) to the bad teeth of a child in William Klein's *Little Italy* photograph (1954), and the 'little boy's huge Danton collar' and 'the girl's finger bandage' in Lewis Hine's image of two physically disabled children from 1924 (50–1).

In some discrete examples from the 1980s and 1990s, Barthes's punctum has been used to argue for a less rational approach to analysing theatre – one that takes into account the audience's emotions, passions and the affective experience of watching live performance. In an essay from 1983, Keir Elam directly draws on *Camera Lucida* when calling for theatre semiotics to take into account the '*punctum*, or *pathos* or if you like audience passion, that compulsion which ... motivates the receiver's active participation in the artistic practice' (269). Theatre semiotician Patrice Pavis was equally critical of the detached and purely analytical approach that had become celebrated in theatre semiotics. In 1997, Pavis called for a more phenomenological approach, writing that 'the problem with semiotics is that in addressing theatre as a system of codes, it necessarily dissects the perceptual impression theatre makes on the spectator' (1997: 212). Pavis also draws on Barthes's punctum to account for aspects of performance's materiality, the 'pre-linguistic impressions' of a performance (210).

In the deconstructive reflections of Herbert Blau in his 1987 book *The Eye of Prey*, Blau attempts to recuperate *pathos* from its denigration in the 'history of the modern' (1987: 84). Blau approaches this through a comparison of the sentimentality of Beckett and Barthes, two figures that Blau argues have a 'heart in [their] head' (ibid.). Blau draws on the associations of the punctum's prick as a 'deadly stigmatum in the brain' to argue for the ways that *Camera Lucida* brings Barthes in relation to Beckett through the 'ecstatic burden of the tragic pathos, its madness, abject, stupid, the nearly forgotten, discredited, old-fashioned emotion' (88). Blau crucially also links the violence of the punctum to Artaud's 'essential drama': 'a jetstream of bleeding image in the cruel service of the violence of thought' (90), and the transcendent 'alchemical theatre', a 'complete, sonorous, streaming, naked realisation' (Artaud 1958: 52).

Over the past twenty years or so, theatre studies has become increasingly interested in how scholarly writing might find appropriate registers to attend to the affective qualities of performance. In the process of translation from live encounter to written account, writers have explored theatre's after-affects (Kelleher 2015), its fleshy remains (Schneider 2011) and the space between documentation and disappearance (Reason 2006). Of relevance here, theatre studies has increasingly (re)turned to Barthes's conception of studium and punctum during this time to articulate affect in theatre and performance: moments in which there is a breakdown in codes of communication, when there is a conflation of sign and referent or a traumatic encounter with the reality of representation. In these instances, the punctum's effects in performance often seem to occur when the 'reality' of live bodies draw attention to themselves in a way that destabilizes the spectator's capacity to interpret the performance.

A very brief, but key, reference to Barthes's punctum comes in Stephen Bottoms's analysis of the dramaturgy of performance company Goat Island (1998; Bottoms and Goulish 2007).[21] Bottoms borrows from Hal Foster's (1996) conception of the punctum (via Lacan) as a traumatic return of the real. For Foster, reading Andy Warhol's car crash prints from the 1960s, the combination of cold and distanced framing of these scenes is contrasted with a disturbing repetition of the image where 'the punctum breaks through the screen and allows the real to poke through' (136). Bottoms argues that in Goat Island's work similar affective/affectless dramaturgies, of insistent repetition and the de-hierarchization of source materials, open up a space for the audience to 'confront and process deeply personal questions and "traumatic realities"' (1998: 444–5).

In *Visuality in the Theatre* (2008), Maaike Bleeker provides a more detailed elaboration of the analytical uses of Barthes's punctum in a consideration of looking in the theatre. Bleeker applies Barthes's term to moments in performance where there is an apparent conflation of sign and referent and we experience effects of presence and immediateness that break the representational frames. Bleeker describes the punctum in performance as the moment where we 'see what we know to be always already representation ... as "just there to be seen"' (2008: 94–5). For Bleeker, though, rather than the conflation of sign and referent leading us back to an unmediated reality, it 'multiplies the frames' producing a perceptual instability that exposes the visual habits of seeing in the theatre (87).

21. Goat Island was cofounded by Lin Hixson and Matthew Goulish, now of *Every house has a door* and contributors in this collection.

Where Bleeker locates the punctum in the instability of framed versus non-framed, Patrick Duggan, in his 2012 book *Trauma Tragedy*, focusses on a similar 'mimetic shimmering' between reality and representation (Duggan 2012: 9). In this book, Duggan follows Raymond Williams's 'structures of feeling' to argue for a contemporary moment of *trauma-tragedy*, in which much contemporary performance is uniquely concerned with 'trying to embody and bear witness to trauma in an immediate way' by evoking 'a sense of being there in an attempt to generate an effect of "real" presence' (42–3). In support of this argument, Duggan examines a series of theatre and performance art moments, from the work of Sarah Kane and Romeo Castelluci to Franko B and Kira O'Reilly. Duggan draws directly on Barthes to identify moments of 'performative *puncta*'. The performative punctum, according to Duggan, occurs when there is either an irruption of the real into the mimetic order (of theatre) or an irruption of mimesis into the perceived 'real presence' (of performance art). Duggan argues that in this process the audience experience can echo the symptoms of trauma (73, 75).

These more recent returns to Barthes's late work provide examples of the ways that his concepts have contributed to a critical language for attending to those moments in performance that escape semiotic analysis. These are questions that have been central to theatre and performance scholars writing about works that foreground the affective encounter – bodily desires, materialities, non/pre-linguistic meaning, trauma, shock and radical pleasure. One wonders if Barthes read Jean-François Lyotard's 'The Tooth, the Palm', first published in 1973, which called for a 'generalised dissemiotisation', a 'theatre of energies' not of meaning but of 'forces, intensities, present affects' (1976: 107, 109). For Hans-Thies Lehmann, Lyotard's essay, and its powerfully affective foregrounding of the body's visceral energies, is 'intimately related' to the kinds of post-dramatic theatre he discusses (2006: 38). Barthes's move away from semiotics in the late 1970s resonates here. And yet Barthes did not examine the avant-garde theatres of the 1970s that Lehmann references (the line from Artaud, Grotowski to The Living Theatre and Robert Wilson), theatre practice that may have provided him with the (im)perfect object for analysis. As demonstrated in the works discussed above, the radical pleasures, bodily energies and affective detail that Barthes explores across a range of other media has been productively applied to contemporary theatre and performance practices from Goat Island to the expressionist dance of Pina Bausch, the visual theatre of Socíetas Raffaello Sanzio, Robert Lepage and live art practices such as Franko B and Kira O'Reilly.

What has been examined much less in Theatre Studies is Barthes's later conception of the Neutral, which runs through texts like *Writing Degree Zero* and *The Pleasure of the Text* but emerges in a more nuanced way through his penultimate lecture course at the Collège de France. Barthes's articulation of a desire for neutral forms that outplay meaning offers an interesting model for exploring the various task-based performance modes that have emerged in contemporary performance. The final section of this chapter elaborates on these neutral forms through the work of Jérôme Bel and Goat Island. An introduction to the Neutral here aims to impress the value of continuing to work with Barthes in theatre and performance scholarship and to emphasize just how rich Barthes's lectures are for thinking through specifically theatrical problems.

From degree zero to neutral dramaturgy

In Barthes's first book from 1953 he identifies the zero degree of writing at the point where there is an absence of style and of language. Barthes locates this neutral writing in Camus's *The Outsider*. For Barthes, Camus's writing approaches a sort of anti-bourgeois absence of style where 'writing is then reduced to a sort of negative mood in which the social or mythical characters of a language are abolished in favour of a *neutral* and inert state of form' (1970: 77, my emphasis). Barthes refers to *Writing Degree Zero* a number of times in his penultimate lecture course on The Neutral at the Collège de France from 1978, terming his lectures a 'remake' of the earlier work (2005: 176). Barthes states that the course examines the word 'Neutral', 'insofar as its referent inside me is a stubborn affect' ever since his first book (8).

As mentioned previously, Barthes's ideas on the zero degree have been developed in performance contexts by conceptual choreographer Jérôme Bel. In the interview with Marianne Alphant, quoted at the start of this introduction, Bel describes his approach to his first performance, *Nom donné par l'auteur*, as one where he 'literally tried to put a boundary round the zero point of dance and theatre … there is no dancing, no acting, nothing except the bare bones of a choreographic production' (2002). Bel explains that in both *Nom donné par l'auteur* and his second piece, *Jérôme Bel*, there was an attempt to strip back the complexity of dance performance in order to find the 'minimum requirement[s] for choreographic-theatrical practice' (ibid.). In *Nom donné par l'auteur*, Bel defines this as 'objects placed in space with set times' and in *Jérôme*

Bel, that it requires 'bodies, music and light' (Bel 2005). Bel quips that in these performances, instead of doing the '1, 2, 3, 4' of conventional dance steps, they did 'minus 1, minus 2, minus 3 ...' (ibid.).

Gerald Siegmund takes up the resonances between Bel and Barthes noting that Bel's work aims to explore choreographic modes at the zero point between language (as a traditional vocabulary of movement) and style (as the dancer's expression). However, as Siegmund points out, style often returns as the kind of 'fleshly double' of language (Barthes 1970: 13), and in Bel's work the materiality of bodies often produces a tension between a desire for neutral forms and the unavoidable references to the body as style in contemporary art and performance (Siegmund 2017: 64–5). For Siegmund this tension is theatricality.

Both Augusto Corrieri and André Lepecki relate the deactivation of the performers in Bel's work to Yvonne Rainer's famous 'NO manifesto' from 1965 ('no to spectacle no to virtuosity no to transformations and magic and make-believe' (in Corrieri 2011: 222). Corrieri and Lepecki separately argue that the task-based modes with which the performers carry out their actions in Bel's work approaches a sort of neutrality. Corrieri writes that Seguette and Bel in *Nom donné par l'auteur* could be described as 'impassive workers' (2011: 217). Lepecki underlines the neutral attitude of the dancer in *Shirtologie* (1997) (usually Frédéric Seguette) when he references Bel's appreciation of Seguette's capacity to 'almost disappear ... from his own presence on stage while performing this piece' (2006: 55, 137 n18).

Contemporaneously to Bel – although in the different geographical context of the performance theatre scene in the United States – Chicago-based company Goat Island developed approaches to performance style that also bear the traces of the Judson Dance Theatre's impact. Director of the company Lin Hixson directly cites Yvonne Rainer's influence on the company's exploration of task-based movement and everyday actions, with non-dance trained performers (Hixson in Bottoms and Goulish 2007: 70). Echoing Seguette in *Shirtologie*, Bottoms argues that the performers in Goat Island resemble automata, exuding a kind of 'anti-presence' where 'the use of a deliberately blank, unemotional facial glazing, means that there is no sense of these movements offering outward expressions of inner selves' (1998: 425).

Discussing *performance theatre* more generally, Sarah Jane Bailes invokes Rainer's concept of the 'neutral doer' in her discussion of performance companies of the 1990s and 2000s 'behaving more like functionary workers within the performance space' (2011: 17). This neutrality is reflected in Goat Island's company member Karen

Christopher's comments on 'acting style', when she comments that 'when I play a character I play a series of gestures and sounds ... what we do is task-based and we do not "pretend"' (Bottoms and Goulish 2007: 84). The result seems again to resemble something of Barthes's/Bel's desire to outplay meaning. Christopher continues:

> In any given moment of the performance, someone just entering the room might see no emotional inflection at all in the delivery of a particular sequence, but for someone bringing with them a chain of connections, built up by the preceding events, that same sequence might seem full of expression. (84)

In this context, neutral performance modes seem to directly relate to Barthes's desire for a parrying of meaning's choice. In the work of Jérôme Bel and Goat Island, this acts as an invitation to the audience to bring their own readings and associations to the work: as Bel says, in order to 'activate the spectator', 'you have to deactivate the actor' (2005). So, neutrality can be thought of as a performance mode in contemporary performance. But, perhaps even more radically, neutral dramaturgy might refer to the way that a performance might be structured to stimulate a certain kind of audience reception, one in which meaning is kept endlessly circulating.

In the practices discussed above, the performers embody a kind of impassive attitude that creates a space for the audience to think and feel in relation to the work. These ideas have been applied in fleeting moments by performance scholars, from Alice Lagaay's application of Barthes's Neutral to explore 'the poetics of negative performance (not-doing, waiting, letting be ...)' (2016: 37); or Matthew Goulish who defends the complexity of *Every house has a door*'s 'neutral' performance style by drawing on Barthes to suggest that the 'restraint' of neutral forms can produce 'infinite potential unfoldings' and 'amplified audience emotion' (Barker and Goulish 2017). However, there is still much to explore between the zero degree, the Neutral and the non-arrogant performance forms that have emerged since Bel's first performance in 1994.[22] These explorations are variously taken up by the contributors to this volume.

22. Not even Siegmund's detailed book on Jérôme Bel from 2017 references Barthes's *The Neutral* – which seems like an oversight given the focus on neutral forms of choreography and their ability to elicit the audience's active participation in meaning-making processes.

In the chapters that follow, a number of practices discussed explore the space that theatre and performance opens up to examine the plurality of meanings, from the workshop practices of Pablo Pakula to Hixson and Goulish's transparent dramaturgies and Simon Bayly's poetic reflections on his experience of Ira Brand's work. Following Bel's application of Barthes to choreography, and Bel's own influence on the forms of contemporary performance discussed in this book, it seems clear that neutral modes of contemporary performance practices offer an enticing space through which to consider Barthes's more recently available ideas around neutrality as a kind of non-aggressive, parrying of meaning and the radical, philosophical and political resonances of these approaches. The meeting points traced in this introduction between Roland Barthes, on the one hand, and theatre theory and practice, on the other, demonstrate a rich generative relationship between Barthes and performance. The contributions to this volume mine that relationship further, to return to Barthes, to think with him and (re)examine his enduring influence – in search of neutral dramaturgies across a range of practices.

References

Arratia, Euridicie (1992), 'Island Hopping Rehearsing the Wooster Group's Brace up!', *The Drama Review*, 36(4): 121–42.
Artaud, Antonin (1958), *The Theatre and Its Double*, trans. Mary Caroline Richards, New York: Grove Press.
Aston, Elain, and George Savona (1991), *Theatre as Sign-System: A Semiotics of Text and Performance*, Abingdon, Oxon: Routledge.
Attridge, Derek (1997), 'Roland Barthes's Obtuse, Sharp Meaning and the Responsibilities of Commentary', in Jean Michel Rabaté (ed.), *Writing the Image After Roland Barthes*, 77–89, Philadelphia: University of Pennsylvania Press.
Auslander, Philip (2007), *Theory for Performance Studies: A Student's Guide*, Abingdon, New York: Routledge.
Badmington, Neil (2016), *The Afterlives of Roland Barthes*, London: Bloomsbury.
Badmington, Neil (2020), 'An Undefined Something Else: Barthes, Culture, Neutral Life', *Theory, Culture and Society*, 37(4): 65–76.
Bailes, Sarah Jane (2011), *Performance Theatre and the Poetics of Failure: Forced Entertainment, Goat Island, Elevator Repair Service*, Abingdon, Oxon: Routledge.
Balme, Christopher (2008), *The Cambridge Introduction to Theatre Studies*, Cambridge: Cambridge University Press.

Barker, Jeremy, and Matthew Goulish (2017), 'Every house has a door's "The Three Matadores": A Dialogue', *Culturebot* website. https://www.culturebot. org/2017/11/27798/every-house-has-a-doors-the-three-matadores-a-dialo gue/ (accessed 10 October 2020).

Barthes, Roland (1970), *Writing Degree Zero*, trans. Annette Lavers and Colin Smith, New York: Hill and Wang.

Barthes, Roland (1972a), *Critical Essays*, trans. Richard Howard, Evanston: Northwestern.

Barthes, Roland (1972b), *Mythologies*, trans. Annette Lavers, London: Vintage.

Barthes, Roland (1975), *The Pleasure of the Text*, trans. Richard Miller, New York: Hill and Wang.

Barthes, Roland (1977), *Image Music Text*, trans. Stephen Heath, London: Fontana Press.

Barthes, Roland (1982), *Empire of Signs*, trans. Richard Howard, New York: Hill and Wang.

Barthes, Roland (1983), *The Fashion System*, trans. Matthew Ward and Richard Howard, Berkeley: University of California Press.

Barthes, Roland (1993), *Camera Lucida: Reflections on Photography*, trans. Richard Howard, London: Vintage.

Barthes, Roland (2002), *S/Z*, trans. Richard Miller, London: Blackwell.

Barthes, Roland (2005), *The Neutral: Lecture Course at the Collège de France, 1977–1978*, trans. Rosalind Kraus and Denis Hollier, New York: Columbia University Press.

Barthes, Roland (2010), *Incidents*, trans. Teresa Lavender Fagan, Kolkata, India: Seagull Books.

Barthes, Roland (2011), *The Preparation of the Novel: Lecture Course and Seminars at the Collège de France (1978–1979 and 1979–1980)*, ed. Nathalie Léger, trans. Kate Briggs, New York: Columbia University Press.

Barthes, Roland (2013), *How to Live Together: Novelistic Simulations of Some Everyday Spaces*, trans. Kate Briggs, New York: Columbia University Press.

Batchen, Geoffrey, ed. (2011), *Photography Degree Zero: Reflections on Roland Barthes's* Camera Lucida, Cambridge: MIT Press.

Bel, Jérôme (2002), 'Interview with Marianne Alphant'. http://www.jeromebel. fr/index.php?p=5&cid=205 (accessed 9 October 2020).

Bel, Jérôme (2004), 'Jérôme Bel – Interview – the Last Performance (1998)', YouTube video, added by Jérôme Bel [online]. https://www.youtube.com/watch?v=ccR4rfoECkg (accessed 9 October 2017).

Bel, Jérôme (2005), 'Jérôme Bel – Interview – *nom donné par l'auteur* (1994)'. YouTube video, added by Jérôme Bel [online]. https://www.youtube.com/watch?v=NtE4Q9fKOxo&t=40s (accessed 9 October 2017).

Blau, Herbert (1987), *The Eye of Prey: Subversions of the Postmodern*, Bloomington: Indiana University Press.

Bleeker, Maaike (2008), *Visuality in the Theatre: The Locus of Looking*, New York: Palgrave Macmillan.

Bottoms, Stephen (1998), 'The Tangled Flora of Goat Island: Rhizome, Repetition, Reality', *Theatre Journal*, 50(4): 421–46.
Bottoms, Stephen, and Matthew Goulish, eds (2007), *Small Acts of Repair: Performance, Ecology and Goat Island*, Abingdon, Oxon: Routledge.
Cixous, Hélène (1976), 'The Laugh of the Medusa', trans. Keith Cohen and Paula Cohen, *Signs*, 1(4): 875–93.
Corrieri, Augusto (2011), 'Watching People in the Light: Jérôme Bel and the Classical Theatre', in Clare Finburgh and Carl Lavery (eds), *Contemporary French Theatre and Performance*, 213–23, Basingstoke: Palgrave Macmillan.
Counsell, Colin, and Laurie Wolf (2001), *Performance Analysis: An Introductory Coursebook*, London: Routledge.
Cull, Laura (2012), 'Performance as Philosophy: Responding to the Problem of "Application"', *Theatre Research International*, 37(1): 20–7.
Derrida, Jacques (2001), *The Work of Mourning*, eds. Pascale-Ann Brault and Michael Naas, Chicago: University of Chicago Press.
Duggan, Patrick (2012), *Trauma-Tragedy: Symptoms of Contemporary Performance*, Manchester: Manchester University Press.
Elam, Keir (1983), 'Much Ado About Doing Things with Words (and Other Means): Some Problems in the Pragmatics of Theatre and Drama', *Australian Journal of French Studies*, 20 (3): 261–77.
Elam, Keir (2002), *The Semiotics of Theatre and Drama*, Abingdon, Oxon: Routledge.
Etchells, Tim (1999), *Certain Fragments: Contemporary Performance and Forced Entertainment*, Abingdon, Oxon: Routledge.
ffrench, Patrick (2018), 'The Afterlives of Roland Barthes by Neil Badmington (Review)', *French Studies*, 72(1): 149–50.
Fischer-Lichte, Erika (1992), *The Semiotics of Theater*, Bloomington: Indiana University Press.
Fortier, Mark (2002), *Theory/Theatre: An Introduction*, 2nd ed., London: Routledge.
Foster, Hal (1996), *The Return of the Real: The Avant-Garde at the End of the Century*, Cambridge: MIT Press.
Foster, Susan Leigh (1986), *Reading Dancing: Bodies and Subjects in Contemporary American Dance*, Berkeley: University of California Press.
Fuchs, Elinor (1996), *The Death of Character: Perspectives on Theater After Modernism*, Bloomington: Indiana University Press.
Gregg, Melissa, and Gregory J. Seigworth, eds (2010), *The Affect Theory Reader*, Durham, NC: Duke University Press.
Heddon, Deirdre, and Jane Milling (2006), *Devising Performance: A Critical History*, Basingstoke: Palgrave Macmillan.
Irigaray, Luce (1991), 'The Bodily Encounter with the Mother', trans. David Macey, in Margaret Whitford (ed.), *The Irigaray Reader*, 34–46, Cambridge, MA: Blackwell.

Kartsaki, Eirini (2017), *Repetition in Performance: Returns and Invisible Forces*, London: Palgrave Macmillan.
Kelleher, Joe (2015), *The Illuminated Theatre: Studies on the Suffering of Images*, Abingdon, Oxon: Routledge.
Kristeva, Julia (1984), *Revolution in Poetic Language*, trans. Margaret Waller, New York: Columbia University Press.
Lagaay, Alice (2016), 'Sleepwalking through the Neutral: With Roland Barthes and Maurice Blanchot', *Performance Research: On Sleep*, 21(1): 37–41.
Lehmann, Hans-Thies (2006), *Postdramatic Theatre*, trans. Karen Jürs-Munby, London: Routledge.
Lepecki, André (2006), *Exhausting Dance: Performance and the Politics of Movement*, Abingdon, Oxon: Routledge.
Lyotard, Jean-François (1976), 'The Tooth, the Palm', trans. Anne Knap and Michel Benamou, *SubStance*, 5(15): 105–10.
Manghani, Sunil (2020), 'Neutral Life: Roland Barthes' Late Work: An Introduction', *Theatre, Culture, and Society*, 37(4): 3–34.
Marranca, Bonnie (2003), 'The Wooster Group: A Dictionary of Ideas', *Performing Arts Journal*, 74: 1–18.
Pavis, Patrice (1985), 'Theatre Analysis: Some Questions and a Questionnaire', *New Theatre Quarterly*, 1(2): 208–12.
Pavis, Patrice (1997), 'The State of Current Theatre Research', *Applied Semiotics/Sémiotique appliquée*, 1(3): 203–30.
Rabaté, Jean-Michel, ed. (1997), *Writing the Image After Roland Barthes*, Philadelphia: Pennsylvania University Press.
Rabkin, Gerald (1983), 'The Play of Misreading: Text/Theatre/Deconstruction', *Performing Arts Journal*, 7(1): 44–60.
Rabkin, Gerald (1985), 'Is There a Text on This Stage?: Theatre/Authorship/Interpretation', *Performing Arts Journal*, 9(2/3): 142–59.
Reason, Matthew (2006), *Documentation, Disappearance and the Representation of Live Performance*, Basingstoke: Palgrave Macmillan.
Savran, David (1985), 'The Wooster Group, Arthur Miller and "The Crucible"', *The Drama Review*, 29(2): 99–109.
Scheie, Timothy (2006), *Performance Degree Zero: Roland Barthes and Theatre*, Toronto: University of Toronto Press.
Schneider, Rebecca (2011), *Performing Remains: Art and War in Times of Theatrical Reenactment*, Abingdon, Oxon: Routledge.
Siegmund, Gerald (2017), *Jérôme Bel: Dance, Theatre, and the Subject*, London: Palgrave Macmillan.
Willis, Emma (2018), '"Against the Tidal Forces of the Day": Idiorrhythmy, Syncopated Subjects and the Non-Assimilative Community in the Work of Erika Vogt and Jérôme Bel', *Text and Performance Quarterly*, 38(1/2): 75–94.
Wilson, Harry Robert (2018), 'Affective Intentionalities: Practising Performance with Roland Barthes' Camera Lucida', PhD Thesis, University of Glasgow. http://theses.gla.ac.uk/30998 (accessed 1 June 2022).

Part I

A DICTIONARY OF TWINKLINGS

Chapter 1

FIVE THESES FOR A DRAMATURGY OF PERFORMANCE

Lin Hixson and Matthew Goulish
with extracts from *Exhibition* by Nathalie Léger

Prologue

I departed Chicago on Wednesday, 5 February 2003, traveling alone to Paris in less-than-ideal circumstances. I would deliver a lecture on the evening of Thursday, 6 February, the day of my arrival. Airfare costs dictated that I then remain in Paris for another two days before the return flight on Sunday morning. It seems like a fantasy now: completing one's obligation immediately, then spending surplus time wandering Le Marais, seeking out the perfect croissant and coffee, visiting the Centre Georges-Pompidou, the inside-out building, just to ride the exterior escalator in its tube. I do share the Parisian infatuation with escalators. In this state, feeling 'unfettered and alive' as it were, with the heightened attentions of aimlessness, I found myself on Saturday afternoon in an exhibit titled *Roland Barthes*. I could not understand the untranslated French texts, but I recall the quality of immersion, the care of collected notes, a video excerpt from Brecht's Berliner Ensemble production of *Mother Courage* exemplifying semiotics of theatre and a collection of photographs that seemed to track correspondences between historical figures and characters in the novels of Marcel Proust. Questions of exhibiting an archive seemed less pressing and more academic than the feelings evoked by this measured, exuberant material translation of tenderness, in which each particular type of paper, pen or card testified to the craft of the office supplies of a past era. On the flight over, the Parisian man in the seat next to me, noticing me writing preparatory notes for my lecture with a pen in the blank book that I carried in its dedicated pocket, suggested that I might like to visit the shops in the Marais. I asked him to write this new word for me on one of my book's pages. I thought of him as I stood before the exhibition's wall covered with index cards of Barthes's handwriting.

Some years later I came to read the novels of Nathalie Léger (2020), three of them published in English translation by Dorothy, A Publishing Project. I pay particular attention to writers born as I was in 1960, believing in the commonality of experience of people, even from different countries, who share the same birth year. I always sensed something of a hybrid humour and ethic for those of us of that precise age, and I came to appreciate Léger's prose constructions as *sui generis* essays in reality, departing from the point of origin of a particular film or photograph. I learned later that she had curated the Barthes exhibit into which I had wandered, in fact had been the director of the Barthes archive. She collected the lecture notes of his final courses and seminars at the Collège de France, in 1978 through 1980, into the volume titled *The Preparation of the Novel*, which included 'the remarkable biographical works and iconographic dossiers on Proust' (Barthes 2011: xxii) that I had seen at the Pompidou Centre.

When Harry Wilson invited Lin Hixson and me to collaborate on a contribution to this anthology, dedicated to Barthes's influence on performance, I had two immediate thoughts at the same time. The first recalled Lin's suggestion in 1987 that I write a manifesto for our style of performance, something I never succeeded in doing (Cull and Daddario 2013; Cull, Goulish and Hixson 2013). I thought I might revisit the directive thirty-plus years later. The second took the form of a transtemporal return to the exhibition on that innocent, rainy Saturday in February 2003, and the sense of occluded, mystical forces guiding one's feet into surroundings that feel accidental, as if they could have been otherwise, but that have an indelible determining effect on the unfolding of one's future life. I came to consider Léger's hybrid autobiographical essays as actualizations of Barthes's unfulfilled aspiration of devising a new novel form. I keep returning to their performative prose, like intricately structured extended monologues, as an exemplary mode, specifically in relation to that recursive aspect of our performance work with *Every house has a door*, that takes as one of its tasks the live retracing of the investigation through which the performance generates itself. I have several times reread the opening pages of *Exposition*, the second novel in Léger's trilogy, and found there the lines that continually reground my thinking about creativity. I have extracted some of those key moments and written five corresponding theses, with the aim of isolating fundamentals. Let us consider a fundamental an element that remains present in every instance. At the same time Lin, the director of *Every house*, has begun passing, from her computer to mine, transcribed notes from years of her directing notebooks. This wealth of material, drawn from her wide readings and processed by her lucid understanding of the spaces of performance and its recodings of time, has for me a distinctly Barthesian feel. Maybe I mean to say post-Barthesian. We speak, it seems then, from a second generation, and only indirectly of Barthes, whose presence suspends over this writing in the form of a horizon, or perhaps, more accurately, an umbrella, sheltering two or three people from the cold Paris rain.

I hope that these three braided intentions might find common transport in this collaborative essay, and that a reader will recognize them in the three discourses and voices woven here in a simple pattern. Although the pentatonic form demonstrates a distinct forward momentum, one need not read the parts in sequence to arrive at some understanding that will hopefully make itself useful in a practice, or range of practices. The passing years have brought about in me a quality of overcoding that this essay's assembly may reflect. Call it, as we must, 'the movement of the subject and of history' (Barthes 1986: 43). That is to say, a reader may begin anywhere.

Matthew Goulish
dramaturg, *Every house has a door*

§

1 – The creation of the performance begins by coincidence

The incunabula, the moment of beginning, exists. One may isolate it, pinpoint it, a pin in a map of the time in one's life. It gives birth to the process which became the performance. It takes the form of an arrested moment, a diversion, a gift of interruption, insisting itself, leaving an imprint. More than once it has happened in a 'dilapidated bookshop'. We recognize it fully only retrospectively. At the time it elicits semi-comprehension, 'a fit of mental mumbling'.

> It begins with some words of someone else. One is not led to philosophical reflection from one's own voice (or what might be

recognized, right off, as one's own voice), but from, as it were, being accosted. (Cavell 1995: 128)

Yet we do not limit this first moment to words and to voices, to those fluent egocentric realms of language. An image may accost us as profoundly, or the gesture of a human or a creature, or even the timbre of a sound, like a school bell in the morning or afternoon. In every case what stops you, and what impels the work of the performance to begin, you recognize only as that which is not already your own. It comes from outside. It belongs elsewhere. You recognize in it some aspect that has been neglected or overlooked, and issuing from this orphaned aspect, as a blank area on the map. You have no right to it, no claim on it, other than your undeniable recognition. Because of this, the blank area calls to you. It has its work to do with you. It will not release you until that labour commences. Is it labour? Is it investigation? Is it sheer multiplication of a closed set of forces? The portrait of this moment, this interruption, the first dramaturgical fundamental – does it provide insights into the subject? No, it is the subject.

> It was by coincidence, at the top of a small wooden staircase in the dilapidated bookshop of a provincial town. (Léger 2020: 8)

> *from the director's notebook:*
>
> To describe how the world is organized may be the same
>   thing as organizing the world
> At every instant, we become other than we were
>
> After reading Édouard Glissant (2020) –
>   Define oneself as much by what is excluded as included
>   Being a kin that touches at the same time that it is touched
>   Limits of knowledge
>   Object always escaping its wholeness
>   Rambling research
>   We think in generalities but live in detail

2 – *The creation of the performance demonstrates boundless unfolding*

The process unfolds and never stops unfolding – a single image, filmic or photographic, or a moment, or a line of text. In the drama of description, we always encounter the necessity of crossing modalities: the photograph that requires language; the poem that requires its own manifestation of clothing, purposefully tailored in patterns and colours, for the speaker; the movement of the body, the choreography, that requires its own accompanying stillness, silence and speech. We discover the closed set of the idea when we simultaneously discover its particular way of opening endlessly.

> And what is a motif? 'A motif, you see, is this...' said Cézanne, clasping his hands. He drew them together slowly, joined them, gripped them, made them fuse together, merging the one into the other, Gasquet recounted. That's what it is. 'This is what you have to achieve. If I go too high or too low, it's ruined.' What is my motif? Something small, very small, what will be its gesture? (Leger 2020: 24)

from the director's notebook:

A cake baked with too much yeast overflows its frame

The work of imagination unfolds in part as the continual threading of the observable—that which one may sense or experience—with the imperceptible.

We gain new understanding of ethics and justice when acknowledging that things are not predetermined but always changing and unfolding

3 – *The material of the performance remains strictly bounded*

The strict boundedness of the material demands that the performance draws nothing from outside of it, from anywhere other than its interior resources. Its boundless unfolding depends on this constraint; limits produce freedom. These boundaries include the fundamentals that the performance, after uncovering as undeniable, reclaims. The performance, for example, includes and encompasses its floor. The ground is never neutral. The performance absorbs it as it does those other features of the room which bound it and inside of which it exists: the air, its properties of circulation or stillness, the temperature and climate, the walls, the windows, the light and its sources; performance turns its material limitations back on themselves. It escapes them to the inside. The accidental transforms into the intentional. This results in part from the acceptance of the performance as never abstract or unplaced, along with the pragmatism that follows that statement. If unactualized, the performance does not exist. Performance defines the joy and the play of the actual.

> Consider the only material that presents itself, as it presents itself. (Léger 2020: 7)

from the director's notebook:

There must be necessity. Otherwise there is nothing at all.

This necessity is a very complex thing.

Limit produces space-time.

We do not invent concepts. We invent blocks of movement time.

If I string all disciplines together that are defined by their creative activity, it is because they have a common limit.

Our discipline communicates at the level of something which never disengages from itself.

4 – *The structure of the performance issues from the bounded source*

As with all of the other elements, the structure that parcels, arranges and organizes the time of the performance issues from the endless wellspring of the bounded source. Only it speaks of and from another dimension: the form given to the experience after the fact. It follows an abstractable pattern, and the genesis of the performance manifests the material in the actualization of the pattern.

Deleuze talks of the event as

> an aggregate of noncausal correspondences which form a system of echoes ... a system of signs. (Deleuze 1990: 170)

The contrast of every unexpected interface of parts speaks to the joy of creation. One may not perceive the pattern as such, as one has difficulty reading codes from the inside of the territory they recode. Immersion has its risks. Yet the progress of structure in time may bypass the senses to some degree and speak directly to the nervous system. Perception allows for more than one channel. In the end, the structure – static or dynamic, complete or decaying – offers its own essay on the material. The structure does the critical work of analysing abstraction.

> Consider the only material that presents itself, as it presents itself, in its disorder and even in its order. (Léger 2020: 7)

from the director's notebook:

> ... historical processes thought to be temporally or spatially distant continue to structure the world.
> —Jaye Austin Williams (2020)

Externalize, move to the outside

Digest things rather than justify them

Make the complex order visible

Defamiliarize belief

Make dance unrecognizable to itself

5 – The performance moves in the direction of the unknown

We understand the problem of the performance as movement in the direction of the unknown. This movement defines the performance through its telos. Because of this, the 'problem' of the performance recedes endlessly as we approach it. As unknown becomes known, unfamiliar turns familiar, a continual horizon opens. One understands the performance as intertwined with the concept of learning, unending and continually universally ungrounding, arising out of the threshold at which pattern emerges from chaos.

> On the radio one day, I heard Jean Renoir's pleasantly booming voice talking about *The Rules of the Game*: 'The subject totally gobbled

me up! A good subject always takes you by surprise and carries you away." For years, I had thought that to write you needed, at the very least, to master your subject. Many reviewers, famous writers, and critics have said that to write you have to know what you want to say. They repeat, hammering it home: you have to have something to say, about the world, about existence, about, about, about. I didn't know then that the subject is precisely what masters you. Or that the littlest thing could swallow you up. That day, I picked up a book at random; it was a book about pythons, how pythons devour things, the gaze of the animal taken by surprise, being swallowed, gobbled up by the still, ferocious subject that makes you spit out whatever you thought you knew; the enormous, hidden subject, incomprehensible, powerful, more powerful than you, tenuous, a detail, an old memory, seemingly insignificant, but it grips you, inexorably you merge with it until slowly you begin to spit out disturbing visions, elusive but insistent ghosts. (Léger 2020: 12-13)

from the director's notebook:

I have always been concerned when making work with how the presence of the unknown hangs onto and imprints the known.

I try to make that visible often by creating an experience that feels both right and slightly wrong at the same time, that breaks the viewer out of anticipating a familiar pattern while also evoking some aspect of the palpable world.

This is done with the intention of making an encounter that has a sense of responsibility and acknowledgement of the state of being other; that articulates presences we have in common and presences of difference.

In relation to animals, we need to set again our priorities and restart our sense of what it means to be human.

When directing I see the experience of performance like a magnetic field of impressions bouncing off one another.

Orchestrating echoes – a vibrating space that is fixed in some way by a frame – the walls of a room or the frame of a film.

1. Five Theses for a Dramaturgy of Performance

I see the performers as entangled events in motion.

The movement through time in the performance materializes, emerges within these relationships not outside of it.

I do not pursue clarity of expression when directing. I pare down elements and put them in relation.

Thinking means something kinetic, building up the surface by prompting different exchanges. Thinking here resembles tracking, a kind of place 'beaten by the activity of thought'.

You don't think with the mind, you think with the entire bodily existence.

Here thought has a temperature, a texture, and an erotics.

I construct modes of passage to trouble existence as we know it.

When doing this, things feel uncertain, not in already-rehearsed forms.

The more I'm able to set aside my own understandings, the more I can listen in an open way.

Performance is always larger than what one person can absorb. I want to gesture toward that largeness.

I see myself as a community.

Leela Gandhi writes about the inner life of democracy. She understands democracy as a shared art of living. She presents a version of democracy defined by inconsequentialism. This lost tradition of global democratic thought dedicates itself to an ethics of undoing, falling short, and making oneself less rather than more. It celebrates self-reduction in forms serious as well as playful, inessential, and superfluous.

How do you create a performance with a life of its own? By creating a container to hold it.

I direct using a combination of intuition and processes that cultivate surprise.

I try to pay attention to what hovers above or behind or beside a performance.

The longer that I create performances the more I trust in strangeness to show me where to go.

§§§

References

Barthes, Roland (1986), 'On Reading', in *The Rustle of Language*, trans. Richard Howard, 33–43, Berkeley: University of California Press.

Barthes, Roland (2011), *The Preparation of the Novel*, trans. Kate Briggs, text established, annotated and introduced by Nathalie Léger, New York: Columbia University Press.

Cavell, Stanley (1995), *Philosophical Passages: Wittgenstein, Emerson, Austin, Derrida*, Oxford: Blackwell.

Cull, Laura, Matthew Goulish and Lin Hixson (2013), 'A Diluted Manifesto', in Matthew Causey and Fintan Walsh (eds), *Performance, Identity, and the Neo-Political Subject*, 119–37, New York: Routledge.

Cull, Laura, and Will Daddario, eds. (2013), *Manifesto Now! Instructions for Performance, Philosophy, Politics*, Bristol: Intellect.

Deleuze, Gilles (1990), *The Logic of Sense*, trans. Mark Lester, New York: Columbia University Press.

Glissant, Édouard (2020), *Sun of Consciousness*, trans. Nathanaël, New York: Nightboat.

Léger, Nathalie (2020), *Exposition*, trans. Amanda Demarco, St. Louis, MO: Dorothy, A Publishing Project.

Williams, Jaye Austin (2020), *Teacher* [online]. http://jayeaustinwilliams.com/teacher (accessed 9 April 2022).

Chapter 2

CEASELESSLY POSITING AND EVAPORATING MEANING: A PERFORMANCE SCORE

Pablo Pakula

Figure 2.1 serves two purposes. On the one hand, it gives a sense of the spatial arrangement required for the score. On the other, it distils its basic components to their simplest formulation and therefore could itself be understood as a kind of Barthesian blueprint which allows space for the reader's interpretation and points towards the score's adaptability and openness.

Timings:

- Minimal set up, with no prior preparation or rehearsal needed.
- The piece[1] should last at least twenty minutes, though it could be longer or even be presented durationally.

Materials needed:

- A room with space to move.
- Some people as spectators, arranged along one side of the room, looking onto the area functioning as the stage: the Audience.
- A small group of performers who will remain upstage [between five and seven people works well, in order to open up possibilities without crowding the space]: the Ensemble.

---

1. Since the score could be used, adapted and presented as either a performance or a workshop exercise, I will simply refer to its outcome as 'the piece'.

- A single performer who will remain downstage: the Scriptor.
- Writing implements: a thick marker pen, and an A4 notebook [alternatively a small whiteboard could be used, though this will not have the same aural or visual qualities as the paper].
- A chair placed at the edge of the stage, downstage, facing the Audience.
- [optional] A few more chairs and a table for the upstage area.

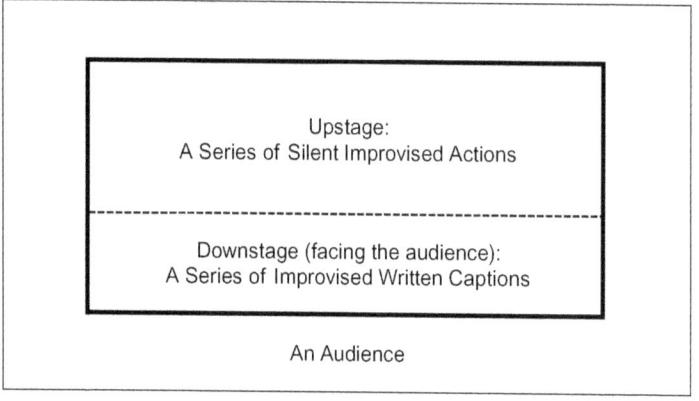

Figure 2.1 Spatial arrangement for 'The Death of the Author' score.

The score:

[NB: Having identified the stage space and where the Audience will watch from, start by drawing an imaginary line to divide the stage in two halves, an upstage and a downstage area. The Ensemble should not cross this line, remaining upstage for the duration of the piece. Optionally, some chairs and a table could be used to give this upstage area some spatial interest for the Ensemble. A single chair should be placed at the edge of the stage, downstage and facing the audience. This chair could be brought on by the Scriptor, but having it on stage from the start creates a sense of anticipation. The piece begins with all performers off stage and the Audience in place.]

1. The Ensemble enter upstage and begin a silent improvisation that involves simple movements or actions. For instance, they could improvise using a restricted vocabulary of simple tasks: standing,

walking, running, sitting down, jumping up, and collapsing to the floor. Individuals may occasionally and briefly leave the stage, as these entrances and exits can add dynamism, but the Ensemble should continue their improvisation until the end of the piece.

[NB: There is no need for characterization or acting from the Ensemble. In fact, the piece works best when expressions, if there are any, are genuine rather than being performed. The Ensemble need only to listen and respond to each other on impulse and in the moment, using the simple tasks with spontaneity. It helps to invoke Anne Bogart and Tina Landau's Viewpoints – encouraging the Ensemble to improvise with a particular awareness of tempo, duration, kinaesthetic response, spatial relationship and repetition.[2] Other movement principles, guidelines or rules could also be employed to help the Ensemble engage in a dynamic and ever-changing improvisation.]

2. After a few minutes for this upstage activity to become established, the Scriptor enters downstage with their writing implements and sits down on the chair facing the Audience.
3. Staying focused on the Audience and without looking upstage, where the Ensemble continues their improvisation, the Scriptor thinks of a caption that could accompany a randomly imagined scenario or image. They write it down in the notebook or whiteboard, hold it up for a moment so the Audience can read it, and then discard it by tearing off the page or wiping off their writing. They then think of a new caption and repeat the process ad infinitum. The Scriptor writes captions in a freely improvised manner so the possibilities are endless. Roughly, the captions will probably do one of the following:
   - refer to time and/or space with varying degrees of specificity (e.g. 1916, a village in Siberia, after the explosion, the moment the lights are turned on in a club, the Oval Office in exactly five minutes);
   - use common expressions and cultural reference points with varying degrees of currency and/or irreverence (e.g. between a rock and a hard place, point of no return, somewhere over the rainbow, the winter of our discontent, Zombie attack, Arnold Schwarzenegger's comeback film, Donald Trump's wet dream); or

---

2. See Bogart and Landau (2005).

- go beyond description and perform an action in themselves (e.g. S.O.S, Help! For Sale).
  [NB: As the piece progresses, the Scriptor can begin to play with the tempo and rhythm of their writing, as well as their relationship with the Audience, in a more deliberate manner – sometimes rushing or slowing down, leaving deliberate pauses or suspensions, sometimes crossing things out or discarding captions before having shown them to the Audience.]
4. The simultaneous upstage and downstage improvisations can last as long as desired, even durationally. To begin to bring the piece to a close, the Scriptor gets up and leaves the stage. The Ensemble should continue their improvisation for a few minutes, thus ensuring the piece ends as it began (i.e. with just the upstage improvisation and no downstage captions). After this final moment, the Ensemble also make their exit and the piece comes to an end.

   [NB: A neat way for the Scriptor to make their exit is to write 'The End' as the last caption, hold it up and then leave – with the option of dragging the chair behind them as they go for added effect. If used in a classroom setting, the score could be followed by a group discussion.]

In the early 2010s, whilst teaching at the University of Kent's Drama and Theatre department, I developed the above score, which I titled 'The Death of the Author' as a shorthand. It outlines the basic instructions for a performance situation and/or workshop exercise composed of two simultaneous yet independent improvisations, juxtaposing movements with written text through chance and without causal relationship. The score was initially an attempt to help students specialising in contemporary performance become more familiar with these practices and vocabularies, whilst at the same time gaining an embodied understanding of the central ideas in Roland Barthes's seminal essay. The score thus aims to destabilise students' oftentight grip on – and narrow conception of – meaning as a singular or fixed entity, and to trouble their sometimes-rigid understandings of authorship and authorial intent. It encourages them to not worry excessively about what things mean/signify and instead work in a more intuitive way, acknowledging the audience's fundamental role as co-authors of any meaning(s).

It is worth pointing out there is nothing original about the score. In line with Barthes, it is a 'a tissue of citations, resulting from the thousand sources of culture'; it 'consists of multiple writings ... entering into dialogue with each other, into parody, into contestation' (1967).[3] The score is indebted to various performance vocabularies and practices: Fluxus's task-based instructions, the pedestrian movements of Postmodern dance, Anne Bogart and Tina Landau's Viewpoints, Forced Entertainment's lists and use of placards, the chance procedures of Merce Cunningham's choreographies or the Surrealists' 'collective writing' of the Exquisite Corpse. In that sense, in putting the score together I have operated like Barthes's Scriptor who 'can only imitate a gesture forever anterior, never original', and whose 'only power is to combine the different kinds of writing' – someone who mixes and samples existing material (1967).

The score is designed in a way that resists hypostases; it 'ceaselessly posits meaning but always in order to evaporate it: it proceeds to a systematic exemption of meaning' (Barthes 1967). Instead of presenting the audience with singular, static or definite readings, these are forever deferred, both generating and dissipating the possibility for meaning(s). In doing so, it makes overt demands on the audience, repositioning them as active participants and co-authors of the piece. Nevertheless, their role is not just to organize or decipher meanings which are already present on stage, waiting to be grasped. Spectatorship, as set up by the score, is not a process of encountering and discovering something fixed but one that keeps the dynamism of meaning open and apparent. Indeed, the score itself 'has no other content than the act by which it is uttered' (Barthes 1967); its primary content is none other than the audience's own dynamic meaning-making processes. The audience has to be understood as 'the very space in which are inscribed, without any being lost, all the citations a writing consists of; the unity of a text is not in its origin, it is in its destination' (Barthes 1967). Indeed, since the score is a multidimensional space that automatically generates a plethora of movements and texts, the audience is the destination

---

3. I am following John Logie's suggestion to cite the original publication of 'The Death of the Author'. This was not the 1968 French publication, but an English translation by Richard Howard which first appeared in *Aspen: The Magazine in a Box*, no. 5+6 The Minimalist Issue. To take this as the urtext allows us to understand Barthes's text, not as a literary essay, but 'as a participant in a collection of artistic manifestos and provocations' (Logie 2013: 510), alongside contributions by Samuel Beckett, William S. Burroughs, John Cage and Merce Cunningham amongst others.

holding together all the different strands which constitute the piece – not only those appearing on stage at any one point, but also those that have come and gone; not only those that appear to make sense with one another, but also those that clash. Therefore, the piece does not play out on stage as much as it does in the mind of each audience member.

References

Barthes, Roland (1967), 'The Death of the Author', *Aspen: The Magazine in a Box*, no. 5+6 The Minimalist Issue. https://www.ubu.com/aspen/aspen5and6/index.html (accessed 15 February 2022).

Bogart, Anne, and Tina Landau (2005), *The Viewpoints Book: A Practical Guide to Viewpoints and Composition*, New York: Theatre Communications Group.

Logie, John (2013), '1967: The Birth of "The Death of the Author"', *College English*, 75(5): 493–512.

Chapter 3

LOOKING THROUGH OLD PHOTOGRAPHS

Andy Field and Deborah Pearson

Dear Deborah,

    It's the end of January 2021, which means that it is exactly 16 years since we first met. I don't have any photographs of that time but maybe you do. I remember you wore cowboy boots and your hair was bleached blonde. I have no memory of what I was wearing. If this sounds like the beginning of a romance then maybe that's intentional. Perhaps it is a sort of romance. An almost romance, and therefore not actually a romance at all.

    I might be straying from the point before I've even started. I think if anything this opening exists primarily to remind you and I and anyone else reading not to be afraid of sentiment.

    Not that I think we ever have been.

    We have agreed to write together about a trilogy of pieces that you made about time and we are already outrageously late in doing so. Those pieces are themselves now past, made between 2010 and 2016 in a period when we ran a venue together at the Edinburgh Festival. A period when your work was very different to the work you make today. A period before you and your husband Morgan had had your first child, Felix. A period before the Coronavirus pandemic. It is an experience of ourselves and of the world that we are now so profoundly exiled from that we might call it history.

    It feels important to locate these three pieces in time, not only because they are themselves about time but because they are also about you, or at least the version of you that existed back then. They spoke to what I think of as preoccupations of yours during that period – time, identity, transit, transience, mortality, memory, loss. Perhaps these preoccupations were partly a consequence of your experience of being a migrant, and the tangible separation this created between your present and your past – a gap as wide as the Atlantic Ocean – and the opportunity that created to reflect on and reconstitute the pieces of oneself.

In *Like You Were Before* (2010) you used camcorder footage recorded on your last day in Toronto before moving to the UK as a means of attempting to understand the distance between the person you were in the video and the person you were on the stage in front of us.

In *The Future Show* (2014) you quite deliberately shifted from looking backwards to looking forward, writing a new future for yourself each time the piece was performed, beginning with the applause that you imagined would end the show and finishing years later with your death, which every time was the same, old, at peace, reaching up to grab a jar of peaches from a high shelf.

In *History History History* (2016), the final part in this informal trilogy, you returned to a story about your grandfather, a comic star of early Polish Cinema, that you'd first tried to tell nearly a decade previously in a play for the Tarragon Theatre in Toronto. This time however you reorganised your telling of it around your own relationship to your grandfather and to the material traces of that story that still remain: old pictures, slides, timelines, audio recordings, and, at the centre of it all, one of your grandfather's original films, which plays out in its entirety across the length of the show.

These pieces might be called autobiographical, in that you perform them, and they are about you. But really, when examined closely, each slips away from this categorisation in its own slightly different way. *Like You Were Before* isn't really a story about you. In some ways it is the opposite of a story – a single afternoon frozen in time, separated from its context and examined, like a pebble plucked from a beach and placed upon a shelf. *The Future Show* is almost but not really an autobiography, in that it is a story about a life you haven't lived yet. Although the person in the story is unmistakably you, the story itself is more like speculative fiction than autobiography. And although *History History History* is a wonderful biographical story about a remarkable life, it is not your life – you sit at the margins of that story, trying with your mother's help to translate the words your grandfather is saying; trying to understand who this man is to you.

Instead, the figure that I think of when I think of these three pieces is that of Roland Barthes in the second part of *Camera Lucida*, his final book, alone in the apartment in which his mother had recently died, looking through old photographs of her, one by one under the lamp 'gradually moving back in time with her, looking for the truth of the face I had loved' (Barthes 1993: 67).

You also, in your three pieces, are I think always looking through traces, in pursuit of something – some truth, some feeling. In *Like You Were Before*, you flick backwards and forwards through the grainy camcorder footage recorded years before, wrapping your mouth around old words, inserting yourself into old conversations with friends who, like you, are no longer the people in the video, in a city that is no longer home. In *The Future Show* you scan through the pages in the binder in front of you, like a diary in reverse, plotting out the significant moments in your life like a pilot plotting a flightpath. And in every performance of *History History History* you watch your grandfather perform his starring role, looking for something familiar, the way he holds his head perhaps, his gait, his sweetness, his fundamental gentleness, something of yourself in him.

'And here the essential question first appeared: did I *recognise* her?' Barthes says. 'I never recognised her except in fragments, which is to say I missed her *being*, and that therefore I missed her altogether.' (1993: 65–6).

What do you recognise in these traces you have assembled?[1]

There was a moment in an early version of *The Future Show* that I once saw, when you performed a note-perfect impression of yourself. Sat at a desk in an outfit that, you slyly point out, we the audience probably didn't realise was a costume, the affectless calm of your delivery (which I hadn't even noticed until that point as either affectless or unusually calm) broke and the chatty, goofy version of you that I have grown to love so much appeared suddenly in your body like a newly-arrived spirit at a séance. It was uncanny. To know yourself well enough to be able to summon yourself like that. To recognise the fragments of yourself and how they are assembled. And how they can be reassembled. To find some truth, some feeling, amidst the fragments.

Barthes quotes Nietzsche's prophecy 'A labyrinthine man never seeks the truth, but only his Ariadne' (1993: 73). The Winter Garden photograph is Barthes's Ariadne – not because it enabled him to discover a secret, but because it revealed the thread that drew him to photography. There is, undoubtedly a thread wound through your

---

1. Can we hear Barthes's distinctions between photography and film? Where photography captures a moment that, in its stillness, is 'ceaselessly drawn toward' the viewer, film 'does not cling to me' but 'flow[s] by' (1993: 87–8) [HW].

trilogy of pieces, slipping between past, present and future – but where or who or what is that thread drawing you on to? And where might it lead those of us in the audience who are following you?

Dear Sweet Andy,

    It feels almost cruel to start with these details, but I must.
    They were not cowboy boots, they were Camper twins.
    It was not reaching for a can of peaches that killed me in *The Future Show* but reaching for dog and cat food. (I never specify which).
    My grandfather was not a Polish comic film star, but a Hungarian one.
    This last one is best, of course. The idea that I would be half Polish and not half Hungarian conjures a wonderful other version of me that could not possibly exist. It's so fitting for *History History History* because it was a show about the ways in which these sedimented layers of seemingly unpredictable occurrences in the past gather into a history that we are so embedded in it's terrifying. You might say that the show is actually about unpicking the fact that without the Hungarian uprising in 1956, I would not exist. This is why I love this alternative impossible insertion of Poland into a memory of the narrative. As I mention in the show, there was a 'mini uprising' against the Soviets in 1956 in Poland as well. Different countries in Eastern Europe are understandably easy to mix up in our memories, but that mix up renders my personal history impossible. It's kind of wonderful.
    But now onto time. I used to be so preoccupied with its breadth and now I want to say I'm preoccupied with its depth. I'm not sure if that's true or not but it sounds good and I want to say it.
    I have a stolen twenty minutes that I've negotiated with my baby's father. That's how long I've given myself to write this. My baby's father doesn't even know that I'm writing, I think he thinks I'm in the other room working on my taxes. Lyn Gardner once told me that everything takes as long as we have for it. If you give yourself a year to write an essay it will take that long. If you give yourself twenty minutes, well, good luck.
    It's amazing that it's been sixteen years that we've known each other. It feels longer yet when I think about the fact that if a baby were born the day you leant me that Bob Dylan CD I never

gave back, they might now be considering having sex or having a lot of sex, well that's weird isn't it? And not just because talking about a baby growing up to have sex is always weird. I think that CD might still be in my parents' basement. Unless I've also misremembered.

Memory is one of the reasons I've always had a slightly uncomfortable relationship with performance theory in general. A literary academic can write an article about a poem, and then the reader can go to that published poem themselves and have something like a common footing to consider the academic's work. The same is true of film theory – if I write about *Touch of Evil*, presuming you're also watching the recut from the 1990s, we can see the same film, and you can read my thoughts about that film armed with the primary source. In performance you are essentially reading theory-based deconstructions of someone else's memory of something. A Hungarian becomes a Pole. Dog food become peaches. The CD in the basement might have been returned to you after all. (I also remember being embarrassed and giving it back to you all scratched up. Did I invent that too?) I think there is something very beautiful about an entire field of research that's really based on in depth writing about each other's flawed memories. What bothers me though is how infrequently that's acknowledged. Or maybe it is frequently acknowledged, but it can never be acknowledged enough really.[2]

Like You Were Before was not my first piece, as you know.

I'd written plays, some of which were sometimes staged at smaller theatres like The Albany in Deptford or Shunt, or staged as readings at places like RADA. I was ever hopeful that someday an agent would see something, pluck me out of one act obscurity, and make an honest woman out of me. It never happened.

I was also making intimate work that I performed in. The beautiful Adrian Howells informally guided me, sometimes mentored me, and I would find myself befriending small

---

2. The *punctum*, photography's wounding detail, is 'revealed only after the fact' in our memory of the image (Barthes 1993: 53). The punctum *develops* through a process that works with (mis)memory, time, feeling. Was Barthes inadvertently giving us tools to understand performance? [HW]

audiences and trying to be both close and far. BAC[3] were paying me for this work, and even occasionally referring to me as a 'mid-career artist' which terrified me because I had no idea what I was doing. They might have just assumed I was mid-career because I'm tall.

I proposed *Like You Were Before* to BAC producer Laura Collier on a bus, on my way to making one of these intimate shows. I really had to sell her on the idea that I could perform in front of a larger audience. I remember telling her I had a lot of experience public speaking from high school and university, and I was sure that would help me through. BAC gave me one of the smallest rooms in the building to develop the show in, and the first work-in-progress audience was about 12 people because that was the largest number of people who could fit in that tiny room. Equally, when the show went to Edinburgh, it was technically a 'hit' but I staged it in the video store where I used to work, and I think I remember around 12 people being almost the most that we could cram in there. It was only when it toured that I found myself in larger rooms, talking to dozens of people at the same time. I still remember a series of texts from Daniel Kitson after a disastrous performance at Arnolfini, where he told me not to be scared of the big room. He told me to only look at the people in the audience rather than the room itself. To try to connect with them. This again, is a tangent though. It's a part of that show's memory I haven't written about before or even thought much about before – its role as a way to help me speak to larger crowds. This is a brand-new memory that has only just been excavated after fifteen years.

The show was mostly developed by me filming myself on my laptop camera and watching the material back. If I found whatever I was doing too boring to watch I assumed an audience would too. I'd worked with directors and actors up until then. I had no idea how to make a show on my own, so that odd filmed process seemed as good as any. The amount of filmed footage that I've probably never revisited on a laptop

---

3. Battersea Arts Centre in London. The venue was influential in supporting and developing intimate and one-to-one performance (see Zerihan [2009] and Heddon and Johnson [2016]) [HW].

that may no longer exist of me as a 26-year-old doing boring things also feels interesting to me somehow. This is because, as you know, the projected video that forms the spine of *Like You Were Before* was nearly never watched again after it was first filmed. And that, my dear Andy, is largely due to you.

You had borrowed my camera to do some research on a project. You'd returned it to me, but lost its charger. It was a North American camera and at the time the terrifying convenience of online shopping had not taken over our lives yet. So, getting a new charger seemed hard, and the camera seemed trapped within itself. Without a way to charge up, it was just this deadened object. I don't even remember how I got a new charger, or if after years of maybe feeling a little bad about it, you got me a new charger. I just remember that I didn't use the camera for five years, and one day I had a charger, and plugged it in, and watched the video that lived inside of it.

It was a video of the first day I'd owned the camera, and the last day I'd lived in Canada before moving to the UK in 2005.

Watching this footage for the first time five years later was the closest I've ever felt to time travelling. And I wanted to make a show about that feeling. I (misremembered?) something from Roland Barthes's *Camera Lucida* about the madness of photography. Something about how there was a kind of inherent madness in modern times that we could look at a photograph and take it for granted. That we wouldn't just spend hours having our minds blown by this captured ghost. That's what I remembered of the Barthes quote, though it's almost certainly wrong. I've gone searching for it in the book since and never been able to really find it.[4]

But a combination of misremembering Barthes and you losing my camera charger are key here. They are the ways in which these sedimented layers of seemingly unpredictable occurrences in the past gather into a history that I am so embedded in it's terrifying. You might say that without them,

---

4. For Barthes, the 'image-repertoire', the circulation and consumption of images in society has the power to tame Photography's 'madness', its ability to produce 'desire without mediation' (1993: 119) [HW].

I would not exist. *Like You Were Before* was not my first piece, but it really started everything, and it might be the touchstone in my work that I return to most frequently. A show about losing time.

Speaking of which, I told Morgan I needed twenty minutes, and now it's been forty.

Dear Deborah,

Are there really no Tinned Peaches at all in the future show?

When I think of that show I think of tinned peaches – soft orange slices in syrup and a green label with a picture of a whole peach on one side, perhaps with a single leaf still attached to the stalk. In my imagination, you are standing alone in a kitchen that looks exactly like my parents' old kitchen (how the kitchen used to look, not how it looks now). You are gazing out of the window at small birds landing on the grass in the garden, and then you turn around and reach for a can of tinned peaches from the topmost shelf in the corner, and as you do so the slightest shift in your equilibrium causes you to fall backwards, hitting your head on the counter behind you.

I agree with you that there is something both beautiful and disquieting about live performance's relationship to memory and remembrance. That by writing it down here my fanciful description of the ending of *The Future Show* now exists as tangibly as anything that was performed onstage. In *The Future Show*, as in any live performance, the author is dead before the audience have even finished applauding. I like to think that someone reading this will, one day many years from now, have cause to remember that show about the future where the lady hits her head and they will ask themselves whether they just read about it or if they actually saw it, and then they will remember the colour of the label on the peach tin and they will think to themselves, yes, it's all coming back to me now.

Performance memory is self-consciously unreliable, but I think if anything this makes it simply more honest than film or literature – or at least, more aware of its fragility and its instability, less misguidedly confident of its immutability. After all, CDs scratch, photographs fade, films are recut, or are lost altogether. Videos get stuck in cameras because inconsiderate friends lose your camera charger and don't buy you a new one for another five years, and when that video finally escapes from the camera, it is no longer the same video that went in anymore. The world around it has changed, and so has the relationship the video has to it.

3. Looking Through Old Photographs

Words wriggle on the page just as the images in a film are constantly shifting in meaning. Who do we see when we watch Rock Hudson and Doris Day now? When the Twin Towers appear in an establishing shot of New York in *Ghostbusters* or *Superman* or *Zoolander* what does it make us feel? I've been thinking about this instability a lot recently, sat at home during lockdown watching movie after movie in bustling cities, bodies packed in tightly next to one another waiting at a crosswalk, or squeezed into a booth in a diner, or throwing punches in a packed bar. These images that were once employed to signify a familiarity, that the characters on screen lived lives much like ours, now speak to me of alienation and of loss. I am estranged from these characters and their lives in a way that the filmmakers never intended. The film has changed.

Michel de Certeau, borrowing as Barthes does from Saussure, talks about consumption as a kind of secondary production characterised 'by its ruses, its fragmentation, its poaching, its clandestine nature, its tireless but quiet activity, in short by its quasi-invisibility' (de Certau 1984: 31). It is this fragmented, clandestine, inexhaustible and yet barely-visible production of meaning that we are all always engaged in when we're watching a theatre show or a film, or reading a book, or listening to a record, or sitting by a lamp looking through a series of photographs. It is a meaning that belongs to us and only to us, that carries no meaning for anyone else.

'I cannot reproduce the Winter Garden Photograph', Barthes says. 'It exists only for me. For you it would be nothing but an indifferent picture, one of the thousand manifestations of the "ordinary"' (1993: 73).

What is I think so beautiful and so rare in your trilogy of time pieces, is that you have in each case found a means of representing this 'quasi-invisible' process whereby we each produce such profound meaning from the 'ordinary' documents – the films, the videos, the stories – we encounter in our lives. As an audience we see both how these documents exist for you, and how they exist differently for us.

Perhaps because of the unusual way you arrived at making them, beginning so intimately, with such small numbers of audience members, your solo performances are structured differently to a lot of other solo work that I have seen. Under normal circumstances, a solo performance is structured around a single relational vector – that between the audience and the performer. Just as you describe Daniel Kitson telling you, the conventional wisdom in such a performance is for the performer to look to and connect with the audience.

But in each of your pieces you are never looking only to the audience. In *Like You Were Before* you return again and again to the video you recorded so many years earlier. In *The Future Show* your eyes are drawn down to the binder in front of you containing the story of your life foretold in chronological order, one concise paragraph at a time. And at points in *History History History* you literally turn away from the audience to watch with us, becoming one of us, as your grandfather's film plays out on the cinema screen behind you. I think in each instance the effect is the same – that the piece becomes a kind of a duet, between yourself and the document, and in a duet our attention is always shared by both partners.

So, we watch you and we see the meaning you have constructed from these documents – we see that quiet, intimate process whereby these films and stories are imbued with the power to transport you. We see the *justesse* of these traces – the truths that they contain for you about who you are and who you might one day be.[5] We see how these fragments have become a time machine. And at the same time we see also what these same objects are to us. We shape our own meanings, full of errors and elisions, projections and distortions, cowboy boots and tinned peaches.

There in those darkened theatres, I could perhaps catch a glimmer, briefly, of all the things that separate my life from yours. I could feel the fundamental unknowability of your experience of the world. I understood that there is no secret to be uncovered in your stories, no greater truth about you or about me, only the thread that draws all of us forward toward one another.

Dear Andy,

It has now been over a month since you wrote me what you described in your email as the 'second and last letter' about my trilogy on time. Meanwhile, my embodied experience of time has been both vast and terse. I am ensconced in the intimate and small pockets of daily childcare time that will be all too familiar to other new parents. Every day is really routine and really not, as that routine breaks down and remakes itself by increments. Complete boredom gives way to sudden jolts of awareness

---

5. '"Not a just image, just an image," Godard says. But my grief wanted a just image, an image which would be both justice and accuracy—*justesse*: just an image, but a just image. Such, for me, was the Winter Garden Photograph' (Barthes 1993: 70) [HW].

of what it means to spend months observing a baby. How impossibly and frighteningly precious that time will soon seem, and already is. On top of which there's a larger social change to our collective experience of time. We are a year into a pandemic and there is somehow time to watch every episode of *Schitt's Creek* three times or more, whilst there is also no time to write an email, to advocate for ourselves, to do anything creative.

I don't know what Roland Barthes would make of this. I don't like to admit that I sometimes think about how he died in 1980 after being hit by a bread truck.[6] I hate mentioning how anyone died, and luckily his life was significant enough that his death is an afterthought. It was quick, unforeseen and random, while his work was certainly not that. But something about my resistance to think about that points me to the fact that even the most critically celebrated writing about time, its passage, the shape of a life, can also somehow get it so wrong. Or get it so right. Frank Kermode writes in his book *The Sense of an Ending* (1967) about how palpable our desire to see things end is, because of the existential hardship of being born and dying *in medias res* – in the middle of history. These conceptions of the passage of time that make sense primarily from within our own lifespan. I guess it's just that I'm thinking about grief lately. The loss of a loved one, the loss of a year, the loss of the ability to write, to watch upsetting dramas, to pay attention, to be present with a growing baby, with ourselves, with our friends, with our laptops. How is grief distinct from memory? Grief is the shock of absence. The gawping and immutable absence of something and coming to terms with how unchanging that is. Memory, however, like all living things is a process. It is about the persistent and mercurial presence of something. A new kind of presence that moves with us.

After 1980 there was no more new writing by Barthes. There may have been some unpublished texts that surfaced, but his work had become a finite thing, a legacy, to be applied to the present moment sometimes adequately and sometimes inadequately. Aware of that same finitude, Barthes is not grieving his mother, but remembering her. He looks through these photographs of her looking for something familiar and yet also looking for a further iteration. To compare the document to his

---

6. A laundry service truck [HW].

present. To facilitate memory through watching how that finite image has changed. I think of the dozens of times performing *History History History* that I watched my grandfather as a young man in the Hungarian football comedy he starred in. When I began making the show I was the same age as he was in that film. Then through touring the show, I got older. Eventually I was three years older than he was, then four years older. The film wouldn't and couldn't change, but my perception of it kept remaking itself, and in that way breathing a life and personal meaning into it for me that, you're right, I invited an audience to witness. Even with these finite records, the way we look at them is always evolving and changing, as long as there are living people who bring themselves to them. A routine self that breaks down and remakes itself by increments. The distance between the finitude of these documents, these tangible objects, and the ways that our perception of them changes, lets the grief they are linked to gradually become a memory that is suffused not with death but with life. Not in the way that we understand life, but in another way – in a way that what is gone can both be static and finite and somehow still change with us.

In lots of ways after this year the person I was feels completely lost to me now. This person is not lost in the gentle drifting way of the 2005 video-self in *Like You Were Before*. This is a sudden and complete shift that feels more like adolescence than anything I've experienced since I was 13 years old. I don't know if it's parenthood or the pandemic, but I routinely look at pictures of myself on holiday in 2017, trying to capture a glimpse of the person I used to recognise.

There's something melancholy and moving about encountering what feels now like this former version of myself in your occasionally impressively accurate and occasionally impressively inaccurate memories of my shows. I see your mis-rememberings as a kind of *punctum* that just goes to reinforce how impressive your recall actually is. Particularly your recall of continental philosophers! Perhaps what I appreciate most is that contradiction in feeling so strongly that I've changed in ways I haven't even reconciled myself to, (the grief), while having a friend stubbornly and joyously carry this continuously adapting memory of who I've been to them. A tie to my past work, to my past selves, to a time we may not have any photographs of, but that we know happened.

It's March of 2021. And the continuity you have brought me through insisting on the *justesse* of your memories feels a bit like hope. For that I would like to say, to you and Roland Barthes and heck to the entire field of performance theory, thank you for trawling those records in search of something to love.

References

Barthes, Roland (1993), *Camera Lucida: Reflections on Photography*, trans. Richard Howard, London: Vintage.

de Certau, Michel (1984), *The Practice of Everyday Life*, trans. Steven Rendall, Berkeley: University of California Press.

Heddon, Deirdre, and Dominic Johnson, eds (2016), *It's All Allowed: The Performances of Adrian Howells*, Bristol: Intellect.

Kermode, Frank (1967), *The Sense of an Ending: Studies in the Theory of Fiction*. Oxford: Oxford University Press.

Zerihan, Rachel (2009), 'One to One Performance: A Study Room Guide on Works Devised for an 'Audience of One', *LADA Study Room Guide*, London: Live Art Development Agency. https://www.thisisliveart.co.uk/wp-content/uploads/uploads/documents/OnetoOne_Final.pdf (accessed 16 April 2022).

Chapter 4

RECIPES/ADDENDUMS/SOUVENIRS

greenandowens (Katheryn Owens and Chris Green)

How these recipes are constructed

Food / Friendship / Care

The recipes that follow are not necessarily ones we have come up with ourselves, however they have been shared together. Like all recipes, these can be taken literally, but they can (and should) be taken and changed to suit. The important thing about the recipes is the potential of them to be shared, but likewise, they may also be eaten alone. The recipes consist of three parts; together offering the things needed to recreate the meals we have had.

1. *Recipes*

The traditional format of an ingredient list, followed by the instructions which need to be followed in order to complete the recipe and cook the food in the way that is intended. These follow a similar structure for each meal. This part of the writing might be considered as a readerly text. However, as some of the recipes are not fully our own invention, we have had to change some of the steps slightly in order not to get into trouble.

Recipes in this way are used often and in a range of settings, they are structurally familiar and easily recognisable. Recipes are cultural artefacts. We have given measurements that may not be suitable for some audiences. We have tried to keep the instructions as clear and as easy to follow as possible. This part of the text can stand alone – someone may choose to only follow this part.

2. *Addendums*

Add-end-ems as is the case with any, and all, recipes there is a level of interpretation which comes here. In this section of the text we highlight the ways that we changed and mixed up the ingredients, the process of making or any extra bits we might have added in or taken away. This is a process of personalisation, for example we will always add double the amount of garlic to any ingredient list, someone else might choose to make something extremely spicy (something that we could not handle).

It is also an invitation; for others to change the recipe to suit their own needs (and those of any other guests they may be entertaining). This section might see people create the meal for people with specific dietary needs e.g. vegan, halal, coeliac etc. People may also wish to change certain spices, flavours or ingredients dependent on availability or budget. This section opens up the recipe to manipulation.

3. *Souvenir*

These are our personal memories and reflections that we associate with the recipes, foregrounded by our first memories of eating the meals. This is the point where we think about and reflect on the relationship between food and memory. This is where we hope to connect to others through the ways that we share food and the things that we remember about what the sharing of the food was like.

In a similar way to section two, we invite those who engage with the texts to reflect on who they were with when they first ate, what the food might remind them of, how the food might help them to care for themselves, care for other people and care for each other.

This section of the text is about the specifics of the performance of cooking (and of eating).

4. Recipes/Addendums/Souvenirs

Smashed Aubergine

Sharing / party

A side dish that can be used as a dip or vegetable accompaniment. This recipe is flavoursome but can look visually unappealing.

1. Ingredients:

   1 kg aubergines
   ½ tablespoon salt
   4 garlic cloves skins left on
   5 tablespoons olive oil, plus extra for drizzling
   ½ lemon, zest and juice
   3 tablespoons finely chopped parsley

   Method: 1. Preheat the oven to 200c / Gas 6. Cut the tops off the aubergines and then cut them into approx 1–2cm sized cubes. 2. Put them in a sieve that is set over a bowl and sprinkle them with salt. Set aside for 30 minutes. 3. Bash the garlic with the flat of a knife to crack the cloves slightly. Lightly rinse the salt from the aubergines and pat dry with kitchen paper if available. If not give them a shake. 4. Toss the aubergine with the garlic, olive oil and lemon zest on a foil lined baking tray. (The aubergine gets quite sticky so can be difficult to clean off an unlined baking tray). Season (a little salt and pepper) and roast it for 30–40 minutes – or longer if required, until it is golden and soft. 5. Remove the aubergine from the oven and squeeze over the lemon juice. Mix it, and gently smash the aubergine with a fork, until it has a chunky consistency like a very thick sauce or dip. 6. Transfer it to a plate or bowl and garnish with parsley. Serve warm drizzled with a little oil.

2. Could mix in other grilled vegetables, like tomatoes, to bulk it out if you don't have enough aubergines (aubergines are kinda expensive). Or it amounts to approx 4 aubergines / Add at least 2 garlic cloves to whatever the recipe recommends / Can measure olive oil by sight, if it looks like enough oil it will do. It does not matter if you forget to drizzle olive oil on at the end, or if you forget about the lemon / Only use the parsley if you want to feel fancy; it's a garnish and not a key ingredient / Salting is because aubergines used to be bitter and the salt draws this out, though most aubergines now have this bred out of them. So, if you are

short on time, skip this step. You could do it for the ritual of it / Bashing garlic enhances the flavour as it releases the oils / Zaatar also makes a nice seasoning / There are lots of ways to adjust or add to the basic recipe. This is a bit like baba ghanoush, but less ingredients, less creamy / You could make this creamier with yoghurt or tahini (with tahini would be more like baba ghanoush) / Or you could blacken the aubergines – grill the aubergines whole until the outsides are blackened, and then cut in half and scoop out the insides. Or could do this if the veg ends up burnt / Apparently aubergine is a good source of fibre.

3. I think this recipe came from the Waitrose food magazine originally, but the magazine is lost, and this is what is written in my recipe book. I used to get the magazine free as a 'perk' of a job I once had. This is literally the only thing I can remember from it and if it wasn't for this recipe, I wouldn't remember the 'perk'.

    I think I first made this when I was staying at my uncle's flat for a couple of months (he wasn't there) in Leatherhead and commuting to work in London (in a department store). This was a strange time in my life, a bit like being on holiday because I was staying in someone else's home. I really enjoyed having sole access to a kitchen and cooked a lot. I was lonely at the time, and I appreciated how taking time with my food gave me a structure to my day. I made this when C and C came to visit for the night. At first, they didn't want to eat it, because it does look unappetising, it looks slimy. But they tried it and liked it (it's honestly really tasty and full of flavour – as long as you like aubergines – and doesn't taste how it looks) and it became a favourite side dish.

    I remember making this for a picnic in St James' Park with Y and C, but I couldn't have, because that picnic predates the Leatherhead meal. I think I've misremembered because I made white bean wafers for the picnic, and the last time I made the wafers I also made the smashed aubergine, so the two have become mixed together in my memory.

    I first remember having this meal for K's birthday one year, we were invited round to her flat in Barking, and a small buffet had been made. I cannot remember though if we also had to bring an item of food, or just drink. The dip was on the table, and I can remember laughing about the way that it looked and not wanting to try it. Once I tried it though I realised it was actually nice and have continued to enjoy it ever since.

I made this for R and M's wedding, where everyone brought food to share rather than having caterers. I argued with my dad because he said we were spending too much on food and can't afford to be so frivolous and I had tripled the amount I normally make, and dad said it would get wasted. I was convinced everyone would want to eat it once they'd tried a little and that I needed to make loads, but I didn't think to put a note next to it on the buffet table saying 'it tastes much better than it looks' and no one touched it.

I last made it for C's birthday, along with the white bean wafers, vegan spanakopita and a massive chocolate cake. I tend to make this as a special occasion party dish, alongside other bits.

Garlic Mushrooms

friends / slow time / comfort

A breakfast dish that can be used as the main portion of the meal, or as a component in a larger breakfast.

1. Ingredients:

   Small onion, finely chopped
   Olive oil
   Punnet of mushrooms sliced
   The best part of a bulb of garlic, finely chopped
   A decent glug of single soya cream, adjust as required
   Few sprigs of dill, leaves picked
   Sourdough toast to serve, buttered
   Salt and pepper to season

   Method: 1. Gently heat the oil, season well and sweat the onions in the oil until soft, without them catching. 2. Add the mushrooms. Stir well and allow to sweat, softening them not browning them. Add more oil if needed. 3. Add garlic, stir well and give time for the flavour to absorb, don't let it burn. 4. Add a smallish glug of cream and a sprig of dill, leaves picked. 5. Let it thicken. Can add more cream as needed. 6. Serve over buttered toasted sourdough, with some more dill as a garnish.

2. White onion might be best, but can use red too, whatever you have / Adjust oil as needed / Use a lot of mushrooms, they'll shrink down a lot / To stop the mushrooms from catching, or to prevent using too much oil, add a splash of water. It can sometimes give the mushrooms a slightly chewier texture, but it makes the creamy sauce more mushroomy / Avoid using too much cream so it's not too rich. If you don't have cream in, use a splash of soya milk. Or if you aren't dairy free use dairy cream / Only use the dill if you're feeling fancy, it's fine if you don't have any / If you want a big meal, wilt in spinach at the end. Or mash avocado on your toast or grill some tomatoes with a little dried oregano and oil.

3. I only recently began enjoying mushrooms as a main feature. I began eating a vegan diet in January 2020 and I think that is when I started enjoying mushrooms more. I remember, early on in the year, going for breakfast with some friends to a vegan café

and ordering garlic mushrooms, and I felt really satisfied. This was a month or 6 weeks or so before the pandemic became part of our daily lives, and we had no idea how shit 2020 would turn out to be. Five out of the six of us at that breakfast all worked together, but now only two of us are still in that job. Most of us had planned to move into a house share together in the summer, but again only two of us (a different two) were able to. I guess these mushrooms remind me of a time when I didn't wake up anxious every morning. I've continued to make them regularly since, with friends or alone, and they are a source of comfort and an indulgence and eating mushrooms makes me feel like I'm caring for myself.

    Before that day, mushrooms were a side. Me and C often make breakfast together and mushrooms would be a little addition on a massive plate of food. We can be quite greedy when it comes to food, especially food we've cooked ourselves. I think having mushrooms as the main part of the meal now somehow makes me feel loved. It connects me to my friends. I really look forward to this now, it makes me want to get out of bed.

    I think we made this together the first time that we were able to meet up together to work after lockdown (for the brief time that restrictions were lifted). I really loved the meal and all of the parts that went into it, I have always really liked mushrooms and I think that this is a perfect recipe to add to a list. I think we may have made this meal a number of times since then.

Spinach and Chickpea Curry

Hearty dinners / house shares / hope

A warming meal for cold evenings that can be served a number of ways.

1. Ingredients:

   A large sweet potato, 1 per person
   200g tinned chickpeas, drained
   2 tablespoons sunflower oil
   2 large onions, thinly sliced
   2 teaspoons ground coriander
   2 teaspoons cumin
   1 teaspoon hot chilli powder
   ½ teaspoon ground turmeric
   About a tablespoon of medium curry powder
   400g canned chopped tomatoes
   1 teaspoon soft brown sugar
   100ml water
   2 tablespoons fresh mint leaves, finely chopped
   At least 100g fresh spinach
   Salt and pepper

   Method: 1. Bake the potatoes using your preferred method. 2. In a pan, cover the chickpeas with cold water, and bring to the boil. Reduce the heat and simmer for 45 minutes or until tender. Drain and set aside. 3. Meanwhile, heat the oil in a wok or large frying pan, add the onions and cook over a low heat for about 15 minutes, until slightly golden. Add the seasoning and stir fry for 1–2 minutes. 4. Add the tomatoes, sugar and measured water, and bring to the boil. Cover, reduce the heat and simmer gently for 15 minutes. 5. Add the chickpeas, salt and pepper and cook for 8–10 minutes, gently. Stir in the mint. Add spinach near the point of serving. 6. Serve over baked sweet potato.

2. The onions should look like burger onions, like how they look at a burger van / It's OK if you forget the mint / To bulk it out use at least double the spinach / This recipe is best with a dollop of natural yoghurt on it. It is also nice with a little grated cheddar / Can serve over rice instead of sweet potato.

4. Recipes/Addendums/Souvenirs 73

3. I don't know where this recipe originally came from, my old housemate N was cooking it (when we lived together) and he gave me the recipe, and I've made it regularly since. I know at some point I have adjusted the seasoning to suit my tastes.

   I remember first eating this meal in the house that we shared together, it was a good house for sharing food and recipes in. I think what I liked about it was that it was really spicy, and I had to keep adding yoghurt to it to eat it. I think the first time I ate it we did not make it, but our old housemate did. I have made it a lot of times since, but I am unable to make with the burger onions usually as D does not like, so I have to adapt the recipe slightly, making it not the same, but still good. I think it is best served with a sweet potato or some bread (naan etc).

   I always eat this with baked sweet potato. Even though I'm sure it would be nice with rice, it wouldn't feel right to me now. I like getting the extra vegetable into it and the flavour works really well. I started doing this because I saw the housemate who gave me the recipe eat his leftovers this way.

   This recipe makes me feel healthy. It reminds me of a time I was unintentionally living a really healthy lifestyle and found day to day life quite exciting. I had moved into a house share with strangers, and it unexpectedly was a really nourishing environment. This came after a period of being isolated. Now when I make this, I suppose it makes me feel there is potential in the future, or like – it's a hopeful meal. Good if you want leftovers and to make the kitchen steamy.

Homemade Birthday Pizzas

sharing / toppings

The traditional mixture of dough, cheese and a range of toppings, sometimes can be made with a thick base or thin, and sometimes a thin one comes with authentic leoparding.

1. Ingredients:

   N.B. This recipe originally came from the BBC.
   For the dough: 650g 00 flour or strong white flour (we used bread flour)
   7g packet easy yeast
   2tsp salt
   25ml olive oil (1floz)
   325ml / 11floz warm water

   1. Mix flour, yeast, salt in large bowl & stir in olive oil. Gradually add warm water to form soft dough. 2. Transfer to floured surface, knead for 5 minutes until smooth & elastic. Transfer to a clean bowl, cover with a damp tea towel, leave to rise for 90 minutes until doubled in size. 3. When risen knock it back & knead again until smooth, roll into a ball & set aside for 30–60 minutes to rise again. 4. Preheat oven to highest, divide dough into 6 balls and roll out onto a highly floured surface until 20cm in diameter. Put on your fave topping and cook for 10–12 mins.

   For the pizza sauce: 2tsp olive oil
   1 small onion finely chopped
   1 fat garlic clove
   2 400g tinned chopped tomatoes
   3 tbsp tomato puree
   1 bay leaf
   2 tbsp dried oregano
   Fresh basil (a bunch)

   1. Heat oil, on a low heat, add onion and generous amount of salt. Fry gently for 15 minutes until softened and translucent. 2. Add garlic & chilli cook another min, stirring continually. 3. Add puree, tomatoes, bay leaf, oregano, and sugar. Bring to the boil and simmer on a low heat, uncovered for 20–30 minutes until thick and reduced. 4. Stir in basil. Does 4–6 pizzas.

2. When making these pizzas, it is important that guests feel they have autonomy over them. The cheese used can be changed depending on specific dietary needs (for vegan cheese for example – however this is not a great substitute for the real thing) / Our preference is towards a thin base, this means that fewer toppings are required as they are unable to be supported / There can be so many different variations here, our suggestion of toppings include; mushrooms, goat's cheese and onion, egg and spinach or simply cheese, tomato and garlic / However, anything goes, feel free to take risks / We like to add additional garlic to the pizza sauce, using 4 cloves here.

3. This is perfect to have with friends and works well for events such as parties. We first tried this recipe for K's birthday party and found that it worked well. There were some parts which required us to perform more labour than the other guests – the preparation of the dough was particularly time consuming, and it is advised that this is done before other people arrive. As it was a birthday celebration, we hosted a number of K's friends, and it was nice as this was one of the first times that I spent with them. Previous to the pizzas we had spent the day out walking, this meant that when we came to eat, we were all very hungry already.

   We spent time together in the morning making the dough; I really enjoyed having this time just us. I thought I'd really love making the actual pizzas, but by then we were starving from our walk, and more people turned up than I expected, and I felt really overwhelmed. C got on really well with my friends, but G had to take over making the pizzas for everyone as I was getting flustered. I'd just gone vegan two weeks beforehand, so I didn't have cheese. I remembered B saying if you have lots of other fats you don't miss the cheese on pizza, so I put on avocado and a drizzle of oil and pine nuts alongside veggies, and it really worked. I felt very grateful for the evening.

Chapter 5

WAYS TO SUBMIT

Ira Brand

This text is a re-visiting of a piece that was originally written for the 2020 edition of Festival Theaterformen, in which *Ways To Submit* was programmed but unable to be presented due to the Covid-19 pandemic. Originally titled *The Practice of Emptying Space*, the project was an attempt to evoke something of what the live work would have been, and to reflect on the conditions of that particular moment of June 2020. It took the form of an audio piece, an image series, and a text, that could be experienced by an audience remotely. You can visit the original project at www.irabrand.co.uk.

—

The rules of this space are:

>   No shoes
>   No socks
>   No jewellery

You can fight in whatever you're wearing right now, but if you would like to get changed there is a dressing room over here, and there are some clothes that you can make use of.

When you are ready to fight you will go and stand there, on that X, and when I am ready to fight again I will stand here on this X.

The aim of the fight – is to fight. We are going to take the fight seriously, but our intention is not to permanently damage or injure the other person.

You can 'tap out' to stop the fight temporarily. If a fighter taps out you separate physically, and then resume the fight until the timer goes.

But there is also a safe word. If either fighter says the safe word, the fight stops immediately and does not resume, and no questions are asked.

Tonight the safe word is:

*

There is a tape-lined square of thick foam mats. The audience sit on three sides. On the fourth side is a bench, a performer, a bottle of water and a light grey towel, a screen. There are two large white crosses taped to the floor.

The space of the theatre both does and does not matter. Like how this space, here – or there, where you are – has the potential to matter and not matter. It's a container. An always different room in which we put the work. Our relationship to the room is fleeting. Yet we spend long periods of time trying to understand each new space. To place the objects, the speakers, the screen, the microphone. To learn how the light falls. To organize the bodies. Every time trying to orient ourselves, towards the room and each other.

At a certain moment the space is also energetic. Energetic with its specificity of who is there and how the bodies compose themselves, and how sound travels, and light travels, and air moves. It becomes hot. It becomes hazy over time. The boundaries blur sometimes, the distance shifts. The space is changeable, and sometimes it is changed. It holds all of the relations of tonight. The space is a container, but another word for contain could be embrace.

*

In the later version of the show, we start to work with sound instead of haze. A different way to play with attention and focus, with what is produced by the bodies that are there that night. We amplify and record the sounds of the fights, and by extension the sounds of things in the space that are not the fights: laughter, vocalisations, shuffles, heckles, silence, breath. On the mat, and off. The boundaries blur.

I have a strange archive now: photos of bodies held in mid-fight and devoid of motion, and audio recordings of bodies in motion with no accompanying visuals. Both materials are inherently incomplete. They are a trace, a suggestion. They are more open to interpretation and also more evocative than the few video recordings I have. In this way I think they are a more 'truthful' representation of the work, in which I have learnt the fights always exist differently for everybody in the room, often in complex, unknowable ways.

Take a moment to listen, or to imagine listening.

Fight #26: Heavy thumping. One body that is audibly bigger than the other. An attack with little hesitation.

Fight #61: The echo of a fall, again and again and again.

Fight #155: Are those the hooves of horses?

Fight #202: Too many noises all at once.

Fight #174: The size and shape of the theatre. The height of empty space above the heads of the audience. The density of the ground beneath them.

Fight #12: You are this thumping body.

Fight #159: Or you are this person sitting in the audience with empty space above you. You are laughing or flinching.

Fight #22: You are holding your breath or just breathing.

Fight #186: You are wrapping your forearm around my throat.

Fight #128: You are pushing your palm against the flat of my forehead to hold me at a distance, it fits perfectly.

*

In the early months of the pandemic, I started running. Not well and not fast, but still.

I started wearing lipstick to the supermarket in an attempt to be seen.

I sat on a park bench in public because I liked being in public. I did not know if this publicness was allowed.

I let the boundaries collapse. I let the mediated online social spaces invade my bed, my bathroom. I let the voices of strangers and semi-acquaintances wake me in the morning and prevent me from sleeping at night. I thought about what these people would think of my behaviour. I let them police me, virtually, and I wondered how it would all be different if we were in close proximity. The possibility of transmission, of contamination, so near. The possibility of a body language. I wondered if we were becoming more or less accountable to each other in these distant, disembodied realms.

I let the boundaries do the opposite of collapse, be built up, maintained. I got suspicious of people I had no reason to be suspicious of, I became judgmental of people I had no right to judge. I did not leave the house for many days. Against my better judgement I let myself feel afraid of touching people. In the presence of fear and in the absence of people, I began touching myself more. Stroking the back of my neck while waiting for the coffee to boil. Fingering my ribs in the shower. Lying with my knuckles pressed into my armpits whilst scrolling on my phone.

I found myself more attracted to people in the street because the thought of being close to them felt even more transgressive than usual. I let the passing smell of unfamiliar perfume turn my head. I remembered, fondly, a fight, and my hands in the wet of another person's armpits.

I ate with my fingers and left sticky prints on the letters of my keyboard.

I let myself project myself into a future where all these statements became about something that had been in the past.

I have never been so good at being in the present moment, and I am getting increasingly worse.

I cried very little, which seemed like an unexpected response to uncertainty. I thought maybe there were already too many people crying and we were burning through tears like fossil fuel.

I used the phrase 'up and down' to describe my well-being, my mood, my motivation, my libido, my spirit, my appetite, my sleep. My internalized neoliberalism, though, was well and truly up.

I saw the faces of friends in large online meetings but did not address them, just smiling at the laptop screen, hoping they would know that I was smiling specifically at them. A desperate kind of performance.

*

I edit photographs of the performance, trying to create silhouetted absences where there were fighters. I spend hours making bodies disappear. Deleting – pixel by pixel – skin, flesh, hair, fabric that clings to thighs, biceps, pubic mounds. The tips of teeth. The toes, the heel. Bones, by implication, the parts of you we don't see. The occasional edge of a wet tongue. A bubble or a string of saliva.

It's hard work. Not hard like heavy labour, not hard like muscle strain. Hard like precision, repetition, detail work.

It feels close to erotic to pay such precise attention to the edges of another person. When we fight we are mostly weight and heat and force and personality. We're all physics and aura, if you believe in that kind of thing. The fights are embodied but they are also fast and – for me – they are many. I rarely think about the arch of the other person's foot, the line where their t-shirt tucks into their tracksuit bottoms.

When I have a philosophical whim, I think: what does it mean to be erasing these bodies? What does it mean to be doing this now? But it gives me something to do.

*

I fight with a friend and afterwards he tells me that he couldn't help but be aware all the time of my nipples visible through my t-shirt. She holds herself low to the ground, making slow and small movements, followed by very rapid holds. Later in the bar she tells me that she has for years been observing how animals fight. I slap him hard in the face and he slaps me back, there is an audible intake of breath from somewhere in the audience. I fight with an ex-lover and they tell me they wish our sex had been more like this fight. She sits still on the mat, refusing to fight, a public protest against what had until that moment seemed inevitable. Power bouncing around the room, like a soft ball of light, or a balloon we are trying to keep in the air. They ask if we can fight with our eyes closed, and I say yes. I hold the back of her neck and use it to push her body to the ground. It feels temporarily and enjoyably cruel. I enjoy being dragged around by my ankles, I enjoy being flipped over. I am talking and they are listening. I get hurt. I get beaten again and again and again and again, and I start to really resent that beating, even though I have asked for it.

Afterwards, I am asked if what they did was okay. I am asked why. I am told they feel bad. I am told I have made them look bad. I am told they feel exhilarated. I am told, several times, that somebody was holding back, and I am reminded that I am small, light, and weak, which I tend to forget. I am asked, always, how I feel, but I think what I am actually being asked is how they are supposed to feel.

In the middle of the performance a woman asks me: how much of this, what you are saying now, is a script? She is asking me to tell her what is real, and what is not.

At a certain point in the tour this starts to happen more and more: people ask questions, and the questions bleed from the after-show bar space into the space of the live performance itself. I realize that I have found a looseness in the text, which is now mostly improvised, and the way I perform, and the way I fight, that makes it possible for people to interrupt, to question, to talk back. Mostly I love that the space is one in which the audience feel able to speak. But I have to teach myself that just because a question is asked, it does not mean that I should answer it.

From inside, the whole thing feels like a thin line I am walking between control and lack of control, tight and loose, holding fast and giving in. Theatre and not theatre, maybe.

*

Both shadow and person pixels are dark, and it is impossible to tell where the shadow ends and the person begins. Things that are in motion are caught in a blur on a photo. So much nuance is lost when you make a body a solid block. The changes in pigmentation as you move along the surface of the skin. The crease between forearm and bicep.

What might fill the space that is left behind? What might we put in there, instead of these heaving bodies? It feels like an opportunity, but I'm still mourning the absent people.

In the later version of the show, there is one fight where I ask if somebody from the audience will 'stand in' for me, to fight on my behalf. I sit, and I watch the fight as part of the audience. It is anxiety inducing and thrilling, sometimes entertaining, surprising, sometimes frightening, boring, predictable. As one audience member fights another, we see two different bodies, suddenly. The constant of my body disrupted. The constant of my strength, or weakness, my shape, my training, my limitations, my gender, my habits, my accumulated exhaustion, my desires, disrupted. And my role disrupted, becoming the person who gets to watch, who has to watch. Sometimes I notice people watching me watching.

I zoom way in. I am looking in granular detail at the shape of an arched body, a loose body, an angry body, a tired body, a surprised body. The task of it is close, it produces an unexpected sense of proximity. A one-sided intimacy, an unrequited love.

I remind myself that pixels are not skin, that photos of bodies are not bodies.

*

One of the side-effects of this practice is that I look at people in public now and imagine fighting them.

> Fight #258: A woman trips and stumbles slightly in the post office queue and I place my hands on her elbows. It's the first contact I've had with a stranger in ten weeks.

> Fight #244: A young couple ask me to take a photo of them, holding a disposable camera in an outstretched hand. I am so taken aback by the request for me to touch the object of their camera that I do it without question.

> Fight #265: We are both running, distracted and looking down, and the right side of my body collides with the right side of theirs. It is hard but does not hurt. We bounce back from each other, and stand out of breath, mouths open, it is unclear how to proceed.

*

5. Ways to Submit

For me the fighting is a practice, and it is a performance. It is a thing I do outside of the frame of the show. But I also make a precise choice to engage in the practice within the space of a theatre, in front of an audience, under lights, framed, amplified. The space of the theatre makes many things possible, as much as it makes some things impossible.

Take a space, empty it. Take everything that was on the inside and put it on the outside. In the process of emptying it, it is likely you will see in a different way what it has been filled with.

And what might fill the space that is left behind? It feels like an opportunity, but I'm still mourning the absent people.

*

The audience are ushered out, gently. Those of us left exhale something, become a bit more relaxed. The music is cut out. The house lights are brought up, the space instantly less aesthetic, and more used. White tape crosses are pulled up off the floor. The sweaty clothes the audience have fought in are piled and put in a bag, to be washed. The unused water bottles too, the half-drunk ones are put in the bin. The microphone is turned down, there is the subtle change of a space no longer being amplified. The ice pack is retrieved from the freezer in the dressing room. The mats are wiped down, cleaned of hair, footprints. They are taken apart, giant puzzle pieces. They are slid four at a time into worn cardboard boxes, and the boxes are taped shut. The towel and wet costume are put in the to-be-washed bag: vest, sports bra, shorts, socks. The chargers are coiled. The chairs are rearranged, or straightened, or stacked.

Tomorrow, the bench is returned to the school gym it was borrowed from.

Chapter 6

ALL THE SENSE OF REAL: A WORLD OF WRESTLING

Simon Bayly

This is how to do it – if you want to do it.

Book to see *Ways to Submit*, a performance by I.B., which will be the second part of a double bill.

Don't read the online programme in advance or the paper programme handed out at the box office, just turn up, take it as it is. No expectations, no foreknowledge, just anticipation.

A long time before that, start talking to someone on a regular basis, preferably every week day in the early morning. Choose someone, call them S., roughly the same age, experienced, but who has perhaps not been working in this particular way for very long, but that should be just speculation. Let the process be taken up with all kinds of wanting, longing and wanting to do and say all kinds of things, murderous fantasies, hopes for blissful romance and everything in between. From early on, repeat cycles of fantasies of fighting and biting, tussling, poking and provoking, both exciting and frustrating. In between those moments of fantasy, there will be others, for example, sitting in S.'s lap. Tell S. all of this.

During the episodes of fighting, the mind will naturally veer towards wrestling, getting it out in the open, there on the floor, release the excitement and frustration. Talk about that repeatedly, similarly exciting and frustrating, because, of course, actual wrestling will not be possible. Any long-term sexual or romantic partner [preferred term: 'life person'], actual or potential, will flat out refuse to engage in any such thing, rightly so, just not interested. Consider friends, even mere acquaintances, as potential wrestling partners – knowing that some have done a bit of this and that in previous relationships – but quickly realize that trying to reanimate past desires could be unwelcome, inappropriate and possibly psychologically harmful.

With S., always return to talking about wrestling, wanting to get into a tussle, moan about the lack of physical wrestling to flesh out the mental wrestling. Don't give up on this topic, keep going back to it, don't be concerned about being boring or irritating. Look up wrestling studios, clubs and societies online, calculate the costs and potential consequences. On the morning of performance day, get taken down: cut off mid-thought with 'it's time to stop there' as the second hand taps out past the fifty minutes. Find a mood and stay in it.

That evening, go alone to theatre, as planned. Don't expect to see anyone in particular. But there in the foyer, will actually be someone, call them R., long time unmet, ordinary and radiant, a quiet familiarity awakened. Talk about how things have been since last encounter, perhaps, say, a cardiac arrhythmia, surgery successful, things were bad but now looking up, or some missed years, some harsh and unshared pain, working, resting, waiting, time passing.

Enter theatre for double act, call them Tim and Tom, who might, for example, be noodling around for a while, with beats, knobs, wires, cables and too many props. Buy R. drink at the interval and make conversation about interesting projects, the way conversations normally go.

After the interval, take the same seat again beside R., notice the marked-out square on the stage floor, the mat, the taped X's, the benches alongside, the 'no biting' projection.

You there, in black, flared shorts (vinyl?), white vest, t-shirt, a red top with a zip.

So some fighting, literal but possibly just metaphorical. All actual stage fighting always metaphorical, that being both the pleasure and the problem of the stage.

Wait for others to sit down. R. will describe a recent performance, two people wrestling and mixing it up by setting various constraints or challenges, taping up an arm or trying to get an actual finger into the other's actual asshole, but not in a sexual way, no not at all. Then silent, in that way that silence must fall before it begins. Feel the presence of R.'s body in the theatre, their breathing, just being there, being side by side the other bodies, not doing anything in particular.

Light is on you now and you're saying something: studying Brazilian jiu-jitsu, always wanting to fight, fighting with friends, lovers, others, being strong or not strong enough or not very good, but still, you want to fight, nine bouts, three minutes each, anyone who wants, change into other clothes in the booth over there, an assistant will help.

6. All the Sense of Real: A World of Wrestling

Looking at you, believing in the contradiction: a light and delicate frame containing an indestructible inner power that can squeeze, crush, choke, incapacitate and hurt. Wrestling, yes, remember saying to S. that the pleasure in it only gained in losing, dominating only through submission. The point being, as suggested, to find ways to submit. Don't stage it, don't make it the product of a tedious theatricality – there must be fighting, actual force and resistance, the possibility of over-reaching, underhandedness and harm, even if accidental.

Looking at you, knowing you already know this.

OK, so here and now, the chance to win by losing, to submit to a greater power under the lights and the judgment of others.

*

get out of the seat, wait barely long enough
the impropriety of enthusiasm
the ugliness of desire that shows its desire
no matter
as usual, be the first to confess
desperate for something

in the early 1980s
remember being stage manager and front of house
at theatre workshop
[long gone]
in edinburgh during festival
[a place you know too, but later]

rose, rose english, performing the beloved

from afar, fall in love with rose almost immediately
or with a persona
harsh, nearly cruel, an analytic austerity
offset with unblushing, unadorned eroticism
despite a taste for feathers, sequins and horsey stuff

late on in the beloved, after an interval
a sequence where rose, dressed in worn white evening gown
asks for a someone to sit in their lap

long sequence, whoever sits in the lap has to sit there for a while

rose not really doing much to or with person in lap
almost a prop: necessary

but specific individuality not at stake and not in question
no humiliation, no jokes
no obligation to do anything in particular

video recording online
of another iteration
at the point where rose asks for a volunteer lap-sitter
no-one comes forward
rose talks around the anxieties that arise for anyone considering
but still no-one
in this instance, they continue without that section

sense of real absence: something omitted
something not happening that otherwise does happen
when someone sits in a lap

first night at theatre workshop, volunteer to sit in rose's lap
from rehearsal, know when the moment is coming
wait impatiently
let the pause after rose asks hang in the air for a few seconds
but not so long as to allow someone else to grab it

don't try to remember what happens while sitting in the lap
except that it is fine just

to sit there

doing nothing

listening to a voice

feeling a body take weight, muscles

adjusting themselves

continuously

under the taffeta

the others out there won't really look, except in passing
but neither ignore
so do not fear being addressed
for the dreadful amusement of others
to sit in a lap: a childhood scene, remembered or wished for
either way, a lap is something that someone both has
and does not have
since a lap is purely accidental to the act of sitting

so, love sitting in the accident of rose's lap
left alone there
in front of everyone

winnicott:
at the core of an emerging, 'healthy' infant subjectivity
a 'cul-de-sac', non-communicative state of going on being
'the true self'
just sitting there
within a world of subjective objects

the inevitable rupture of this isolate state
by either internal or external disturbances
demands communication proper
addressed to objective subjects [other people]
communication that requires another dimension of subjectivity
'the false self'
a necessary prop

> there seems to be no doubt that for all its futility from the observer's point of view, the cul-de-sac communication (communication with subjective objects) carries all the sense of real. per contra, such communication with the world as occurs from the false self does not feel real; it is not a true communication because it does not involve the core of the self, that which could be called a true self. (Winnicott 1984: 184)

leave aside worries about notions of true and false selves
instead, concentrate on the phrasing:
cul-de-sac communication carries 'all the sense of real'

neither 'all the sense of reality'
nor 'all the sense of the real'

and so an absence of anything definitive
the real or reality abandoned, for a time

sit in rose's lap
all the sense of real
or some of it, for a bit

winnicott again:
to become a person, a subject, involves 'establishing a private self that is not communicating, and at the same time wanting to communicate

and to be found […] a sophisticated game of hide-and-seek in which
it is joy to be hidden but disaster not to be found.' (186)

sit in rose's lap
feel found
hidden in plain sight
without disaster

back in the yard
in its theatre

put on yellow t-shirt in dressing cubicle
remove boots and thick walking socks
of soft brown merino wool
clipped from an animal
take off watch and belt
give glasses to assistant

step into the light
hear the instructions
accept the arrangements
fight you

fighting you, feel the presence of a want of weight
a subtracted resistance
even as you press hard and push back
something like strength, withheld
yeah, you can be carried, without effort
yeah, just like hoisting up a neighbour's kid last week

even a scarred heart will not give out as you lie on top
a forgiving blanket of warm flesh and panting breath
take all of you from a standing position
holding you up like a prize
or a sacrifice
that does not feel right

grab your ankles and pull the rest of you across the floor
no struggle or surrender
because you can't
it seems
barely held
yet you won't escape

6. All the Sense of Real: A World of Wrestling

head wedged between thighs
resting on vinyl-covered ass
classic scissor choke-hold
wait for the pressure
but you offer nothing
except the gift of inertia

lie entwined on the floor
breathe heavily
feel OK
alone together
there, around and among some limbs, without orientation
no sense of what is where

then realize this:
want to fight but need to fight
to take care, take care of you
because you can be hurt
but will not believe in hurt
or will not believe a want
to hurt you
could take care to hurt you
or hurt you by not taking care

disclaimer in the dressing area asks:
take responsibility for whatever may happen
before fighting, you ask if that's been read and agreed
agree, without thinking, bow respectfully, just do this
but be responsible for what happens to you

after the pause, make to grab a thigh again
take you down
but partially resist the performance of the action
to keep you standing
therefore there is now acting, not fighting

which is disappointing
because of wanting to fight
to actually fight and not act fighting

[when fighting, no communication
more like going on being
but just more intensively]

now, there is acting fighting
there is good communication
watching and laughing
eyeing each other
eyed by the others who laugh

now, both you and I are here
they have arrived together
in front of them

now, I have a reasonable sense of what your body can do
and what it cannot do
whereas before that sense was unreasonable
now, I can clearly understand your body as yours
a moveable object
with boundaries and limits
with which I can respectfully communicate
to which I owe respect

what a shame
there is shame here because
as you become an objective subject
with which I can communicate
I become an I
saying this
riveted to myself once again
writing this
with knowledge of what I can do and cannot do
which I can communicate
to you and to them

as the seconds tick away
I understand your winning strategy
to lose
by giving away this knowledge
to which I must submit
ashamed of the longing
that thought it could be otherwise

that we could fight
with all the sense of real
or some of it, for a bit

6. All the Sense of Real: A World of Wrestling

and now it's time to stop

*

they fight you, younger and lighter
fairer fights perhaps
but you tire
fatigue the unforgiving victor
no contest

toward the end
the volunteers stop forthcoming

you're finished really
just going through the motions
walking it down
winding it down
you're done

then A., who looks like a man I might like to have looked like,
steps up

'grudge match', they announce, gently, in jest
introducing a neat complicity, some kind of prior understanding

you fight, kind of, they laugh and you smile
good communication

as the timer approaches zero
they move towards you
extending arms as if to make for a last move
to take you down

a lure: it's an embrace
and you return the embrace
fighting gives way to love and respect, mutuality and equality
played out

sat in my seat, a shame, I think again
and feel ashamed for thinking so

*

Outside in the bar, R. will announce they're going home, although, in theory, staying would have been equally possible. Karaoke will start up, a champagne supernova in the sky. In the yard, there'll be a hesitation,

R. will ask what it was like to fight you. Tell R. the story told above, or a draft of it, more partial and incoherent than this version, without Winnicott's essay or Rose's lap. They will listen intently, smile and laugh, saying that now there's a real story to tell. R. will mention the final embrace with A., seeing it as a dramaturgical defeat for you, something in its balanced resolution that upstaged the delicate asymmetry of what had gone before – or that is at least what it seems they will have meant but said simply.

Drift with R. towards the train station. Their train leaves in a few minutes, from the other platform, going in the opposite direction. Move towards each other awkwardly and place a cheek next to theirs for a moment, feel their breath and then, goodbye.

Stand alone in the station entrance, feel something missing without knowing what it is. Return to the theatre, only a few steps away, perhaps not wanting to stand on the cold platform for twenty minutes. Hesitate at the door and follow the bouncer's gesture into the bar, where the karaoke will be in full swing and the air will be warm.

Look around, thinking to tell you this story right now, during these minutes of not really being anywhere. Catch sight of you, in close conversation with someone, remember that it is a belt that's left behind, which is why jeans fall down.

Enter the theatre. It'll be empty, cold and dark, the mats and benches will all be gone, apart from someone in the far corner, looking at a phone. They will look up, but won't react, they will go back to the phone.

Inside the dressing cubicle, the belt lies under the chair.

There it is, by itself.

Grasp it and leave the empty theatre without putting it on.

You'll still be in the bar, still talking over there with the other person, there is good distance between you and good communication. Decide it would be creepy to approach, holding a belt, disturbing the conversation, to tell this story.

Put on the belt outside in the yard and walk back to the station.

On the platform, someone else will be pacing furiously up and down its entire length, over and over. Get into the train, they will continue pacing, moving rapidly back and forth between the busy carriages.

See the only empty seat and at the same time as seeing the seat, see that the person sitting in the next seat is someone familiar, perhaps a doctor, the partner of a neighbour going home [they don't live together].

Sit down, say hello but at first they won't recognize who it is, then they will and they'll ask what's been happening tonight. Tell them about going to the theatre, they'll ask what was it, tell them this story, or at least a much shorter version of it, including S., but without Winnicott's essay or Rose's lap or R.'s grace and tenderness or the belt or the person with the phone in the empty theatre. The other person will still be pacing the length of the carriage. They, the neighbour's partner, will smile and laugh and say, well now there's a real story to tell for tomorrow.

Arrive home, the house will be dark. A son will be making tea in the kitchen before returning to oil painting on small blank cards. The life person, if there is one, will be nearly asleep, the bedroom lights will be off. Undress and lie down. A question will come: how was the theatre? Tell this story, in an even shorter version because they will have to get up at 6am, don't mention any supporting characters, just the basic facts: that you wanted to fight and that people fought with you for a few minutes. Well that's a shame, the life person – if present – will say, why, because there's something lost when fantasy becomes reality, however exciting it may be, something is lost in the acting out: say, yes, but still, there is reality and then there is all the sense of real, they are different, aren't they, then stop talking and try to sleep.

Today, tell this story. Even though it won't have taken long, keep checking the time so as not to be caught out by being cut off again at the end. S. won't immediately say anything. [That is how it often goes.] Start off with another thought about how S. sometimes says that something that's been said gets ignored or skipped over whilst at the same time S. often does something similar, usually by remaining silent.

After a long silence, S. will say, not in these words, these are different words and there are more of them, so this is not what will be said, nothing like it, but still something like:

> you seem to want to fight at the moment
> a moment when we seem to have arrived at
> something intimate
> something private
> something that only you and I share
> but no-one knows what it is
> but, when we get there
> to the moment where there is just you and me
> a piece of work
> just sitting here
> lying there
> no open lap
> no close choke-hold
> you introduce a scene

for example, a fight
or sitting in a lap
and in that moment
you seem to think that someone will get hurt
and so you have to protect them from that possibility
by immediately telling a story about it to other people
even before the thing has finished
and so in the story itself there are suddenly more people to whom
you are telling the story
while it's happening
people who seem to be very important
without whom the story is nothing
not worth anything
because it can't be told
because there is no-one to listen
and without them, it can't happen

in making a drama out of a fight or a lap
out of what involves just you and me
wanting to tell the story of the drama
as it happens
you imagine that whatever is just us is being damaged,
and lies there left behind: a broken thing, unfound and unsayable.

For a long time, don't say anything, because the pressure to say anything has disappeared. Just lie there, where S. is out of sight, no glance to catch, nothing in particular to communicate, just the breathing and the sound of some small movements.

On the way back, stop off in a café. It will be 9.25am, so it's just stopping for a coffee, perhaps a small breakfast and then get on with the day, there's so much in the world left undone. While waiting for the coffee to be made, start writing. At 4.30pm, it will be getting dark, in the same seat in the café, write the paragraph above, they are starting to lock up, battery is at 2%, then save the file.

Wonder if this document should be sent to someone, as if it was a letter, or rewritten or just deleted, or whether to send it first to R., just in case they might not want to be represented in this version of events or even to be identified from it, which might cause some unanticipated slight, even to someone somewhere else, unconnected to R.. But then think, what about S. or A. or the neighbour's partner on the train, the people in the theatre or on the platform or on the train, or the person pacing on the platform, the other one sitting in the empty auditorium, or the neighbour's partner, or the other neighbour's kid, or you or Winnicott or Rose, or the life person, the son?

The café owner says no need to leave now, we are just fixing the lock, but leave anyway, step out into the rain and go home.

If you get this, perhaps you'll be asked to keep it to yourself.

Live, fight another day, in some other arena, hope for all the sense of real.

Reference

Winnicott, Donald Woods (1984), *The Maturational Processes and the Facilitating Environment: Studies in the Theory of Emotional Development*, 1st edn, London: Routledge.

Chapter 7

PRACTISING NEUTRAL DRAMATURGY(IES)

Will Daddario and Harry Robert Wilson

A dictionary not of definitions but of twinklings {*scintillations*}
—Roland Barthes 2005: 10

In the early stages of editing the essays assembled in this volume, Harry and I noticed that we had received an unexpected gift,[1] albeit a gift that first looked like a problem (and ultimately revealed itself precisely as a problem, but a problem in the most generative and benevolent sense).

The gift was this: several of the contributions weren't really about Roland Barthes. Discussing this phenomenon, we generated a few

---

1. Upon re-reading what I had written here, I noticed that I had written 'grief' instead of 'gift'. Well. Surely this grief twinkles. 'Between the moment I chose the subject of this course (last May) and the moment I had to prepare for it, there entered my life, some of you know it, a serious event, a mourning' (Barthes 2005: 13). In the space of a couple of short paragraphs, Barthes moves from that disclosure to the annunciation of a second Neutral, one that dwells behind the first.

> In the end, its essential form is a protestation; it consists of saying: it matters little to me to know if God exists or not; but what I know and will know to the end is that He shouldn't have simultaneously created love and death. The Neutral is this irreducible No: a No so to speak suspended in front of the hardenings of both faith and certitude and incorruptible by either one. (Barthes 2005: 14)

Barthes appeared to both Harry and me during periods of intense grieving. Grieving is perhaps the motive force of this second Neutral and the desire of neutral dramaturgy.

questions: Is it possible to assemble a book about Roland Barthes, theatre, performance and dramaturgy without necessarily discussing Roland Barthes? Might it be advantageous to do this? Might it, on the contrary, constitute an opaque or illegible gesture to make such a move?

Admittedly, we went down 'the wrong' path at first, which is to say that we adopted a non-Barthesian approach to this gift-problem. We replied to several of the drafts – which you now see collected in this dictionary of twinklings – with requests for the authors to speak more directly to the specific writings of Barthes, thereby contextualizing and even explaining (which now feels embarrassing to say) how certain writerly and/or artistic choices tie back to Barthes.

To call this 'the wrong' path is to say that such an editorial approach misses the disruptive and even salutary beauty of what Barthes calls 'the Neutral'. Furthermore, by missing the Neutral we also missed an opportunity to draw attention to the evanescence of neutral dramaturgy not only in the performance practices referenced in this book's contributions but also in the structure of the book itself.

And so here's the next problem. Wouldn't it be equally un-Neutral to explain all of this in a short section about neutral dramaturgy embedded in this dictionary of twinklings? Yes. Yes it would. The generative and benevolent dimensions of this problem, however, offers a splendid opportunity to *not* explain anything while also emphasizing something that appears in the periphery of our vision, something dealing with the desire and need for neutral dramaturgy in the present moment, where the 'emphasizing' would be like gently holding a butterfly beneath one's big toe in such a way that we neither crush it nor let it float away.

Here it goes.

The Roland Barthes who performs the lectures on The Neutral is also a scenographer who makes visible the epistemic conditions that enable him to speak of the Neutral, thereby rendering, albeit negatively, the setting of his performance. This setting is the matrix of paradigmatic thinking:

> where there is meaning, there is paradigm, and where there is paradigm (opposition), there is meaning → elliptically put: meaning rests on conflict (the choice of one term against another), and all conflict is generative of meaning: to choose one and refuse the other is always a sacrifice made to meaning, to produce meaning, to offer it to be consumed. (Barthes 2005: 7)

Barthes recognizes himself to be speaking from (quite actually standing in) a position where meaning-making is not only highly prized but also given as, de facto, precisely *the* purpose of thinking. Yet, if he makes this setting visible, he does so only to resonate dissonantly within it. The Neutral, after all, is not at home in this setting: 'temptation to suspend, to thwart, to elude the paradigm, its menacing pressure, its arrogance → to exempt meaning → this polymorphous field of paradigm, of conflict avoidance = the Neutral' (ibid.).

As such, we would not say that the lectures that follow from this point are *about* the Neutral. Rather, the lectures reveal occasions on which the Neutral has appeared, and thus the lectures are *of* the Neutral.

Transposing Barthes's situation to our own begins with acknowledging the paradigm in which we were initially enmeshed. The conflict between 'writings about Barthes' and 'writings not about (or maybe not *enough* about or about *in the right way*) Barthes' was the opposition we wrestled with. But why wrestle in this way? What other activities might we rehearse? These questions were the wrapping paper around the gift.

Barthes is quite clear about the non-methodology that presented certain texts to him, texts that he would eventually make reappear in the lectures on the Neutral. The texts were all dwelling beside one another on the shelves of his personal library. They were there. Barthes visited them. Barthes perused. The books enticed him. Barthes read. The Neutral, at times, twinkled. And then, when it came time to arrange the twinklings into a series of lectures, a problem (again, generative, benevolent) presented itself:

> It's fine to discuss the concept of fragment, it's fine to have a theory of fragment—I am regularly interviewed about it—but no one realizes what a problem it is to decide in what order to put them. There is the real problem of the fragment … For me, still in the stage of infancy: "electronic" change = solution. (2005: 12)

That is, Barthes relied on a John Cage–like chance operation to order his twinklings and even preserved a scent of the chance operation's *ad libitum* through his semi-improvised lecture performance that was tethered to written notes and textual fragments but never entirely scripted by them.

A book that speaks of a desire – a la Barthes – for neutral dramaturgy can neither be about nor not about Roland Barthes. Such a thing would need to baffle or outplay that paradigm and, instead, assemble itself alongside the ongoing performance of (maybe *with*?) the Neutral that Barthes began so many years ago.

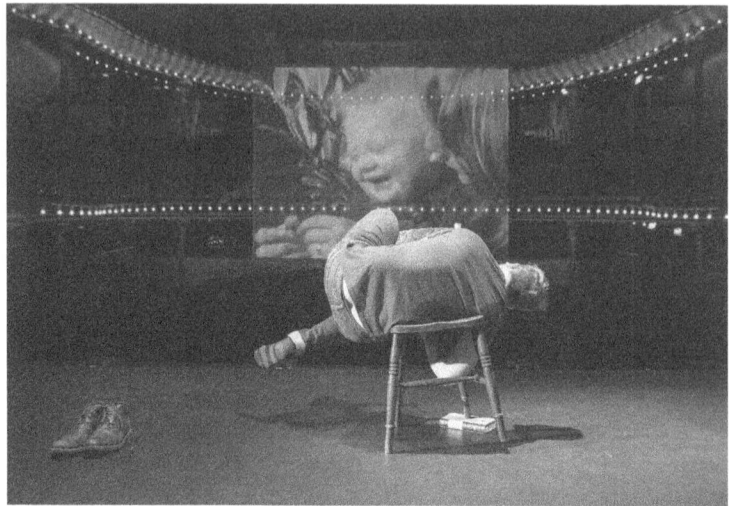

Figure 7.1 *After Camera Lucida*, 2017. Citizens Theatre, Glasgow. Harry Robert Wilson.
Source: Photograph: J. K. Bauer.

Performances of/with the Neutral

For Barthes the Neutral is all about 'side stepping assertion' (2005: 44). With this in mind, rather than offering a direct definition or analysis of what neutral dramaturgy is and where it can be found, what follows here is a series of shimmers. We offer a few fragments, some moments where neutral dramaturgy twinkles at the edges of a series of performative encounters. There is something liberating about this method – it allows for a certain kind of *kairos*, a timeliness of capturing thoughts in process. Less like an essay and more like a lecture, perhaps, which can be written and delivered in a relatively short space of time and is contingent – waiting for an audience, for the moment of its performance.

Action

Barthes on Wou-wei, the Taoist notion of 'non-action': 'Act as if you were good at nothing' (179). Wou-wei shimmers within Yvonne Rainer's 'No Manifesto' when she calls for 'no to virtuosity' (Rainer 1965: 178). Wou-wei baffles Western drama's privileging of action in favour of suspension. I think of performances that suspend action and slow down time such as Grace Schwindt's sculptural film performance *Tenant* (2012). Here untrained performers read text carefully but without inflection. They are not representing characters in the story so much as voicing the text. Performers in the film move very slowly or hold frozen poses. The staging does not always correspond with the spaces and characters described in the text. There is slippage between what we hear in the narrative and what we see the performers 'enacting'.

Or in my own piece *After Camera Lucida* (Figure 7.1), a performance installation in response to Barthes's book about photography, I slowed down two minutes and forty seconds of home movie footage of my mother holding me as a baby so that it lasted twenty-seven minutes. Installed in the nineteenth century auditorium of the Citizens Theatre in Glasgow, I invited thirty audience members to watch me perform a series of slowed-down gestures and movements in response to the film. The suspension of action, movement and meaning in order to explore suspended feelings of grief.[2]

Or in Mamoru Iriguchi's *At the Ends of the Day* (2021) a geographically dispersed audience gathers on zoom, in the dark, with a lit candle, to experience the last hour of the day together (in the time zone in which the piece is programmed). Nothing 'happens', in the conventional sense, but we are passed between a series of 'host DJs', zooming in from a range of countries, who play soundscapes recorded on the street during the last hour of their day. The video-conferencing platform is repurposed as a space of reflective calm, suspending the constant movement towards productivity and efficiency. The piece exists in the virtual space between geographical locations, at the end of one day and the start of the next, between waking and sleeping, a space of 'negative performance (not-doing, waiting, letting be …)' (Lagaay 2016: 37).

Arrogance

Arrogance: 'discourses of intimidation, of subjection, of domination, of assertion … that claim authority, the guarantee of a dogmatic truth' (Barthes 2005: 152). Neutral dramaturgy, then, as a non-arrogance, as a thwarting of this dogma. Here I think of Nic Green's *Cock and Bull*, first performed in May 2015 on the eve of the general election in the UK. In *Cock and Bull* (see Figure 7.2) Green, along with performers Rosana Cade and Laura Bradshaw, take verbatim text from Conservative Party conference speeches and pattern, loop and repeat it to exhaustion, transforming it into a kind of live exorcism.

2. I discuss this performance in more detail in Wilson (2019).

Figure 7.2 *Cock and Bull*, 2015. Laura Bradshaw and Nic Green. *Source:* Photograph: J. K. Bauer.

Dressed in men's suits, with gold painted hands and mouths, Green, Bradshaw and Cade accompany the repetitive Tory slogan-speak ('hard working people, people who work hard') with robotic gestures borrowed from the political speeches of David Cameron, George Osborne (and others) only to deconstruct and reconstruct the movements into a semi-naked choreography of tenderness.

The trio of performers reference the intimidation, domination and assertion of Tory dogma to empty it of meaning, stripping it of its effects. *Cock and Bull* thwarts the political authority of right-wing politics – neutralizes it – in favour of something more humane.

Beside-the-point

Barthes discusses the use of 'beside-the-point answers' as a way to resist the logic of 'serious' or 'noble' philosophical questions. His description of the 'beside-the-point answer' recalls some of the linguistic strategies of the early Dadaists or absurdist playwright Eugene Ionesco's use of nonsensical language in *The Bald Prima Donna*. Barthes writes:

> Imagine for an instant that to the large , pompous, arrogant, pedantic questions, of which our social, political life is excessively woven, the

stuff of interviews, of round tables etc. ... imagine that someone answers ... 'The sky is blue like an orange,' or that if this question is put to you in public, you stand up, take off a shoe, put it on your head, and leave the room. (Barthes 2005: 117)

Suspension of meaning as perhaps the only solution to arrogance. And here there are also resonances with the strategies of post-dramatic theatre where, as As Liz Tomlin notes, 'language is used, not to wield an invisible and ideological authority as in dramatic theatre, but rather to expose its own indeterminacy' (2018: 65). Or as Tim Etchells discusses in relation to his own performance writing tastes, he favours 'language at the point of breakdown, at the edges of sense, on the edge of not coping at all. A writer of nonsense. A writer of shapes that only look like letters. A writer of filthy words' (1999: 102).

Kairos

Kairos as opposed to Chronos: the ripening of time, the opportune moment, like a serendipitous photograph or when a grape is ready to harvest. See Maurya Wickstrom on Kairotic time in performance artist Cassils's *Terisias* (Wickstrom 2014). Kairos as a time out of time, the logic of the 'perishable moment' (Barthes 2005: 175). Kairos is the fragility and contingency that links performance to a lecture from Barthes. Neutral dramaturgy as a dramaturgy of timely moments.

In my piece *Kairos* (2016; Figure 7.3), inspired by Barthes's chance methods of organizing his lectures in *The Neutral*, I developed a series of twelve one-word figures made in response to some of the ideas circulating in Barthes's late texts (e.g. absence, grain, haiku, kairos, ecstasy etc.). I developed movements and task-based performance material in response to each of the figures and performed them each four times over the course of four hours. The audience could come and go for the duration of the performance. Each time I performed the sequence in a new random order dictated by the shuffling of 'title' slides in an old 35mm slide projector. I hoped to create a dramaturgy of chance moments whereby audience members might attach a unique and individual significance to each section of material and the contingent sequence(s) in which they encountered them.[3]

---

3. For a more detailed description of the format of the piece see Wilson (2017).

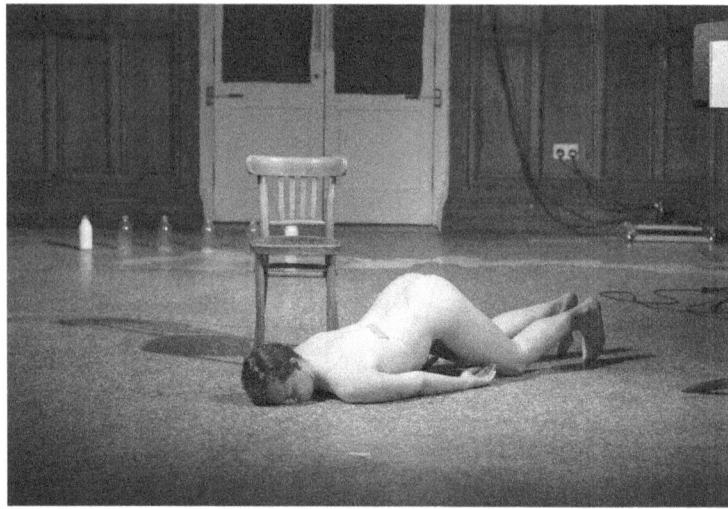

Figure 7.3 *Kairos*, 2016. Buzzcut Festival, Pearce Institute, Govan. Harry Robert Wilson.
Source: Photograph: J. K. Bauer.

Neuter

Grammatically speaking, neither masculine nor feminine, or better 'both at once', 'at the same time' (Barthes 2005: 190). For Barthes, 'The neutral is a question of gender' (186) because, in French, the paradigm of language forces us to choose a gender. For Barthes the grammatical neuter allows 'the possibility of another logic to resonate, another world of discourse' (79). Barthes is using gender as a grammatical category and yet we might draw links to Rachel Hann's application of the term 'nonbinary thinking' in relation to trans performance and scenography. Borrowing from Arturo Escobar's notion of the 'pluriversal', Hann argues that nonbinary thinking resists binary models that 'produce definitive categories of experience that impact upon all aspects of a culture; from gender to knowledge, social value to ecological awareness' (2021: 8). Instead nonbinary approaches can 'alter the conditions of "the possible"' whether by 'challenging world narratives or reconsidering gender as process-based and generative (rather than definitive)' (ibid.).

Live artists and lovers Rosana Cade and Ivor Mackaskill's *The Making of Pinnochio* (2021) borrows from the story of the puppet who wants to be a real boy to share and respond to the autobiographical experience of living through Ivor's gender transition. In the digital edition of the performance, which was made for Take Me Somewhere festival in May 2021, Rosana and Ivor playfully blur the lines between genders, between cinema and live performance, between the real and the fake, the possible and the impossible. Their 'wildly queer utopic imaginings… where everything can change and everything can connect' (Take Me Somewhere 2021) not only presents gender as a hybrid and fluid in-between space but also the form of the piece takes place in between film and theatre; it is 'both at once' 'at the same time'.

Queasiness

The 'dramaturgy of the neutral tone' is glimpsed by Barthes as a 'powerful queasiness' (2005: 76). Pain is a strong state, one that is easy to describe; queasiness is harder to say, harder to describe. Queasiness, for Barthes, is an 'intense but never verbalised pathos' (ibid.).

Rebecca Schneider (2011) talks of the queasiness evoked by moments in performance where past and present seem to touch. This 'cross-temporal slippage', as she terms it, can produce queasy sensations in the spectator when they start to feel the jump of time – its theatricality (60).

In Vivian Chinasa Ezugha's *Mammies and Jezebels* (2016) Ezhuga draws on the recognizably racist iconography of the mammy and the jezebel stereotypes to examine and confront their place in the cultural memory of her (mostly white) audience. For *this* white body, the piece is a kind of confrontation (and to say this performance elicited a queasiness that was hard to describe would certainly be accurate).

Ezugha embodies these racist caricatures, gliding between the sexually promiscuous Jezebel and the submissive mammy, via the 'twerk', reminding us that these stereotypes persist and inform current representations of Black women. As Ezugha states, in her performances her black body 'serves as a reminder of historical and social prejudices' (2016): 'The hauntingness of history, its literal in-bodied articulation, the boisterous and rattling ghosts of ancestors, and the queasy "something living" of the pastness of the past' (Schneider 2011: 60).

References

Barthes, Roland (2005), *The Neutral: Lecture Course at the Collège de France, 1977–1978*, trans. Rosalind Kraus and Denis Hollier, New York: Columbia University Press.

Etchells, Tim (1999), *Certain Fragments: Contemporary Performance and Forced Entertainment*, Abingdon, Oxon: Routledge.

Ezugha, Vivian Chinasa (2016), 'Stereotype Dramaturgy: Vivian.C.Ezugha @ Buzzcut', *The Vile Blog*. http://vilearts.blogspot.com/2016/03/sterotype-dramaturgy-viviancezugha.html (accessed 15 April 2022).

Hann, Rachel (2021), 'On Atmospherics: Staging Stormzy and nonbinary thinking', *Ambiances*, 7 (2021): 1–22. http://journals.openedition.org/ambiances/4172 (accessed 15 April 2022).

Lagaay, Alice (2016), 'Sleepwalking through the Neutral: With Roland Barthes and Maurice Blanchot', *Performance Research: On Sleep*, 21(1): 37–41.

Rainer, Yvonne (1965), 'Some Retrospective Notes', *The Tulane Drama Review*, 10(2): 168–78.

Schneider, Rebecca (2011), *Performing Remains: Art and War in Times of Historical Reenactment*, London: Routledge.

Take Me Somewhere (2021), 'The Making of Pinnochio: Digital Edition, Cade & MacAskill'. *Take Me Somewhere* [online]. https://takemesomewhere.co.uk/cade-macaskill-1 (accessed 15 April 2022).

Tomlin, Liz (2018), *Acts and Apparitions: Discourses on the Real in Performance Practice and Theory, 1990–2010*, Manchester: Manchester University Press.

Wickstrom, Maurya (2014), 'Desire and Kairos: Cassils's "Terisias"', *TDR: Drama Review*, 58(4): 46–55.

Wilson, Harry Robert (2017), 'The Theatricality of the Punctum: Re-Viewing Camera Lucida'. *Performance Philosophy*, 3(1): 266–84.

Wilson, Harry Robert (2019), 'The Theatricality of Grief: Suspending Movement, Mourning and Meaning with Roland Barthes', *Performance Research*, 24(4): 103–9.

Part II

RETHINKING ROLAND BARTHES, THEATRE, PERFORMANCE

Chapter 8

WE'VE NEVER MET BUT WE MAY HAVE FOUGHT

Simon Bayly and Ira Brand

On 16 Aug 2019, at 23:29, Simon Bayly wrote:

Dear Ira,

We've never met, but we may have fought – like the outcome, it's undecided. I came to see *Ways to Submit* at the Yard earlier this year. I met a friend, whom I think you also know, at the show by chance and we had an interesting conversation afterwards, I told her a story – which she told me I should write up. So I did. When I saw her a few weeks later, also by chance, she told me that she had already told the story to someone else and did I mind? I imagine she thought I might have minded because the story contained some intimate and somewhat disorganised feelings, but I didn't mind and perhaps I was even glad, since she had managed to [orally] 'publish' the story without involving me, which I regard as an ideal form of authorship. Anyway, the writing has remained sitting on my computer for a while and I forgot about it until recently. I looked at it again and it seemed OK to send it to you, though I had never intended to do that at the time of writing. […] No obligation for you to respond, to like it or anything else really. But if it in some way contributes to the conversations or the show's future iterations, then that will be a good outcome.

With best wishes,
Simon

On 10 Feb 2020, at 13:35, Ira Brand wrote:

Dear Simon,

This is a super delayed response, but maybe that's also fine. Maybe it's a nice length of time between your coming to see the show, and you sharing your writing, and me actually getting round to reading it. I realised that last week was exactly a year since the shows at The Yard.

I received your email when I was in the middle of a super intense project, which meant everything else fell away a bit, and then I part forgot, part put off reading what you had written. I guess I was really pleased to receive it and that you had taken the time to articulate something in response (partly) to the work, but was also a bit nervous and feeling a bit vulnerable at that time. Today I find myself on a long, disrupted train journey and I realised I had two texts that I had been sent by audience members that I had never read, and it felt like a moment where that would be possible.

Anyway, I just wanted to respond to thank you for writing this and for sharing it with me. It was really great to read, and has given me a lot to reflect on. It is also just beautifully, intimately, and rigorously written so I feel like my tedious train journey has been improved by being taken on your journey.

Thanks very much, and all the best,

Ira

On 12 Feb 2020, at 16:40, Simon Bayly wrote:

Dear Ira,

Thanks so much for your reply – especially after such a long time. I'm glad that you found something interesting in the writing. I'm intrigued by a state of mind in which one might wait so long before reading and responding to something like this – which you describe obliquely – perhaps something like receiving an unsolicited gift at a complicated life stage and not being sure of the what the consequences of opening it might be. I get that. Anyways, good to see you're still performing the piece – it's a lovely, thought-provoking thing. If you ever thought there might be any mileage in some sort of publication that involved audience responses to the work and perhaps to that of other artists who've gotten involved with similar things recently and historically, then I'd be up for that.

All the best,
Simon

On 17 Feb 2020, at 20:48, Ira Brand wrote:

Hi Simon,

That's kind of funny, that was my first thought when I read both these texts last week, how nice it would be to compile something of these kinds of reflections. I find it particularly interesting because of how different the responses are, and I assume would be, and this makes me think about how much of the work actually happens or is shaped in the mind and body of an individual audience member, rather than necessarily a shared experience. I guess that's always the case but feels heightened here.

Well, I'll keep musing on that – and if I think of the right frame I'll be in touch!

All the best,
Ira

On 26 Nov 2020, at 13:33, Simon Bayly wrote:

Dear Ira,

I'm just getting back in touch to ask you something. Earlier this year, just after our email exchange, Harry Wilson, who works at Glasgow University, put out a speculative call for a proposed edited book of essays about Roland Barthes and performance […] A bit on a whim, I sent in a very short abstract for an 'essay' based around the writing I'd sent you, given that Barthes's first 'signature' essay for an English-speaking readership is 'The World of Wrestling'. And he has been a figure who has kind of shadowed my work in and out of the theatre ever since I was 19 or so. […]

The publishers are now moving ahead with the proposal and first drafts are due 18th Jan … I haven't quite figured out what to do with the writing in terms of publication, but before doing anything I wanted to see what you thought. […] I'm wondering if there might be an opportunity here to 'compile something', as you suggest, or for you (and perhaps others?) to contribute to that compilation, if that was of interest – and it would also be fine if it wasn't. On that front, I wouldn't want to move further with putting what I've written into the public domain without you being OK with that, as a bare minimum. But I guess in sending it to you, it has already gone 'public' in some way? And this rather blurry distinction between private/public – which seems a redundant binary today – seems very much part of Barthes's legacy to writing, which makes it perhaps all the more relevant to the proposed essay collection. Anyway, I just wanted to hear your thoughts before doing anything else.

    Best,

Simon

On 4 Dec 2020, at 17:34, Ira Brand wrote:

Dear Simon,

Sorry for the slight slowness (although not as slow as last time!), I've just started a new part-time job so have been finding my feet with that this week.

    This sounds great, and I'm really happy for you that the text might have another more public outing.

    In a way, I'd love to think about a compilation of texts as you suggest, though my hesitation would be that the texts that are already written about *Ways to Submit* might not relate enough to Barthes to fit here. […] If you think that's not the case, I'd be super happy to chat more to understand what could be possible, and certainly I'd be up for writing something if you think it would add some interesting context to – or exchange with – your essay. […]

    Very best,

Ira

On 10 Dec 2020, at 14:25, Simon Bayly wrote:

Dear Ira,

Thanks – I'm glad you're up for this. […] I think there might be space for anything between 1500 and 3000 of new material.

    That said, you've already written something around/about the work – which feels just about perfect as it is. There is a sense of longing for something in your writing – for a certain type of presence, contact, intimacy – which, while it might be responding to the additional distance of 'socially distanced' life, also speaks to a more primordial distance (or perhaps a fantasy of the absence of it) that gives shape to a kind of eros of the everyday. Barthes's iconic essay on wrestling, which seems to also be an essay about the theatre, is all about its radical *intelligibility*:

> There is no more a problem of truth in wrestling than in the theatre. In both, what is expected is the intelligible representation of moral situations which are usually private … In wrestling, nothing exists except in the absolute, there is no symbol, no allusion, everything is presented exhaustively … What is portrayed by wrestling is therefore an ideal understanding of things; it is the euphoria of men [sic] raised for a while above the constitutive ambiguity of everyday situations and placed before the panoramic view of a univocal Nature, in which signs at last correspond to causes, without obstacle, without evasion, without contradiction. (Barthes 2009: 7 and 14)

But it seems to me that *Ways to Submit* implicitly 'wrestles' with Barthes's reading of wrestling and theatre, saturating it with a kind of sensual *unintelligibility*, messing with its exhaustive theatricality, reasserting the non-ideal, 'constitutive ambiguity of everyday situations' but without being able to fully abandon the vice-like grip of theatre and theatricality. In fact, they become the conduit or means to access or engage with what is unintelligible, but nevertheless experienced and understood […] This seems to resonate with the themes of the proposed book – and perhaps more so for not being 'signed', i.e. made clearly intelligible or directly correlated to Barthes's own work.

Anyway, I'm wondering if there's a possibility of (re-)working what you have already written so eloquently about the show, alongside what I have written? […]

All the best,
Simon

References

Barthes, Roland (2009), 'The World of Wrestling', *Mythologies*, trans. Jonathan Cape, London: Vintage, 3–14.

Chapter 9

FOR THE LOVE(RS) OF DRAMATURGY: ON ROLAND BARTHES'S AMATEUR

Swen Steinhäuser

Part one: Mixtape for Roland Barthes

Lookout mountain, lookout sea

Is this a picture of the student's sanatorium at Sainte-Hilaire-du-Touvet in the Isère in the Alps between Grenoble and Chambery? The same sanatorium where a young Roland Barthes spent his days reading and writing between 1942 and 1945 after suffering a relapse of pulmonary tuberculosis, a condition he was first diagnosed with in 1934? Or is it a picture of the university sanatorium at Leysin above Aigle in Switzerland, where he spends another year convalescing in 1946? (Figure 9.1) In any case, between Leysin, Sainte-Hilaire-du-Touvet and the village of Bedous in the Pyrennees – to which he briefly relocates from Paris in 1934 for the benefit of the mountain air – Barthes will have spent a total of some eight years convalescing in medical isolation. Disrupting his studies for the baccalauréat in 1934 and depriving him of the chance of sitting the entrance exam for the École Normale Superieure, the condition painfully diverts him from the traditional academic path to which he had aspired. Far from the customary institutional routes of the French elite, Barthes is forced to forge a different path towards writing and publication by substituting the formal contexts of higher education with a concentrated time of solitary reading and writing 'at a distance aloof from the uproar of life' (Barthes 2005: 164).

Deprived of the institutional benefits of Higher Education, his medical isolation in rural refuge nevertheless provides him with certain favourable conditions for a *desiring* reading, that 'absolutely

Figure 9.1 Perhaps the student's sanatorium at Sainte-Hilaire-du-Touvet in the Isère in the Alps between Grenoble and Chambery or the university sanatorium at Leysin above Aigle in Switzerland.
Source: www.geneanet.org

separated, clandestine state in which the whole world is abolished' (Barthes 2005: 38–9). When burrowing through the sixty volumes of the complete works of nineteenth-century historian Jules Michelet on top of a mountain in the Swiss Alps, he first develops what is to remain a lifelong working method of compiling index cards filled with fragmentary notes, quotations and drafted thoughts that accompany his reading. Advancing a kind of '*intelligence of the mole*' (emphasis added), he 'scratch[es] out the details', or perhaps more caringly selects and assembles the fragments, and indexes the *flakes*, against the contrasting backdrop of the panoramic setting (164). Closely entangling the gestures of reading and writing in an elaborate system of note-taking, filing and the shifting combinatorial re-assemblage of parts into the singular constellations of works, the young Barthes unwittingly stumbles upon a gesture and attitude of production that is to concern him in a more self-reflective manner later on. Letting his reading and writing practice be knowingly and demonstratively traversed by quotations, references and the echoes of cultural languages, he rehearses a modality of thought that begins to *think in other heads while in his own others beside himself are thinking* (Barthes 1989: 213). An avid collector of fragments with a keen eye for the cut and the seam, he is devoted to a gesture of production that resembles 'the original art of the courtier': 'pieces, fragments are subjected to certain correspondences, arrangements, reappearances' (281). The autodidactic and artisanal quality of this scene becomes a more and more legible trace within the lapidary tone of Barthes's style, which selects, turns and shifts the pieces of disparate genres, disciplines and sources with the lightest of touch, gathering fragments with the near pressureless 'gesture of the chopstick' into singular constellations of assemblage (Barthes 1982: 15).

*

What brings and holds together the various elements of Barthes's works and oeuvre is not the disciplined rigor of the expert in pursuit of a narrowly scoped out field of accumulated knowledge – paying his respects before the itinerary of some tightly pre-prescribed menu – but the idiosyncratic trajectory of the cruise: a self-reflective mapping of the stroll of an idle subject without precise destination. Suspicious of the 'arrogance of theory' (Hollier 2005: 35) his research is saturated with a 'joyous dilettantism', the obsessive love and admiration of recurring sources and the recently discovered (Barthes 2005: xxiii). True to his claim, as Jacques Derrida has recalled it, 'To be looking for what comes *to him* and suits him, what agrees with him and fits him like a garment' (2001: 39; emphasis in the original), the 'Preliminaries' to his lecture course on 'The Neutral' eschew the usual bibliographical ambition or pretence of objectivity and totality of a staked-out field of research in favour of 'nothing more than a list of the texts whose reading, in various ways, has *punctuated* the preparation of this course' (Barthes 2005: 1; emphasis added). Limiting himself solely to works found in his personal library in Urt, 'a place-time where the loss in methodological rigor is compensated for by the intensity and the pleasure of free reading' (9), his working 'method' – if we can still call it that, given that it lacks systematicity and orderliness, and therefore, precisely, method – embraces chance, accident and an unabashedly personal and forever tenuous logic of consistency as valid structures for a project of public research driven by an attraction for *advenience*, if not adventure (Barthes 1989: 285). Deeply involved with, as well as more or less committed to, various intellectual currents that sweep throughout his oeuvre, he remains an 'amateur' before them all – borrowing, mixing, more or less adopting but above all testing their respective 'language' from a position of theatrical distance, the kind of 'distance' he so much admired at the heart of Brecht's 'revolutionary dramaturgy' and the

Japanese puppet theatre *Bunraku* (Barthes 1982: 54). Demonstratively gathering a *heterology* of knowledge marked by a discontinuity of the codes, he denies his discourse the illusory ground of a stable, masterful site of origin (Barthes 1989: 109). Unable to account in his own person for what he is never alone to write, he follows the Brechtian dictum to let citation rule, allowing himself to be traversed and somewhat tossed about by a wide range of sources and influences, finding serenity in the midst of disorder, sustained by a contradictory immobility in movement of the drift (1982: 55). Carried whilst himself carrying, his is a paradoxical productivity in a state of passive relaxation, taking up that 'most relaxing position of a body' that *floats*, that is, 'live[s] in space without tying oneself to a place' (2005: 19), not unlike the image of the '*halcyonian*' bird, which builds its nest on water to labour on a momentarily calm sea (164–5, emphasis in the original).

*

No master

When Barthes finally does end up – via the detours of convalescence, librarianship and journalism – with a 'chair' at the Collège de France and the status of public intellectual, he does so not without a cultivated attitude of reluctance. Placed into unavoidable structures of institutional hierarchy and authority, he is perpetually to be found contemplating the limited possibilities of eschewing an accredited mastery. During the April 29 session of his lecture course on 'The Neutral', he draws up a detailed breakdown of various ways to dodge a question and baffle the arrogant request for a good reply. Assembling an inventory of possible gestures of evasion, he recounts the examples of various 'beside-the-point answers' – 'hairbrainers' – subversive, provocative and unsettling texts, gestures and acts. In thrall to the example of Eurylochus, who 'once in Elis ... was so hard pressed by his pupils' questions that he stripped and swam across the [river] Alpheus' – taking his leave upon proffering nothing but the flippant word *Ciao* – Barthes dreams of emulating his claim to 'the right ... of knowing nothing, of thinking nothing, of saying nothing' (2005: 111).

*

Elsewhere, Barthes reflects and tests out other, less drastic ways of avoiding mastery, 'the stake today of all teaching, of any intellectual "role"' (1989: 176). Stylistically stretched between positions of reading

9. For the Love(rs) of Dramaturgy

and writing, assimilation and exposition, he can be found to demonstrate 'that he is teaching himself what he is supposed to be communicating to others' (ibid.), cultivating the habit, as Derrida observes, of 'explaining what he is doing by giving us his notes', 'describing his way of proceeding, … giving us an account of what he is doing while he is doing it' (2001: 42). The exposed impossibility of speaking from a position of mastery puts him in the position of a subject who no longer allows himself to speak merely *about* something – a given object of knowledge and information, an irreducible content extracted from a mere ornamental form, the finality of some signified freed from the play of and with signification – but one who assumes the experimental attitude of a (demonstrated) *practice*. Producing 'messages' that cannot be summarised once and for all – destroying thereby, as he points out, their nature as message – by adhering to a type of knowledge production that he associates with the figure of the amateur (Barthes 1989: 312).

*

In a lecture at the Collège de France, which takes up a reflection on the stylistic innovations of Marcel Proust in the context of an imagined future of his own work, Barthes associates the amateur with writing in the emphatic sense of a practice. Anxious over the possibility of a 'foreclosure of … Adventure (that which "advenes" – which befalls me)', he evokes the cruelty of feeling doomed, in the middle of his life, with no time left to try out several new ones, to the endless repetitions of an acquired mode of doing (1989: 285). Compelled to transform a habitual way of doing, disrupting the comfortable security of an acquired status, non-conforming with an instituted expectation as well as abandoning the drowsy familiarity of an acquired knowledge, he speculates on a projected process of un- and re-learning that were to put him in a favourable condition for the adventure of some coming innovation. Interrogating a coming style from the position of somebody who acts *as if* he were to write a work that he does not yet know and master but 'expect[s] to break with the uniformly intellectual nature of [his] previous writings', Barthes 'put[s] [him]self in the position of the subject who *makes* something, and no longer of the subject who speaks *about* something' (289; emphasis in the original). Instead of 'studying a product, [he] assumes a production', by which 'the world no longer comes to [him] as an object, but as a writing, i.e., a practice'. Doing so, he 'proceed[s]', as he puts it, 'to another type of knowledge', namely, 'that of the Amateur' (ibid.).

*

Although the projected possibility of this adventure must in its structure remain radically uncertain and without actual referent, the 'utopian novel' that it tentatively evokes is circumscribed as a possible offshoot of that 'third form' he recognises in Proust and with which we indeed have more or less come to identify Barthes's own late style. Its 'mixed, uncertain, hesitant form, both fictive and intellectual', is neither that of the essay nor the novel, saturated with 'a certain indecision of genres' (1989: 279). Its collections of diverse fragments are 'shielded from the ancestral law of Narrative and Rationality', out to establish 'another logic' that rests on the provocative principle of a disorganisation of Time (of chronology) – 'of Vacillation, of Decompartmentalization', and above all, *of rhythm* – that force of consistency in disorganisation (281).[1] This rhapsodic 'novel' imposes itself on Barthes as the possibility of a more neutral form, breaking with the paradigmatic 'terrorism' of discourse and its brutish pressure to enter conflict, to choose – one term, concept or argument over another. Refraining from the assertion of a thesis it 'exerts *no pressure* upon the other (the reader); its power is the truth of affects, not of ideas', aligned, as he puts it according to a Nietzschean typology, 'with art and not priesthood' (289, emphasis added).

*

Barthes daydreams of a mode of inhabiting language that thwarts the structural violence of assertion. Unsurprisingly, his dream of eluding the paradigmatic injunction to produce meaning, to enter conflict, to 'take responsibility' becomes a problem for the situation of teaching that his professional role bestows on him (2005: 7). In his programmatic reflections on the seminar, 'To the seminar', he circumscribes the utopia of a non-hierarchical learning community of desire rather than of science. In an echo of what he elsewhere designates as the knowledge of the amateur, he insists on the need to resist the authority of a discourse sustained outside of praxis. In other words, not to say merely what he knows, but to set forth what he is doing (1989: 333). Here, the situation of teaching, traditionally understood as the transmission and reception of a pre-existing knowledge content, is foreclosed and disappointed. Instead, knowledge

---

1. An organizing principle of rhythm that also lies at the heart of a dramaturgical know-how of devising as the process of a structural weave of heterogeneous elements that leaves palpable the cracks within a weak whole. Rhythm, in other words, turns out an important dramaturgical modality of care for the minimal consistency of an essential fragility of world.

must persistently and demonstratively be (re-)produced. Either, by someone working, seeking, gathering, writing in the other's presence, or by a collectively shared incitement to produce a circulating object of knowledge passing from hand to hand (336). This will also be the scene of learning at Dartington College of Arts as I recount it below. What here remains of the teacher's responsibility is an initial initiation, putting the object of knowledge to be produced into circulation. Such an attitude of participation in the circulation and dissemination of knowledge foregoes the authoritarian claims to copyright and filiation that are the traditional hallmarks of author- and professor-ship. Whereas 'the Father is the Speaker: he who sustains discourse outside praxis, severed from all production', as Barthes notes, 'the one who shows, the one who states, the one who shows the statement, is no longer the Father' (340).

Put differently, he is the amateur.

*

Part two: Notes on amateur dramaturgy

Elegy for Dartington College of Arts

Like so many others working with or on experimental structures of contemporary theatre, performance and choreography, I have had my fair share of formative experiences in more classical forms of drama (most notably, participating in the brilliantly melancholic, funny and somewhat sexy 1997 production of Georg Büchner's *Leonce und Lena* by Theater AG Helmholtzschule under the ingenious direction of Katrin von Plotnitz). By the time, however, I left Germany for England on a Eurobus from Frankfurt Hauptbahnhof in September 1999 to take up my place on a BA course in Theatre at Dartington College of Arts, I was eager to learn how to construct performance works without the foundations of a play-text or the strictures of a traditional narrative structure. Inspired by the live encounter with works of the late 1990s by Robert Wilson, Forced Entertainment, Gob Squad, Christoph Schlingensief, Drei Wolken and William Forsythe, as well as saturated with a multitude of stimuli taken from film, literature, critical theory and the visual arts – arriving at Dartington at the turn of the millennium – I found myself less interested in re-rehearsing the structural break with a dramatic tradition of theatre than in taking the leap into the void of an uncertain methodological field of experimentation without narrowly defined origins or anticipated outcomes of form. Dartington, at least as

I remember it today, was more than able to facilitate this experimental leap with the kind of broad, unsystematic, inter-, cross- and transdisciplinary outlook that facilitated the discovery of what suited me. At that time and place, the word 'dramaturgy', with its Germanic resonance of a certain bookish guardianship over the repertoire of dramatic texts and structures, felt more than a little out of place.

*

When the word returns to me today, it is precisely in close proximity to that methodological field *without narrowly prescribed way of doing*, that method without method, which at Dartington in the early 2000s was called 'devising'. If the latter term has perhaps since fallen out of fashion and retreated to the margins of disciplinary concern – especially since Hans-Thies Lehmann's influential formal classification of the 'postdramatic', with which it shares a considerable pool of practitioners and works – it nevertheless warrants saving as an emphatic designation of a mode of practice, process, gesture and ethos rather than the classification of a type of work.

*

This practico-ethical dimension of the dramaturgy of devising is a tentative, experimental know-how of structuring (the) time and space (of a performance-event). Its defining trait is a lack, as well as active refusal, of readymade blueprints for a pre-programmed work. 'In devising', David Williams notes, 'dramaturgy is uncovered, worked and articulated *through the process of making and rehearsing*, rather than being predetermined' (2010: 198; emphasis in the original). In gestures of fragmenting, collecting, de- and reconstructing, citing, assembling, juxtaposing, relating, responding, improvising, composing, choreographing, scoring, rehearsing and recalling, it facilitates the construction of a fragile field of consistency of an assemblage or (livable) 'world'. Eschewing a definitive map of a narrowly preconceived terrain, it resembles a labour of (dis)orientation within a weak structural field. Amateur dramaturgy would thus be the know-how of passage through the crisis of knowledge and meaning 'towards' a work's unpredictable *coming*. It rehearses the *nuance* of looking, listening and thinking irreducible to seeing, hearing and knowing.[2] Perhaps its most gentle,

---

2. For a more concentrated account of dramaturgy in the context of devising 'nested' in an experience of working at DCA, see David Williams's 'Geographies of Requiredness: Notes on the Dramaturg in Collaborative Devising' (2010).

most tactful approach would amount to adhering to the task of memory alone (with or without the help of external substrates: notebooks, index cards, scores, video recordings etc.). Allowing with time for the possibility of return and the repetitions of rehearsal, saturating each mark with the gentle gravity of accumulated layers of time. Marianne Van Kerkhoven has spoken of dramaturgy as a gesture of guardianship over the history of a process, 'in order, occasionally, to restore [it] to memory' (1994: 144). But beyond the patient (re)collection of the memory of a process, the dramaturgy of devising might also designate that gesture of tentative projection towards an unknown future (work) from within a given set of assembled materials and conditions (one of the possible German translations of 'devising' being *entwerfen*, with its Heideggerian resonance of the *geworfene Entwurf* (thrown projection) (Heidegger 1993). As the experimental know-how of a practical cunning – that is, the ability to operate from within an uncertain field of procedure impossible to master in advance – the dramaturgy of devising becomes synonymous with the knowledge and ethos of an amateur, who loves what Williams calls the 'fragile imperfect life' of a 'made thing still being made' (2010: 201). An ethos as it lay at the heart of my experiences of learning at Dartington College of Arts: paradoxical institute of higher education in the rigorous training in amateur know-how.

*

Today, I look back on those experiences, situated somewhere between memory and myth, with a degree of amazement and near disbelief in face of the kind of loose, idiosyncratic and often performative

---

At several points of his essay, Williams can be found to associate the ethos and practice of dramaturgy with the figure of the amateur as it resonates with my present concerns, whether by championing 'a pragmatic educational philosophy of learning by doing' (200), by valuing the cracks, fragility and imperfections of 'a made thing still being made' (201) or by cultivating a broad, trans-disciplinary and largely 'scavenged' dramaturgical know-how unfounded in real expertise (199). I am grateful to Harry Wilson for pointing me in the direction of Williams's writings on dramaturgy after reading a first draft of my essay. Suffice to say that, given the profound influence of Williams's work on my own experiences as a student at DCA and beyond, their general ethos already lay implicitly at the heart of the relation of dramaturgy, devising, Dartington and the amateur as I here explore them within the context of Roland Barthes.

modalities of teaching I encountered there. Notwithstanding some form of structured engagement with an admittedly complex history of contemporary performance since at least the 1960s and the multiple, undecidable origins of its bastard lineage, what I remember most about my education (apart from simply providing me with certain favourable conditions to experiment, *aloof from the uproar of life*) are not the well-meaning but often tedious and somewhat anxious attempts to appropriate various forms and genres by tracing their lineage within the crude -isms of intellectual and art historical periodization, but the many idiosyncratic details and fragments difficult to fully subsume under the auspices of some well-structured syllabus: seeds of confusion, irritation, reflection, inspiration and above all desire. Walking out of a lecture theatre at Dartington was never far from the experience of leaving the theatre at the end of a performance – a bit hit and miss, to be sure, but never without some strong sensation on the level of affect. At its best, this was a feeling of astonishment and desire, feeling interpellated as a practitioner called to participate in a collective production of knowledge rather than to passively receive some readymade piece of information. A lit candle in a darkened lecture theatre, a lecturer in a wedding dress, some personal account with maps tracing the journey through a Paris graveyard, a long list of fires, a projected film of night time shots of American suburbia accompanied by a brooding Leonard Cohen soundtrack that continues to play as I leave the auditorium – these are the kind of strange fragments of education that have *pricked* me. Unable to let go of or lightly subsume under some recallable body of knowledge, they put me to the task of a response to this day, leaving me to continue to think, make, write and teach in their wake.

*

At Dartington, knowledge was something that was produced there (or not), but never hierarchically transmitted. Passed around people passionately at work alongside each other, it failed to ever come to rest as an accumulated possession. Following an ethos of experiment and rehearsal unburdened by the weight of disciplinary regimes and narrow fields of specialization, Dartington offered the uncertain ground for a *training* – in the Brechtian sense of *Übung* (exercise, practice) rather than the goal-directed disciplining of a body and brain – for how to become and, what is more, how to remain, an amateur (dramaturg).

*

Towards a society of amateurs

Learning how to remain an amateur does not here mean to accept lightly the socio-economic status of a semi-professionalism in constant danger of petering out into a hobby – such as it is the cruel and alienating reality for many artists and researchers working on the institutional fringes of an ever more closed, underfunded and (structurally) competitive landscape of the arts and humanities. The ethos of a generalized amateurism as it concerns me here does not correspond to a social division of status and institution, plays no part in the reductive opposition between doing something for the love or the money and can be practiced on and across both sides of a structurally fragile divide. To 'remain' an amateur in this context means precisely to stay outside of mastery and 'the will-to-possess' in spite of crossing some institutional threshold of education or employment. This was also the story of Roland Barthes, who had an unfailing taste for the ethos of a certain amateurism on both sides of a socio-institutional divide – whether painting as a 'Sunday painter' or lecturing from his 'chair' at the Collège de France. Instead of reaffirming an oppositional paradigm, the know-how and gestures of a generalized amateurism cut across, if not subvert, the socio-institutional split between amateurs and professionals, consumers and producers, readers and writers. Pointing towards the social utopia of what Barthes calls 'a society of amateurs', they engage in a critical practice of eroding, scrambling and rendering porous the existing limits and divisions of contributory participation in the (re)production of knowledge and culture. Limits and divisions that are at once structural *and* political, that is, both ineluctable as well as given over to the possibility of an endless transformational critique.

*

In Barthes's writings, a latent, discontinuous thematic concern with the amateur stops short of a macro-political engagement with a broad, socio-historical analysis of the regression of knowledge and contributory participation in capitalist industries of material and cultural (re)production. In other words, Barthes refrains from pursuing the opening of the theme of the amateur onto what he himself evokes in passing as 'a problem of civilization', that is, the history of 'technical development and the evolution of mass culture [that] reinforces the division between producers and consumers to a frightening extent' (1992: 217). Despite abstaining from a detailed account of such a macro-political perspective, his expression of fear in face of the troubling reality that 'we are a consumer society and not at all a society of amateurs' nevertheless bespeaks a critical concern with the underlying conditions of such a state of affairs. What he does pursue instead is the micrological perspective onto a body's (failed) modalities of adoption of a 'logosphere', that 'biological ambience' of language, as he calls it, 'within which and through which [man] lives' (2005: 86). Drawing out the nuances of contact and entanglement between a body and the pre-individual fund of collective memory, the 'I' and the 'We', Barthes's intricate concern for practices of socio-individuation in gestures of (self)writing across a diversity of media remains firmly rooted in his own bodily experiences of pleasure, bliss, pain, desire and taste (1989: 32). Uninclined therefore to merely speak *about* the amateur from the safe distance of a theory, he himself begins to stammer *as* amateur, dedicated to a (dis)orientating practice of writing irreducible to the transparent (re)presentation of ideas. The depths of his demonstrated bodily involvement in writing as a practice embodies what he designates as a defining trait of the figure of the amateur, namely, that 'contact between [his] body and his art is very close' (1992: 217). An intimacy between body and art, or body and techne, which springs from a demonstrated involvement in processes of assimilation and adoption. Caught up in a perpetual desire for the (ex-)appropriation of a given 'logosphere' without the will to possess, the amateur turns out a virtuoso of the repetitive rhythms of the rehearsal, able to perpetually 'renew his pleasure' with regards to a practice: '(*amator*: one who loves and loves again)' (Barthes 1994: 52; emphasis in the original).

*

Amateur dramaturgy perhaps begins here, with the demonstrated involvement in a non-possessive process of assimilation of a pre-individual fund of knowledge – scavenging, accumulating, transforming and re-circulating a stock of traces, materials, gestures and compositional models across time and space. Far beyond the narrow context of the arts, this paradoxical expertise in the modality of rehearsal turns out a model ethos for a much broader task of inheritance. In its expanded sense of a general know-how of contributory participation in the perpetual (re)weaving of a shared intertext, amateur dramaturgy begins to resemble a gesture of loving care. What it loves and takes care of is the essential fragility of a shared ethos and habitus – a made thing still (forever) being (re)made.

*

Part three: Index cards

'Writing *seems* like the ultimate magic trick', the photographer, filmmaker and writer Moyra Davey notes with a degree of appropriate uncertainty, 'of making something from nothing' (Davey 2020: 61; emphasis in the original). An uncertainty that brings to mind the need of dramaturg Matthew Goulish to counter a false impression that his devised work with the US performance company Goat Island has sprung from a similar act of conjuring. 'People have told us', Goulish relates, 'that our work starts with nothing and builds something. But I have never been convinced about the "starts with nothing" part' (Bottoms and Goulish 2007: 55). For the company's devising processes have indeed grown from something – a question, a task, a carefully selected array of fragments from a range of pre-existing source materials – raised from their 'original' contexts before gently placed and patiently woven into a unique new spatio-temporal assemblage.

*

Yet despite the material certainty of the sources, something might still be said to appear from nothing in the process of their re-assemblage. For the discovery of an absolutely unique relation between the assembled parts necessarily springs from the radical absence of its preconception. In other words, it is an emptiness of the future rather than of the past that here enables the possibility of newness to enter the world.

*

The beginning of each new process of devising opens the void of an empty futurity. An opening onto uncertainty and unknowing most difficult to bear when least grounded in the features of an as yet to be established precondition. Entering the generic 'emptiness' of a rehearsal studio at the beginning of each process, saturated with an ambivalent mood of excitement and anxiety, one is bound to experience in equal measure the exhilarant possibility of adventure mixed with an oppressive lack of pre-direction. Because 'anxiety arises', as Barthes notes, 'not from having to choose between two paths but from having all the paths and thus no "path" open before one', it is necessary to start from somewhere, to draft the location of some minimal ground, a preliminarily staked out field of limitation (2005: 145). In other words, one must bear and patiently negotiate the experience of an uncanny uprootedness at the threshold of its potential vanishing, fending off the starkest of deprivation of the minimal security of a ground from which to project, however tenuously, into an unknown future, whilst remaining distractively attentive (i.e. open) to its unpredictable coming.

*

The virgin space of an *open field*, Barthes notes, lacks the necessary landmarks to imbue it with the topicality of a *livable place*. (Amateur) dramaturgy would be that cunning know-how of passage through the crisis of knowledge, meaning and institution in search of the topicality of a (livable) place. It is the gesture of assemblage that reconstructs out of little (but not nothing!) a weakly erected ensemble of spatio-temporal markers of the possibility of return that make up a 'world'. It rules tactfully over time and space in the manner of the Japanese concept of *ma* according to Barthes: a spacing of space and time that is 'neither crowding nor "desertification"' (2005: 147). Between a sense of unbearable disorientation at the extreme end of overcrowding and the emptiness of the open field, it invents myriad ways to (re-)construct the livable place of an ethos according to a diversity of tastes, styles and temperaments – from hoarding to decluttering, from pairing to constellating, from focusing to blurring, including those paradoxical states of liminal grace when 'the sharp seizes the blurry' ('what one could call', as Barthes notes: 'the consciousness of mist') (2005: 98).

*

Every world is made from the ruins of another. Its perpetual (re)construction passes through the task of inheritance as a practice, not an accumulated wealth of ready-made goods. (Amateur) dramaturgy, as a practice of facilitation of the passage from past to future via the crisis (of knowledge, meaning and institution) in any given present, is fundamentally linked to gestures of collecting, indexing, gathering, safekeeping and recollecting. As dramaturg Marianne Van Kerkhoven has pointed out, such gestures are essential to the field of dramaturgy as an everyday attitude of encounter with the world. 'One of the essential axes on which the practice of dramaturgy turns', Kerkhoven relates,

> is the accumulation of a reservoir of material – amassing knowledge in all fields: reading, listening to music, viewing exhibitions, watching performances, traveling, encountering people and ideas, living and experiencing and reflecting on all this. Being continuously occupied with the building up of a stock which may be drawn from at any time. Remembering at the right moment what you have in your stockroom. (1994: 146)

*

Davey's book, *Index Cards*, resembles such a stockroom. Full of accounts of the many processes and adventures of gathering its content, she inflects her uncertainty about writing's conjuring trick in the context of a reflection on the difference between the gestures of writing and photographing. In response to Susan Sontag's observation that the former 'has to reach and is constantly aware of how basically it comes from inside' while for the latter 'the world is really there', she advances a beautiful, personal and fitting counterpoint: 'Perhaps I still "write" like a photographer – I go out into the world of other's people writing and take snapshots … "word-pictures," … from [which] I can make something' (Davey 2020: 61).

*

The title of Davey's book evokes a certain stocking of 'snapshots' and resonates with the obsessive practice of note-taking developed by Roland Barthes. Beyond Davey's 'snapshots' of Barthes's work within her own, her text puts into practice the kind of deep imbrication of the gestures of reading and writing within an endless chain of desire as Barthes has analysed, practiced and advocated it throughout his work. 'In order to write I must keep reading', Davey says in an echo of Barthes, for what she writes is 'about being deformed and remade by the things I read' (2020: 136). In thrall to a Barthesian gesture of relating a personal history of *reading while looking up from a book*, it is difficult to pronounce with certainty where reading stops and writing begins here. Like Barthes, she transcribes the flow of ideas, stimuli and associations that grow from the intermittent suspension of a reading, 'at once insolent … and smitten', perpetually interrupting and returning to its object of distracted attention (Barthes 1989: 29). This text-as-reading, as Barthes calls it in contestation to the autonomous, untouchable and policed property of the work of an author, has become a kind of work in its turn. A *weak* work, to be sure, 'at once cohesive and detachable', happily coming undone at the seams upon the faintest touch of another's reading, 'destined to be … recomposed' according to the rhythm of its 'consumption' (Barthes 1982: 11).

*

Davey's text, which is strewn with reflections on the working methods of others and her own – a veritable treasure chest of 'dramaturgical' know-how across artforms and disciplines that include practical advice and self-reflection from novelist Virginia Woolf, sculptor Thomas

Hirschhorn, cultural theorist Walter Benjamin, video artist Matthew Buckingham, filmmaker Jean-Pierre Gorin, architect Aldo Rossi and many more – seemingly follows the programme of Barthes's 'third' adventure of reading, namely, reading as 'a conductor of the Desire to write' (Barthes 1989: 40). 'In this perspective,' Barthes states,

> Reading is a veritable production: no longer of interior images, of projections, of hallucinations, but literally of *work*: the (consumed) product is reversed into production, into promise, into desire for production, *and the chain of desires begins to unroll, each reading being worth the writing it engenders, to infinity*. (41, emphasis added)

*

Without mentioning the amateur by name other than by what we might read as its metonymic substitution as a lover, Barthes goes on to relate the intimate pleasure of the adventure of a writerly reading. Here, an amateur's pleasure of adventure, which springs from an instance of contributory socio-individuation – that is, the reciprocal becoming of an I and a We through processes of adoption and the shared relaunching of a cultural inheritance – is linked once more to what Barthes calls 'a problem of civilization' (Barthes 1989: 41).

> Is this pleasure of production an elitist pleasure, reserved only to potential writers? In our society, a society of reading, seeing, and hearing, and not a society of writing, looking, and listening, everything is done to block the answer: lovers of writing are scattered, clandestine, crushed by a thousand – even internal – constraints.
> This is a problem of civilization: but, for me, my profound and constant conviction is that it will never be possible to liberate reading if, in the same impulse, we do not liberate writing. (Barthes 1989: 41)

*

Here is not the place to address this immense problem in more detail. Instead it seems to me worth noting that it remains almost undecidable for Barthes's text, were it not for the opposition of a passive reading and active writing, if 'seeing and hearing' as opposed to 'looking and listening' are the traits of a disenfranchised consumer deprived of know-how and initiative, or of an arrogant master that rests on a possessive relation to the already-known. Both would be equally prone to miss, for however divergent structural reasons, what we might call with Barthes the *shimmer* of the *nuance*. Becoming legible only through a practical 'effort towards slight difference', the nuance, 'that whose aspect/ meaning is subtly modified according to the angle of the gaze', belongs to the clandestine lovers (of dramaturgy) (Barthes 2005: 51) – those, for instance, that endeavour to stay with an essential fragility of knowledge,

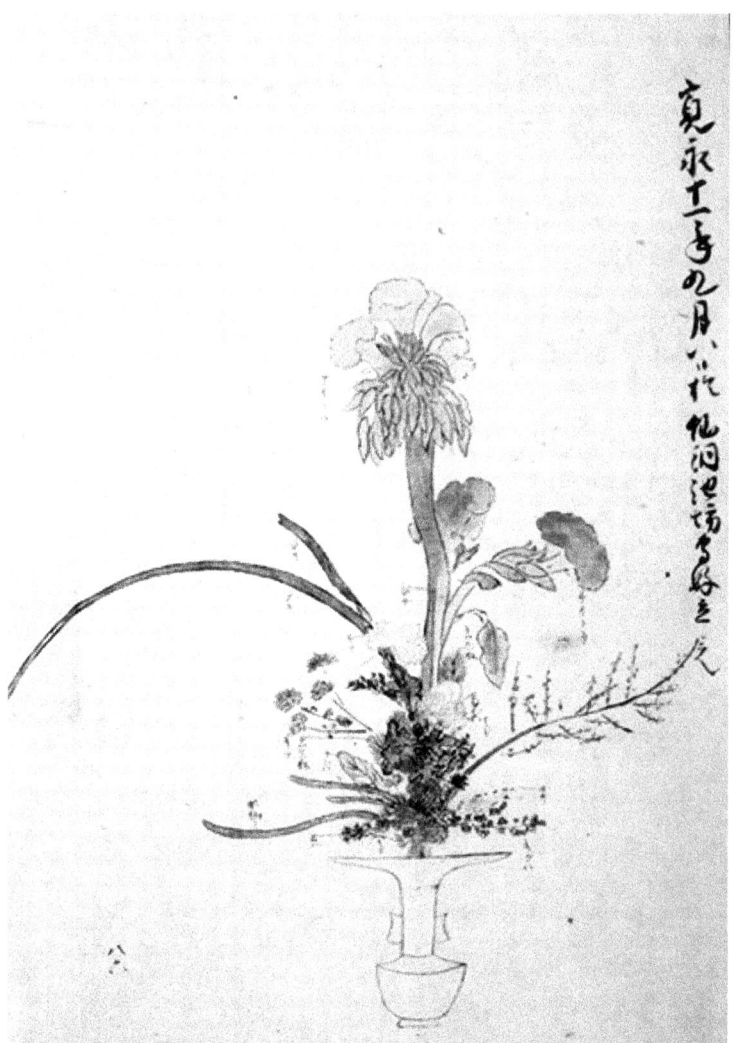

Figure 9.2 Illustration of a rikka work from the *Rikka-no-Shidai Kyūjūsanpei-ari (Ikenobō Senkō Rikka-zu)*, by Ikenobō Senkō II. Between 1628 and 1635. *Source:* Public Domain.

meaning and institution by committing to a perpetual reworking of a made ethos forever being (re)made. Involved in some process of devising or other, whether in the context of the arts or beyond, these amateur dramaturgs are able to 'entertain the life of an image/action' (text/architecture/assemblage etc.), as Williams puts it, without the need to own or readily subsume it within the logic of a larger whole. 'Staying close' to the 'excess' and 'alterity' of the nuance, they 'encourage its multiplicity and growth *without* seeking to explain it away, or to restrain its development by harnessing it within an authoritative discourse that will rob it of its otherness' (Williams 2010: 200).

*

The lover of dramaturgy is not an enemy of the work. But the work remains close to a production of 'the circulation of air'. However 'rigorously constructed' and imbued with symbolic intentions, as Barthes observes in his knowingly uninformed, or else 'amateur' reading of the art of Japanese flower arrangement *Ikebana* (Figure 9.2),

> You can move your body into the interstice of its branches, into the space of its stature, … to follow the trajectory of the hand which has written it: a true writing, since it produces a volume and since, forbidding our reading to be the simple decoding of a message, it permits this reading to repeat the course of the writing's labor. (1982: 44)

References

Barthes, Roland (1982), *Empire of Signs*, trans. Richard Howard, New York: Hill and Wang.
Barthes, Roland (1989), *The Rustle of Language*, trans. Richard Howard, Berkeley: University of California Press.
Barthes, Roland (1992), *The Grain of the Voice: Interviews 1962–1980*, trans. Linda Coverdale, New York: Hill and Wang.
Barthes, Roland (1994), *Roland Barthes by Roland Barthes*, trans. Richard Howard, Berkeley: University of California Press.
Barthes, Roland (2005), *The Neutral: Lecture Course at the Collège de France, 1977–1978*, trans. Rosalind Kraus and Denis Hollier, New York: Columbia University Press.
Bottoms, Steven, and Matthew Goulish (2007), *Small Acts of Repair: Performance, Ecology and Goat Island*, London: Routledge.
Davey, Moyra (2020), *Index Cards*, London: Fitzcarraldo Editions.

Derrida, Jacques (2001), 'The deaths of Roland Barthes' in *The Work of Mourning*, trans. Pascale-Anne Brault and Michael Naas, Chicago: The University of Chicago Press, 31–68.

Heidegger, Martin (1993), *Sein und Zeit*, Tübingen: Max Niemeyer Verlag.

Hollier, Denis (2005), *Notes (on the Index Cards)*, *October*, 112: 35–44.

Kerkhoven, Marianne Van (1994), 'On Dramaturgy: Looking Without Pencil in Hand' *Theaterschrift*, 5–6: 140–48. http://sarma.be/docs/2858 (accessed 15 April 2022).

Williams, David (2010), 'Geographies of Requiredness: Notes on the Dramaturg in Collaborative Devising', *Contemporary Theatre Review*, 20(2): 197–202.

Chapter 10

THE DISTURBANCE OF ONE SYSTEM BY ANOTHER

Claudia Kappenberg

An approach

Roland Barthes's *A Lover's Discourse* (1978), a collection of short, visceral linguistic outbursts, was a catalyst in the development of my performance practice at a time when I was trying to articulate and define concepts and strategies. I was – and still am – largely concerned with the fact that the everyday has become infiltrated by a credo of productivity and purpose that hugely constrains the lives of individuals, and that the performing arts tend to be largely complicit with this hegemony; however critical the intention, performances tend to consist of physical endeavours, spectacles and achievements large and small. I was curious as to how performance could resist this productivity whilst nevertheless constituting works of art, and how it could challenge the associated, ubiquitous and moral imperative to be useful.

Looking for allies, I was drawn to Roland Barthes's writing and his commitment to challenging the work of writing and of literature, that is, by his experimentation with form and with the construction of meaning, and by the sense that his writing was portraying language as process; 'Language is a skin', writes Barthes in *A Lover's Discourse* (1978: 73), and the physicality of this metaphor is striking. In my reading, this is not skin as layer or laminate, but skin as that which constitutes a temporary appearance of a body that is otherwise largely unknown and unknowable. I am drawing here on Elisabeth Grosz's writing on subjecthood and embodied presence, and her proposition of the three-dimensional shape of a Moebius strip as a metaphor for the Self. With this she implies an 'inflection of mind into body and body into mind, the ways in which, through a kind of twisting or inversion, one side becomes another' (1994: xii). With this model, an exteriority can fold to become an interiority, and an interiority can fold to become an exteriority, meaning that subjectivities are neither purely driven by inner impulses nor fully determined by external conditions. This also means that language may fold to become body, and body may fold to become language, together constituting what we call discourse. This discourse is therefore process and both an outer appearance and the folds and folding. In the process intensities emerge.

Exploring the discourse of desire Barthes writes, 'I rub my language against the other. It is as if I had words instead of fingers, or fingers at the tip of my words. My language trembles with desire' (1977: 73). In Barthes's discourse of desire, words and bodies are interchangeable, neither pertain to a surface but form embodied presences and movement with and between bodies, conjuring pathways and processes which in turn constitute relations. As Sunil Manghani argues in 'Barthes/Bataille: The Writing of Neutral Economy' (2018), the writings of Roland Barthes and of his fellow thinker Georges Bataille sought to articulate intensities which take the reader on a journey. Their philosophical bodies of thought resist classifications, practising writing as operation and movement rather than as a way to determine meaning. Much like Bataille, Manghani contends, Barthes's writing is dedicated to challenging conventional forms of knowledge production and it doubts language as a system that ensures meaning (195–6). Barthes dedicated his work to 'outplay' the consolidation of meaning, devising literary strategies that would facilitate a composition of text whilst challenging expectations as to the production of meaning, coherence and resolution.

My encounter with Barthes's strategies and resistance to meaning in writing was a kind of crossroads for my endeavour to outplay 'doing' in performing, that is, the kind of doing that colludes with expectations of productivity and purpose. In particular, Barthes's writing on the amorous dedication in *A Lover's Discourse* and key terms such as 'disruption' and 'silent expenditure' informed the making of a performance entitled *Flush, or the possibility of moving towards an impossible goal* (Kappenberg 2002), a site-specific intervention in Geneva, Switzerland. Key strategies developed for *Flush* also underpinned much of my later work including *Swan Canal* (Kappenberg and Seror 2011), an unofficial intervention in the city centre of Venice that was part of a city takeover initiated by an association of performance artists under the name of *Infr'Action*. This chapter will focus on these two performances and the questions they raised, namely, how interventions in the street could both enchant and challenge the passers-by and how this work could promote non-activity in resistance to a systemic oppression of the individual for the sake of wealth creation. Barthes's *A Lover's Discourse* will be consulted with regards to the first question, and his late lecture *The Neutral* with regards to the second. I have a sense of kinship with Barthes and a deep respect, but there is also an inscription at play within this relation; at the end of this chapter Barthes emerges as a fellow artist trickster and his literary oeuvre will be connoted as strategic and disruptive performative interventions rather than as an intellectual, critical, analytical or essayistic contribution.

The chapter partially draws on reflections of mine that constituted an aspect of my PhD (Kappenberg 2017), but has been written long after the fact, digging into a creative process that was not as explicitly formulated at the time. On one hand, this creative process spans years and, on the other, creative decisions sometimes happened with astonishing speed. In an excursion through Western philosophical bodies of work, the French philosopher and novelist Catherine Clément investigates this dazzling capacity of thought. Gathering lapses in rational thinking and dialectic constraints, she reviews for example Kierkegaard's *The Seducer's Diary*, in which thought is briefly equated with a young girl's leap (Clément 1994: 86). Leaving aside the gendered clichés and exploitative tenor of this narration, which Clément humorously describes as a 'plot for a bad film', Kierkegaard's text offers an intriguing comparison between a girl's agility and the calculating man's inability to leap into the unknown. Kierkegaard writes,

> Her leap is a gliding. And once she has reached the other side, she stands there again, not exhausted by the effort, but more beautiful, more soulful than ever; she throws a kiss over to us on this side. Young, newborn … she swings out over the abyss so that everything almost goes black before our eyes. (Clément 1994: 87)

I am interested here in both the suggestion that the leap was effortless and that it can be hard to follow. This instance is a metaphorical black out, a moment where insights and decisions occur that are not determined by conscious effort. A choreographic and devising process is, by and large, formed of many turns and twists but some conceptual leaps are effortless and hard to comprehend, even for oneself. Reading Barthes all those years ago, some sentences in his writing facilitated a leap within my process which leaves me with a challenge with regards to the present endeavour: how to retrace my steps? As I discovered in my practice, there is however the possibility of moving towards an impossible goal, and this text will endeavour to do just that.

A dance at noon, disturbance and silent expenditure

In 2002, I was invited to devise a project for an exhibition entitled *[Un]bemerkt in Genf, [Un]noticed in Geneva*, hosted by the Centre D'Art en Île, a gallery located in the city centre of Geneva on a small island in the Rhone which flows right through the city. I conceived a site-specific performance for a narrow footbridge, which leads from the small island down the middle of the river to the higher bridges that span the river, in parallel to the riverbanks. Being lower than the main bridges and the surrounding roads, the footbridge resembles a stage in the centre of an urban amphitheatre. The intervention was entitled *Flush, or the possibility of moving towards an impossible goal*.

The gallery had advertised the exhibition and performative interventions but there were no public signs at the actual location indicating that art was taking place, and no instructions as to how to negotiate the intervention on the narrow bridge. Over four days, around lunchtime, two female performers in long black rubber dresses with fluorescent green and pink sleeves walked onto the bridge with a bucket each. They engaged in a ritualistic activity, which suggested an un-obtainable goal: to scoop water with a bucket on one side of the bridge and pour it out into the same river on the other side of the bridge whilst working in opposition to each other.

The performance proceeded in a slow and measured way; the performers stood at some distance from each other, each looking out to one side of the river and the banks of the city, holding a bucket that was tied to a long rope. They dropped the buckets over the railing on their side of the bridge, waited for the buckets to fill up with water and hauled them up when full. Holding the buckets, both performers turned to cross the bridge, rested the buckets on the opposite railing and poured the water back into the river. When the buckets were empty, the performers lifted the buckets up high as if to pour out even the last few drops, paused and began a new cycle, dropping the buckets into the river below and waiting for them to fill up and so on (Figure 10.1).

As I discovered some time later, the costumes and buckets echoed the history of the bridge as suggested by the name of the walkway, La promenade des Lavandières (Passage of the Washerwomen), marked

Figure 10.1 *Flush, or the possibility of moving towards an impossible goal.* Kappenberg, 2004.
Source: Photograph: Andrew Downs.

on a street sign. At this point in time, however, the footbridge served as a path for the urban passers-by, as a means to get from one place to another. The persistent activity and repetitive gestures of the performers mirrored the sense of direction and purpose of the daily commuters, somewhat like clockwork, but it also played with the conventional economic logic: each cycle of buckets led to another cycle, but without producing anything and without leaving any traces at the site. Furthermore, by working in opposition, the performers cancelled each other's efforts, adding an absurdist note to an already seemingly irrational undertaking. The intervention constituted, above all, a generous squandering of effort and time.

Additionally, the steady rhythm of the activity was periodically suspended by sudden freezes of the performers, adding a confusing and disruptive element: after a certain number of cycles the performers suddenly froze in mid step. Standing still they held their buckets while the city around them and the waters below continued to flow. This sudden absence of movement stood in a marked contrast to the constant current of the river and the adjacent city traffic with its relentless noises of cars, buses, trucks and trams. As the performers stood still the walkway fell silent, invoking an absence as in the ghost note of the bass player, a missing beat.

When conceiving of *Flush* as a kind of unannounced street intervention, I wanted to work both with and against the specific location, to both echo and disrupt the physical, urban and economic patterns that occupied the site and to both enchant and challenge the passers-by. I needed to draw in the urban passers-by to gain their interest, that is, to get past a fleeting glance on their part and to enchant them.

Barthes's writing on the amorous dedication in *A Lover's Discourse* draws on Pasolini's film *Teorema* (1968), in which a mute stranger quietly inserts himself into a family and makes everyone fall in love with him. For Barthes, this dynamic compares to what occurs during an amorous dedication, when something is presented to a lover, be that a material or immaterial gift (1977: 75–6). Love will seek whatever forms of expression it can, Barthes writes, be that song, work of any kind and writing such as a dedication to the lover. Barthes includes here offerings that are not solicited and perhaps not even wanted or expected, and that may constitute an imposition of some kind. Such offering would not necessarily be kind to the other and might possibly oppress the other, potentially constituting a demonstration of one's own mastery (78–9). Barthes surmises that that which masquerades as a dedication is instead an inscription whereby the one who gives inscribes himself into that which he gives, the song, the dedication, the text, the gesture, and he inscribes himself into the one to whom he gives. Speaking of the loved one, the object of love, Barthes adds,

> Your presence within the text, whereby you are unrecognizable there, is not that of an analogical figure, of a fetish, but that of a force which is not, thereby, absolutely reliable. Hence it doesn't matter that you feel continuously reduced to silence, that your own discourse seems to you smothered beneath the monstrous discourse of the amorous subject: in *Teorema*, the 'other' [the stranger] does not speak, but he inscribes something within each of those who desire him – he performs what mathematicians call a catastrophe (the disturbance of one system by another): it is true that this mute figure is an angel. (79)

Teorema's stranger, the other, the mute figure, Barthes writes, inscribes himself into those who come into contact with him. Drawing on mathematical modelling, by which a sudden change or 'catastrophe' can occur following a change in a system's parameters, the stranger causes a commotion, a rupture in relations, which Barthes summarises as 'the disturbance of one system by another'. Barthes's writing echoes Pasolini's intention, in that the latter devised *Teorema* as a response to the increasing power of the society of prosperity and its ubiquitous bourgeoisie, which, according to Pasolini, leaves no opportunity for a different existence beyond or outside of its confines (Merjian 2019: 38). According to Ferdinando Camon, *Teorema* furthermore suggests that revolution is impossible and that only miracles could intervene or break up this oppressiveness (Rowiński 2019: 181). The mute stranger or angel is therefore a kind of surprising event or catastrophe, which manages to intervene in the family's vacuous lives and break up its monotony.

Teorema, and Barthes's transposition of this dynamic into the context of an amorous relation, provided me with a model or a blueprint for the kind of uninvited performance I was aiming for. It gave me a sense of how we could be in relation to the passers-by and how they might respond to us while we were performing for them and amongst them, despite the fact that we were imposing ourselves. The monotony of bourgeois life determined the routines of the passers-by in Geneva, and the society of prosperity formed the straitjacket that dictated their pace and behaviour. The arrival of the angel in the family and the disturbance that this constituted in the family's routines mapped onto the appearance of the performers on the bridge and their seemingly suitable but strange activity. Barthes's mute stranger, in other words, compared well with the performing figures who did not speak; the performers inserted themselves quietly into the locality and performed the catastrophe, the disturbance of one system by another, substituting an economic clockwork in which all activity is designed to maximise profit, with an absurdist endeavour and squandering of effort and time.

The intervention had its own internal logic; contravening market economies that are built on scarcity, the performers had an infinite supply of river water that was borrowed and recycled ad infinitum. Instead of demonstrating efficiency, the intervention performed excess in the sense of a sustained dedication to an activity that was devised to be useless, a uselessness doubled through the two performers who worked in opposition to one another. Instead of serving scarcity, the scene revelled in abundance. The responses of the passers-by to this intervention tended to be physical and immediate, they would halt their progress over the bridge and observe, then hurry away, or respond with an erratic combination of both. Perhaps they 'fell' for this other presence that appeared in their midst somewhat like the family in *Teorema* who fall in love with the mute stranger, and perhaps they were also weary of its proposition and what it might demand of them. There is a change of scale between *Teorema*'s family crisis, Barthes's catastrophe and the visually poetic intervention of *Flush*, but the patterns and dynamics echo each other. In each case, nothing is known about the intention of the intervening agent, *Teorema*'s mute stranger, Barthes's lover and the performers in *Flush*; nothing is known about the performing figures as they appear on the bridge, dressed for the occasion, placing themselves in the midst of the passers-by and inserting themselves into the coming and going on the footbridge. At the heart of these interventions is a mathematical modelling by which a sudden change occurs following a modification in local parameters.

Barthes's discussion of the dedication as an unsolicited offering or gift references Marcel Mauss's seminal 1925 publication *The Gift* (1966), as well as Georges Bataille's subsequent reading, or rewriting, of the notion of the gift in 'The Notion of Expenditure' (Bataille 1985), 'The Gift of Rivalry: "Potlatch"' (Bataille 1997a) and 'On Nietzsche: The Will to Chance' (Bataille 1997b). As discussed widely in structuralist and post-structuralist discourse, both Mauss and Bataille undertook an analysis of the gift-economy in indigenous societies and of the American Indian ritual of potlatch in particular, albeit with somewhat different conclusions. Barthes drew on this research in that he understood the gift as something excessive and therefore disruptive: 'The gift is not

10. The Disturbance of One System by Another

necessarily excrement, but it has, nonetheless, a vocation as waste', wrote Barthes; a gift is disruptive because it does not fit into existing patterns or arrangements, it 'is more than I know what to do with, it does not fit my space' (1977: 76). To further elaborate on the disruptive potential, Barthes differentiated between the gift that is declared as such and which becomes part of an exchange economy, and that which he termed silent expenditure:

> A typical argument of a 'scene' is to represent to the other what you are giving him or her (time, energy, money, ingenuity, other relations, etc.) ... To speak of the gift is to place it in an exchange economy (of sacrifice, competition, etc.): which stands opposed to silent expenditure. (76–7)

Silent expenditure here stands for gifts that are not declared or made explicit, that do not come with an expectation of a return. Barthes's silent expenditure speaks to the gift's potential as an irrational, disruptive gesture, as an excessive element that exceeds established relations. Barthes's reading also corresponds to notions of the gift in Indian rituals, discussed more recently by Carl Olson in a comparative study between Hindu and Western concepts. Drawing on the work of Jonathan Parry on the giving of gifts by pilgrims in the city of Banaras, Olson proposed that 'the best form of a gift is secret and without a recipient. A good example of a secret kind of gift is money that is surreptitiously thrown into the Ganges River' (Olson 2002: 365). Such a gift would constitute perhaps the ultimate loss, not even be witnessed and not secure any kind of status or power like the gift-expenditure that takes place in the context of an exchange. Olson's idea of a secret gift resonates with Barthes's proposition of silent expenditure as a gesture or activity that is without representation.

Flush was not a secret activity but it was nevertheless a surprising intervention and combination of gestures that was silent in the sense that it was devoid of explanatory signage and not instrumentalized as part of any predetermined exchange. The performers were doing their thing, proceeding without explanation, perhaps seen and perhaps not. Outside of any given narrative, the scene could potentially inscribe itself onto the passers-by, challenging the work patterns that control their bodies and identities as employees of a global and pervasive enterprise in which everything is designed to contribute to productivity and wealth creation. Perhaps the scene facilitated some recognition on the part of the audience as to this possibility of excess in alternative regimes and relations that are motivated by different paradigms and values.

As an ephemeral event, a live performance is not a gift that can be touched, but, as Barthes proposes in the case of language, it can be dedicated: 'The gift is exalted in the very voice which expresses it, if this voice is *measured* (metrical); or again: *sung* (lyrical): this is the very principal of the *Hymn* or *Anthem*' (1978: 77; emphasis in the original). *Flush* as a gift is not a song but a *dance* dedicated to its audiences, an equivalent formalized gesture that is measured and lyrical, and devoid of functionality. 'Song means nothing', writes Barthes, 'it is in this that you will understand at last what it is I give you; as useless as the wisp of yarn, a pebble held out to his mother by the child' (ibid.). What may be a pebble for a child is a bucket full of water in this dance at noon, held out to the passer-by. *Flush* is a choreographic gesture and useless in its status as a dance; it is wasteful/ excessive with regards to dominant economic values and their moral underpinnings. Uselessness, however, is not meant to suggest that it is without purpose; rather, the intervention is devised to produce a jolt and an inscription.

Feathers tossed in the air, and indistinction

Barthes's exploration of the amorous dedication as silent expenditure provided one of the theoretical frameworks for *Flush* and subsequent street interventions, clarifying my relation to audiences and allowing me to formulate an approach to site-specific performance in which the performers constitute a kind of mute angel and inscribe themselves into those whose attention they catch. This concept, and its associated strategy of a 'disturbance of one system by another', came to define my approach to performance. Occurring unannounced in the middle of the everyday and without representation, this kind of intervention offers some form of resistance and a possibility of protest against the values that dominate the urban sphere.

My artistic project and investigation had found an ally in Barthes although I did not realize at the time how much of his work concurred with the trajectory I was on. A subsequent encounter with Barthes's late writing in *The Neutral* revealed his own interest in non-activity as part of a wider search for alternatives to the socialist, confrontational and dialectic framework that had informed so much of his own work and of the French intellectual life around him. Barthes appears to search for a way out of confrontational modes which confine individuals to an ongoing struggle that is perhaps not their own, distancing himself in his late work even from the desire-driven subject he had explored in *A Lover's Discourse*, the subject that is motivated by a will-to-possess (Lübecker 2009: 128). In *Early Barthes/Late Barthes*, Nikolaj Lübecker argues that Barthes's rejection of dialectical frameworks and their adversarial character also extended to seeking a different approach to writing that was beyond the conflictual mode of address (126). This is evident in Barthes's lecture series *The Neutral*, where he turns East for inspiration and examines the possibility of non-activity through the Taoist notion of Wou-wei. He introduces the concept as follows:

> The Wou-wei: obviously, it's not the opposite of the will-to-live: it's not a will-to-die: it's what baffles, dodges, disorients the will of life. It's therefore, structurally, a Neutral: what baffles the paradigm. (Barthes 2005: 176)

The statement signals that Barthes's interest in Wou-wei lies in its potential to intervene systemically. As a principle, Wou-wei proposes not-to-act as a way of living and also implies inspiring others not to act, constituting a subject that is free of will and choice, very much the opposite of the Western subject that is defined through action and autonomy. Lübecker remarks on the fact that Wou-wei is scandalous for Westerners, whose very idea of civilisation is defined by activity: 'No subjects are therefore more dissimilar than the Tao-subject and the Western political subject with its dogmas about action and engagement' (2009: 125). The West does not have an equivalent for the principle not-to-act and neither do we know how not-to-act. The original choreographic question in *Flush* was concerned with precisely this conundrum: how to imagine the possibility of a suspension of doing and making. When working on *Flush*, my solution was to build a momentum and to periodically disrupt this very motion, in Barthes's terms to devise an event which is disrupted through minimal effort, effectively framing one through the other, playing one off against the other. In *Flush*, the unexpected stopping and starting, the contiguity between life-as-action and the intent not-to-act became the very core of the work, that which baffles, dodges and disorients the passer-by, almost literally, constituting the work's arresting quality.

In 2011, I had an opportunity to revisit these ideas when I was invited to join the international performance collective *Infr'Action* to perform in Venice city during the previews of the Venice Biennale, as part of an independent takeover of public space. The occupation had been devised as a provocation to the exclusive international art event that takes place behind closed doors and is unaffordable and inaccessible to the average Venetian. The takeover and performances were intended to undo this institutional arrogance, to perform outside of the actual and metaphorical walls of the institution and to be part of the city and its spontaneous flow of passers-by. This was an ideal premise for a site-specific performance and called for interventions which occur unannounced in the middle of the everyday. I collaborated with performance artist Dorothea Seror for this project, and we joined many other performers in Venice for the duration of four days to choose a site, devise and perform.

The resulting intervention was *Swan Canal*, another dance at noon, this time making use of the steady Venetian winds which travel through the city along the canals towards the open sea. On one sunny afternoon, passers-by came across a white feather pillow that was ripped open on one side and suspended over a canal (Figure 10.2), its four corners tied to two long ropes which stretched across the water and which in turn were held in place by two performers who were counterbalancing on either side of the water. The ends of the ropes had been tied to either end of two broom sticks, so that each performer could step into the contraption and lean back against the horizontal sticks to maintain the tension of the ropes. As expected, the winds swept along the canal and over the pillow, with small and large gusts picking up clumps of feathers and tossing them into the air before dropping them in the canal and taking them out to sea. Drawing in parts on *Flush*, the performance was staging a non-activity, this time placing a domestic object at the centre of attention within the public place with the two performers at some distance, counterbalancing across the canal. A gentle dance of feathers commanded by the wind played off an otherwise busy canal with people walking this way and that, crossing the water at a nearby bridge. The scale of the contraption contrasted with the light and mellow dance of feathers that emanated from the domestic pillow suspended in space.

The nearby bridge served as a viewing platform for passers-by who tended to stop on their way over the canal and observe. The intervention was again silent, and no explanation was given anywhere as to what this was or why it was happening now. The unusual ensemble of urban architecture, public square, domestic objects, performed and natural elements gave the work a poetic quality and played with, or outplayed, the different functionalities that normally define this site. In *The Neutral*, Barthes describes the poetic as 'a structural, paradigmatic

10. *The Disturbance of One System by Another*   149

Figure 10.2 Image with performer in black dress in counterbalance: *Swan Canal*. Kappenberg and Seror, 2011.
Source: Photograph: Brian Conolly.

game ... set between qualities' (2005: 54), as an endeavour to unravel classification. Barthes leads up to this statement in Supplement II where he recounts the occasion he bought some bottles of pigments and spilled one labelled 'Neutral'. To Barthes's disappointment, this Neutral turns out to be a 'colour' like all the other colours and is both classifiable and marketable. 'All the more reason', he writes, 'for us to go back to discourse, which, at least, cannot say what the Neutral is' (49). Looking for other manifestations of indistinction, Barthes considers grisaille painting as a genre that skips the paradigm of colour by working with differences or nuances of light and dark instead, and he identifies grisaille as an equivalent for the Neutral due to its endlessly nuanced and shimmering space; if something shimmers, it makes it difficult to pin down the differences. Searching further for non-differentiation, Barthes quotes the German theologian, philosopher and mystic Master Eckhart's dictum that 'the distinction between the indistinct and the distinct is greater than all that could separate two distinct beings from one another' (quoted in Barthes 2005: 51). For Barthes, the Neutral has these almost mystical aspects of signalling an (ur) paradigm of distinction and indistinction and claims that this is what makes the Neutral so 'difficult, provocative, and scandalous' (ibid.). Barthes also acknowledges that to remain indistinct is a constant struggle also in discourse, as 'language and the coded practices that flow from it always reframe the Neutral as colour' (52). For a performance artist, this fascination with the indistinct is familiar ground, and the performative is frequently teetering on this edge in its attempts to challenge codes and to disrupt or suspend the categorisations that form, inform and deform our subjectivities. Perhaps this is also the most scandalous aspect of performing, when it touches on the potential of indistinction. All of which suggests that Barthes's Neutral is itself performative and that, somewhat like *Swan Canal*, it intervenes in the field of literature and discourse through an imposition of the possibility of indistinction; it performs a disturbance of one system by another whilst, of course, refusing to be any kind of system. However, reframing the Neutral as performative is also problematic in that it undertakes the kind of linguistic coding that Barthes seeks to undermine; an equivalence is nevertheless proposed here in the sense that the performative is not a thing but an intervention engendering process in the tradition of Bataille's 'formless', a term which he devised in 1929–30 as part of his *Critical Dictionary* and which is 'a term serving to declassify' (Bataille, Lebel and Waldberg 1995: 51). Barthes's Neutral is above all something which intervenes in and unsettles a sphere of literary and philosophical conventions and could in that sense be described as performative.

It is interesting that Barthes brings in the notion of a game when he describes the Neutral as 'structural, paradigmatic game ... set between qualities', implying a combination of rules as well as chance. In several passages in *The Neutral* Barthes references John Cage, the master of chance, as in the passage which begins by considering organization and routines and leads via the notion of small ownership to a consideration of personal objects which have a mnemonic charge, objects that are almost 'a gesture of my body' (2005: 143, 144). Barthes also notes variations in the individual and social relation to space, referring to situations where spacing is left to chance or feeling, and those where it is culturally determined. A combination of rules and chance also make up *Swan Canal*, in that the work started with a domestic feather pillow, no doubt a bodily gesture, that is brought into a public square and suspended in mid-air above a waterway, intervening in somewhat unexpected ways in a traffic system and a complex – and mostly invisible – organization of control and access to the Venice Biennale.

10. The Disturbance of One System by Another   151

Swan Canal combined a strategic approach to performance with a set of chance elements that led to unforeseen consequences.

Surprising endings

Dorothea and I set up the contraption by meeting in the middle of the bridge, tying the pillow to the ropes in situ and slowly unfolding the ropes as we walked down the bridge towards either side of the canal, maintaining a tension throughout to make sure that the pillow did not drop into the water. None of this was rehearsed. We had chosen this particular canal as it seemed to be a dead end with no police presence, but the canal turned out to be a VIP access way for the Biennale. When a first police boat came along, we improvised a response by lifting the contraption and the pillow as high as we could; the policemen on the boat ducked under and drove by without comments. Their compliance was funny, and passers-by were laughing and clapping. A couple of hours passed, the wind did its thing picking up feathers and boats came and went. Then, however, a boat came down the canal with someone on a megaphone shouting at us aggressively in Italian, most likely telling us to get out of the way. Mindful of the delicate balance of the contraption, we couldn't just undo the setup. Perhaps emboldened by the acquiescence of the police, we lifted the contraption again and moved closer to the bridge, waiting to see what would happen. The boat came closer and closer and, after further shouting, pulled in on Dorothea's side; an armed guard jumped from the boat onto the pavement, grabbed Dorothea and tried to pull her away from the canal, thereby pulling me towards the water edge on my side of the water (Figure 10.3). I tried quite desperately not to fall into the canal in order not to escalate the situation. Within minutes a spatially expansive act of counterbalancing had turned scary and unpredictable. Unable to push us away, the guard produced a knife and slashed the ropes with which the pillow fell into the water to the loud protest and boos from the audience. The guard took no notice of the response, got back on deck and the boat drove past the soaking pillow and ropes and vanished. The encounter left behind a general sense of astonishment and incomprehension over this brutal termination. Someone suggested that the Argentine Prime Minister had been on the boat, visiting the Biennale, which would at least explain the armed security guards. Dorothea had several bruises on her arms and one passer-by shared a couple of photos of the wrestling scene, which

Figure 10.3 Image with police wrestling with the performer: *Swan Canal*. Kappenberg and Seror, 2011.
Source: Photograph: Kin Waa Lee.

serve as a record of the confrontation. Gradually the crowd dispersed while we watched the pillow drifting out to sea and also left.

The fact that the intervention was not part of an institutional agenda and had not been authorised by the Biennale made it vulnerable to being shut down, but the contrast between the dance at noon and the violent response was bewildering. What precisely led the security guards to respond in such a way, and might their violence mirror something that was in the work? Why did the police duck under and the security guard reach for his knife? Elsewhere, Barthes wrote about the 'violence' in a photograph, 'not because it shows violent things, but because on each occasion it fills the sight by force, and because in it nothing can be refused or transformed' (Barthes 1981: 91). The notion that a sight is filled by force describes essentially a takeover or an imposition, the experience of which could be a sense of arrogance or violence. In Venice, the intervention had forcefully taken over the site and embedded itself into its architecture in a somewhat parasitical mode. This was an imposing bodily gesture of a domestic pillow hovering very publicly in the square, lost to an entropic game and clashing no doubt with a whole range of less visible directives, constraints, by-laws and agents. One can only speculate as to what exactly triggered the intense violence of the security guards, but there was little possibility of negotiation through this counterbalancing across the canal as the performers could not be pushed away. Nothing of this intervention 'could be refused or transformed' which left the boats with essentially two options, to give in and surrender or to demolish. The police seemed happy to play along, the security guard resorted to slashing the ropes and destroying the whole thing.

This possibility of a violence in a photograph by dint of how it imposes or inscribes itself on the viewer puts forward a pattern that can also be mapped onto Roland Barthes's own concept of the Neutral; the term is an imposition, which by its sheer indeterminacy plays with antagonistic histories and puts an end to the kind of violence that is embedded in dialectic discourses. At the same time, it is itself violent as a takeover that imposes itself on a discursive paradigm. Barthes acknowledges this conundrum in the first of the lecture series, when he writes that the Neutral 'stages a paradox: as an object the Neutral means suspension of violence; as desire, it means violence' (2005: 13). The Neutral as object is the term which invites the possibility of indistinction and distances the reader from wilful dogmatism; the Neutral as desire is aligned to artefacts such as images or performances, which impose themselves and cannot be refused or transformed. At the end of his revision of *Early Barthes, Late Barthes*, Nicolaj Lübecker comments, however, that Barthes never quite quits the dialectic framework because, 'it would just prolong the dialectic movement: only as literature (in the largest sense of the word) can this derailment of "Hegelian" logic take form' (2009: 138). Lübecker's notion of a derailment is very apt, suggestive of trains of thought that are set into motion but lose balance further down the line. The notion of derailment also evokes films of resistance fighters, in which a couple of guys would sabotage major operations with very little means, and it recalls trickster strategies. The late critic and writer Jean Fisher has written about the artist as trickster, a mythological figure which can be found in cultures around the globe, and which serves to provoke change when change is not possible from within. The trickster is to some extent an opportunist, but he intervenes in ways that unsettle a particular context or situation, kicking up dust so to speak, and then disappears (Fisher 2013). In the Preface to *The Neutral*, Thomas Clerc assigns Roland Barthes the title of artist-professor and highlights Barthes's desire for the lectures to be a 'work' and a divagation that partakes in discourse, not in language (Barthes

2005: xxiii, xxv). This proposition of the lectures as a work and a divagation chimes with artist trickster mythology; Barthes did indeed kick up dust while his unexpected death added a dramatic note that was probably not intended. Fisher originally drew on trickster mythology to think through the complexities and vulnerabilities of those artists who seek to challenge colonial powers and who may need to rely on tricks and cunning to claim agency and voice. As an eminent figure of the French intellectual establishment, Barthes fought a different kind of battle; in the case of the Neutral his cunning is directed at the Hegelian dialectic which has dominated so much of Western thought.

I never intended to go into battle, and my creative practice of street-based interventions was not intended to be violent or to provoke violent reactions, but it addresses a society of prosperity that is inherently violent, resorting to violence to maintain the status quo. A bodily gesture such as a feather pillow suspended in public space therefore has the capacity to trigger the powers that maintain the given order. The Taoist Yang-tzu recommends in *accord*ance with Wou-wei: 'Do nothing evil, for fear of being punished; do nothing good, for fear, having acquired a good reputation, of being charged with time-consuming and dangerous functions ... Act as if you were good at nothing' (Barthes 2005: 179). Barthes knew that acting as if you were good at nothing would find fierce opposition in the political maximalism of market-driven societies: 'There can be societies where it becomes immoral to do nothing and where the useless and sacred oaks are cut down' (Barthes 2005: 179, 200).

Dancing at noon touches on the immoral and it risks being cut down like useless and sacred oaks.

Bibliography

Barthes, Roland (1978), *A Lover's Discourse: Fragments*, trans. Richard Howard, London: Vintage.

Barthes, Roland (1981), *Camera Lucida: Reflections on Photography*, trans. Richard Howard. New York: Hill and Wang.

Barthes, Roland (2005), *The Neutral, Lecture Course at the Collège de France (1977–1978)*, trans. Rosalind E. Krauss and Dennis Hollier, New York: Columbia University Press.

Bataille, Georges (1985), 'The Notion of Expenditure', in Allan Stoekl (ed.), *Visions of Excess, Selected Writings 1927–1939*, 116–29, Minneapolis: University of Minnesota Press.

Bataille, Georges (1997a), 'The Gift of Rivalry: "Potlatch"', in Fred Botting and Scott Wilson (eds), *The Bataille Reader*, 199–209, Oxford: Blackwell.

Bataille, Georges (1997b), 'On Nietzsche: The Will to Chance', in Fred Botting and Scott Wilson (eds), *The Bataille Reader*, 330–42, Oxford: Blackwell.

Bataille, Georges., Lebel, Robert., and Waldberg, Isabelle, eds (1995), *Encyclopedia Acephalica*, London: Atlas Press.

Clément, Catherine (1994), *Syncope, The Philosophy of Rapture*, Minneapolis: University of Minnesota Press.

Fisher, Jean (2013), 'Tricksters, Troubadours – and Bartleby: On Art from a State of Emergency', *In Print*, 2 (1): 13–28. https://arrow.tudublin.ie/inp/vol2/iss1/3 (accessed 26 June 2021).

Grosz, Elizabeth (1994), *Volatile Bodies, Towards a Corporeal Feminism*, Bloomington: Indiana University Press.

Infr'Action (2011), 'Venice'. http://teatromagico.us/performance/INFR-ACTION/Infr-Action_Venezia_2011/index.html, http://www.infraction.info/en/projets.html. Vimeo https://vimeo.com/24914074 (accessed 14 December 2022).

Kappenberg, Claudia (2002), *Flush, or the possibility of moving towards an impossible goal*. Centre D'Art en île Geneva, Switzerland, 4–6 April 2002. Performed by Claudia Kappenberg and Elgin Clausen. Devised by Claudia Kappenberg. The work was later reconfigured and presented in form of a video installation as part of *Controlled Democracy*, White Space Gallery, London UK, 1-18/09/2004. http://www.ckappenberg.info/flush-performance (accessed 14 December 2022).

Kappenberg, Claudia (2017), *The Use of Uselessness as Strategy for Contemporary Performance Practice*, PhD Thesis, University of Brighton.https://research.brighton.ac.uk/en/publications/the-use-of-uselessness-as-a-strategy-for-contemporary-performance (accessed 14 December 2022).

Kappenberg, Claudia, and Dorothea Seror (2011), *Swan Canal*. Part of: Infr'Action, Venezia. Devised and performed by Claudia Kappenberg and Dorothea Seror. https://vimeo.com/24914074 (accessed 14 December 2022).

Lübecker, Nikolaj (2009), *Community, Myth and Recognition in Twentieth-Century French Literature and Thought*, London; New York: Continuum.

Manghani, Sunil (2018), 'Barthes/Bataille: The Writing of Neutral Economy', *Theory, Culture & Society*, 35 (4–5): 193–215. 10.1177/0263276418769998 (accessed 9 January 2021).

Mauss, Marcel (1966), *The Gift: Forms and Functions of Exchange in Archaic Societies*, London: Routledge and Kegan Paul.

Merjian, Ara H. (2019), ' "Howls from the Left": Pier Paolo Pasolini, Allen Ginsberg, and the Legacies of Beat America', in Luca Peretti and Karen T. Raizen (eds), *Pier Paolo Pasolini, Framed and Unframed: A Thinker for the Twenty-First Century*, 37–62, New York: Bloomsbury Academic.

Olson, Carl (2002), 'Excess, Time, and the Pure Gift: Postmodern Treatments of Mauss' Theory', *Method and Theory in the Study of Religion* 14 (3–4): 350–74. https://brill.com/view/journals/mtsr/14/3-4/mtsr.14.issue-3-4.xml?language=en (accessed 9 January 2021).

Pasolini, Pier Paolo (1968), *Teorema*, Italy: Aetos Produzioni Cinematographiche, 98min.

Rowiński, Krzysztof (2019), 'From Accattone to "Profezia": Pier Paolo Pasolini and Productive Failure', in Luca Peretti and Karen T. Raizen (eds), *Pier Paolo Pasolini, Framed and Unframed: A Thinker for the Twenty-First Century*, 177–94, New York: Bloomsbury Academic.

Chapter 11

BAFFLING DRAMATURGY: BETWEEN THE OBVIOUS AND THE OBTUSE

Mischa Twitchin

Since, as I have tried to suggest, this teaching has as its object discourse taken in the inevitability of power, method can really bear only on the loosening, baffling, or at the very least, of lightening this power.
—Roland Barthes 1979 [1977]: 15

If you allow your mind to guide you,
Who then can be seen as being without a teacher?
—Chuang Tzu 2006: 11

That was our conundrum.
—Alvis Hermanis 2014: 187

In 1979, Roland Barthes published two texts that addressed the work of Cy Twombly: one under the title 'Cy Twombly – works on paper' and the other 'The Wisdom of Art' (at least, as they appear in their English translations). Although different, both essays not only share their ostensible subject but even many of the same sentences and it is precisely between the same and the different that the ground of their relation – that of the neutral – becomes legible. This legibility is not necessarily proposed by the essays' author, but by what one might call (in the context of dramaturgy here) their 'staged reading'. Barthes offers an image of both the writing and the writer as gauche or obtuse, counter-pointed – in a key thought-image for reflecting on modes of knowledge (as practices of power) – with the disciplining of children. In Barthes's celebration of baffling systems of expertise and authority, both the Twombly essays include, for example, identical observations on the kind of graphism commonly associated with children. In 'Works on paper', we read,

> In Twombly, the letter – the very contrary of an illuminated initial – is produced without deliberation. Yet it is not childish in form, for the child applies himself, presses down, rounds off, sticks out his tongue in his efforts; the child works hard to join the code of the grown-ups. Twombly draws away from it, loosens. (Barthes 1991: 158)

While in 'The Wisdom of Art', we read,

> In Twombly, the letter is the very contrary of an illuminated or printed letter; it seems to be formed without deliberation, and yet it is not really childish, for the child is diligent, presses down, rounds off, sticks out his tongue in his efforts; he works hard to join the code of the grown-ups; Twombly draws away from it, loosens, lags behind. (1991: 188)

Through the evocation of Twombly, then, we are offered a scene of writing – a relation between image and thought, effort and code, child and adult, discipline and practice (not to mention, of course, punishment) – that may seem more or less 'obvious'. That this example of writing was worth repeating indicates how much Barthes appreciated such a drawing away from the 'code of the grown-ups', especially with regard to that code's pretentions to defining knowledge as 'right', whether in distinction from wrong or, as we shall return to, left – in a dynamic of the 'obtuse' running counter to the 'obvious'. This 'loosening' offers an alternative to that discipline to which, in its own way, the very application or deliberation of the child expresses a resistance. Between the tightening and the loosening in this example of composing letters by hand (rather than using a pre-formed type on a keyboard or of gilding the initial letter of an illuminated authority), we see Barthes's concern with what – in the words of his friend Jean Louis Schefer – 'opens up (or, strictly speaking, invents) the emotional body' (1995 [1980]: 61). Rather than the recognition of learning or discovering, institutionalized practices of knowledge – disciplines – typically define themselves by the standards of the pre-formed, as those of the correct (or the correctable), as the assertion of generic 'methodology' over the surprise of the particular – or, indeed, the baffling. Barthes evokes, by contrast, an experience that may be profound as if 'without deliberation', without the expected attributions that govern disciplinary knowledge and its objects (together with their academic reproduction in an essay such as this one) – including claims concerning 'dramaturgy'.

The desire of both of Barthes's essays on Twombly 'to situate an ethic' that eschews a sense of 'possession' with respect to the work being discussed (or to its 'subject') is explicitly signalled by another shared pair of references – to Webern and to the *Tao Tê Ching*.

The Webern quotation (which, indeed, provides the subtitle of the first essay in French) is from a dedication of his six Bagatelles for string quartet (Op.9) to Alban Berg: *Non multa, sed multum* [*not many but much*]. (The more explanatory, or less enigmatic, English version of the essay's title refers to the fact that it first appeared in a catalogue raisonné of Twombly's works on paper [1982: 162].) The aphoristic condensation of Webern's dedication – consonant with the Bagatelles themselves, which expressly avoid anything expansive – might be taken as a variation of the famous dictum that 'less is more'; itself offering a modernist reformulation, perhaps, of Gertrude's advice to Polonius to present 'more matter with less art' (Shakespeare 2016: 2.2.95). If not a criterion of dramaturgy necessarily, this dictum is standardly applied by critics – at least in the UK, where the implications of the post-dramatic are largely decried by the literary management of what is called 'new writing'. That this claim for the 'new' is, nonetheless, all too often produced by means of the 'old theatre' attests to a sense that what might be experimental in this theatre remains literary rather than, precisely, theatrical (where 'writing' is still read, predominantly, in terms of the 'dramatic'). Barthes himself glosses the modernist sense of 'art' not in terms of more or less, but through a relation between 'density' and 'rarity' (1991: 193), as this generates a sense of enigma – or, one might say, of bafflement. Indeed, he remarks on his own expanded sense of 'literature' that 'because it *stages* language instead of simply using it, literature feeds knowledge into the machinery of infinite reflexivity' (1979 [1977]: 7, emphasis in the original). In Barthes's sense of 'writing', the scene of legibility *concerns* the 'emotional body' as it resists the demands of what is already codified institutionally.

The quotation from the *Tao Tê Ching* appears as the final gesture of both the Twombly essays and raises its own questions of and for reading, displacing 'comprehension' (let alone 'conclusion') into the domain of the enigmatic. Reference to the *Tao* is part of Barthes's later course at the Collège de France on the Neutral and my discussion here begins again with the potential of this ending. After all, enigma introduces a question of textuality and 'signifying' (*signifiance*) – through the suspension of any anchoring in the signified (whether by denotation or connotation) – with which a reading of Barthes becomes necessarily engaged. Here then is Barthes's closing paragraph on Twombly, common to both essays, with its citation of the *Tao*:

> There are paintings which are excited, possessive, dogmatic; they impose the product, give it the tyranny of a fetish. Twombly's art – this is its morality, and also its great historical singularity – *does not want to take anything*; it hangs together, it floats, it drifts between desire, which subtly animates the hand, and politeness, which is the discrete rejection of any desire to capture. If we wanted to situate this ethic, we could only go looking for it very far away, outside painting, outside the West, outside the historical period, at the very limit of meaning; we would have to say with the *Tao Tê Ching*:
>
> > He produces without taking for himself,
> > He acts without expectation,
> > His work done, he is not attached to it,
> > And since he is not attached to it,
> > His work will remain. (1991: 175–6; 194)

Although one might suppose that Barthes is speaking here not only for, but also of, himself, the ostensible subject of these lines obscures its own potential questions of translation. I am not competent to trace the complex relations between the Chinese 'book of five thousand characters' and its transformations in – and between – French and English. However, in situating 'this ethic' of art between these two European languages, there is an interestingly enigmatic play between the 'what' and the 'who' of its apparent subject. The French in Barthes's citation (which is, typically, uncredited[1]) – *Il produit sans s'approprier* (1982: 162, 178) – could as well be translated by 'it' as by 'he', referring

---

1. The translators of *The Neutral* note that

   > as he will do most of the time during the course, Barthes quotes Lao-tzu from Jean Grenier, *L'Esprit du Tao* (Paris: Flammarion, 1973) ... Grenier himself uses Henri Maspero's French translation of the *Tao te king* (*Le Taoisme*), vol. 2 of *Mélanges posthumes sur les religions et l'histoire de la Chine* [Paris: SAEP, Publications du Musée Guimet, 1950]), a book that Barthes also consults occasionally. (Barthes 2005: 213)

to 'the deed' or 'the teaching' rather than 'the sage' (evoked in the lines preceding those quoted by Barthes).

In D. C. Lau's English version of this second verse of the *Tao*, for instance, we read, 'It gives them [creatures] life yet claims no possession;/ It benefits them yet exacts no gratitude;/ It accomplishes its task yet lays claim to no merit./ It is because it lays claim to no merit/ That its merit never deserts it' (1963: 6). Alternatively, in Ursula Le Guin's translation (evoking, in her concern with the powers of language, 'a present-day, unwise, unpowerful, and perhaps unmale reader' [2019: x]), the creativity of the impersonal is taken even further: 'To bear and not to own;/ to act and not lay claim;/ to do the work and let it go;/ for just letting it go/ is what makes it stay' (5). Undoing the relation between communication and subjugation that Barthes identifies in language (1979 [1977]: 5), the key to the *Tao* is a teaching that is undemonstrative and undidactic – one that is, in its appeal to the Neutral, 'undramatic'.[2]

Despite Barthes's hyperbole, then, concerning 'the very limit of meaning', one could say it is the 'discrete rejection of any desire to capture' that 'subtly animates' his own sense of writing, producing a body of work that will itself 'remain' in its own testimony to an encounter with its readings, evading the 'tyranny of a fetish'. As against the 'code of grown-ups', Barthes's writing unfolds with what he calls an 'erotics of the Tao' (1991: 193) – an erotics of that writing itself as it permeates a dramaturgy of the Neutral (of non-possession). Through the analogical theatre of Twombly's painting (at least, in the reading of Barthes), we discover an account of dramaturgy that is obliquely (or bafflingly) interwoven with an invocation of 'the wisdom of art'.

*

2. One might hear an echo of this, for example, in Alvis Hermanis's interest in a dramaturgy that is not invested in conflict, exemplified by the theatre of revenge in Shakespeare:

> When someone has a problem the solution for Shakespeare is to *kill* somebody. Our question was, at the outset of *Sound of Silence*: is it possible to invent dramatic forms without conflict? How to show happiness in the theatre would be, perhaps, the most boring thing for the theatre. And that was our conundrum. Another challenge would be for the professional actor to pass across the stage unnoticed. This would be the highest form, or quality, of acting we would say. (2014: 187)

The two essays on Twombly were republished in a posthumous collection, *L'obvie et l'obtus* (1982), translated by Richard Howard and published in English as *The Responsibility of Forms* (1991 [1985]), from which they are quoted here. In this collection, the essays are presented under the separate headings of 'readings of gesture' and 'readings of art', albeit as both engaged with what the editor, François Wahl, calls ('for want of a better term') the 'writing of the visible' (1982: 5). Between writing and reading, then, as between gesture and art, we discover Barthes's analysis of dramaturgy between the obvious and the obtuse. (Wahl's collection also includes a second part on 'the body of music', where both fields of research – the visible and the audible – are distinguished from Barthes's responses to literary questions [ibid.] in essays collected subsequently in *The Rustle of Language* [1986], which was also translated by Howard.)

The change in the terms ('the obvious and the obtuse') by which Barthes's (or, perhaps, Wahl's) volume of essays (concerned with 'writing the visible'[3]) is known in English – 'the responsibility of forms' – is itself of interest. Beyond the 'childish' scene of making writing visible, the English title echoes, perhaps, the Brechtian critique of 'commitment' or 'engagement' – looking back to the (Sartrean) cultural politics against which Barthes's earlier semiotic project was working in the 1950s, rather than looking forward to the concern with 'signifying' (*signifiance*) in the work of the later 1960s. Here the question of and for dramaturgy appears to oscillate between erotics and responsibility—'led astray [as Barthes suggests in his inaugural lecture at the Collège de France] not by the message of which it is the instrument, but by the play of words of which it is the theatre' (1979 [1977]: 6). Wahl's commentary in the Preface to the English edition of his volume, indeed, alludes to 'the double movement – focusing and also transcending semiology – [that] develops a method of "reading" which governs the subsequent essays' (1991: v) – that is, 'subsequent' to those already included in the earlier English-language collection, translated by Stephen Heath, *Image Music Text* (1977a).

This history of translation into English has a parallel with that of Julia Kristeva's work, where these 'subsequent essays' belong to a

---

3. This is Howard's translation of 'l'écriture du visible', which (given their close friendship) one may suppose was made in consultation with Barthes (and which, perhaps 'childishly', I gave as 'the writing of the visible', citing Wahl earlier).

11. Baffling Dramaturgy 163

context that relates particularly to Barthes's reading of (and with) Kristeva, to whom he described himself as being indebted (1986: 168). In a review of her book *Semeiotike*, for instance, he encapsulates this debt in terms of the reflection that '*any semiotics must be a criticism of semiotics*' (169, emphasis in the original). To use a famous formulation of his own, Barthes's work at this time was oriented by the sense of 'a change in the object itself' – much as occurred with the idea of 'drama' in dramaturgy, not least, with the emergence in Anglophone academia of *performance* studies. Echoing again the scene of the emotional body in 'childish' writing, we might relate Barthes's 'change' to what he called (in the Preface to the re-publication of *Mythologies* in 1970 [1973: 9; 1977a: 167]) 'semioclasm', or, later, to 'semiotropy', as his analysis turned away from simply 'the destruction of the sign' (1979 [1977]: 14). In an essay of particular relevance here (evoking what he called 'the third meaning'), Barthes also refers to this as 'an authentic mutation of reading and its object' (1991: 62); all of which is to give some sense of a genealogy to what often seems baffling to dramaturgy (at least, in reference to Barthes). In terms of 'reading theatre' (to echo the title of a contemporary project by Anne Ubersfeld [1999 (1976)]), this 'change' or 'mutation' in the sense of an 'object' – in this case the legibility of theatrical signifiers (or of what signifies 'theatre') – also involves a staging (or writing) of the visible obliquely by way of painting, or, more specifically, by way of Twombly's art of gesture, in a writing of the event 'transcending' (Wahl) the earlier analyses of, and with, Diderot and Brecht.[4]

Although the 'responsibility of forms' (with its echo, perhaps, of Brecht) remains a vital context for reading (with) Barthes, this title – in the English translation – obscures the guiding distinction (in the French title) between 'the obvious' and 'the obtuse'. (Although it might seem as if the citation of these two terms simply transliterated their Latin derivation, this would itself collapse the distinction in favour of the obvious. The apparent neutrality of transliteration obscures questions of difference in translation, not least as concerns the specific distinction of these terms already at play in the French text.) Chosen by

---

4. Barthes's work in this respect both echoes, and is echoed by, Jean Louis Schefer's, whose own journey from analyses of the framing of mise-en-scène to the disturbances of colour – specifically that of red – offers a comparative (and companionate) example to Barthes's own. Indeed, Schefer also wrote on Twombly in terms of the 'childish' and the 'left-handed' (1995 [1986]: 148–55).

Wahl as the title for his collection, the distinction between 'obvious' and 'obtuse' is the subject of an essay (as already mentioned) on 'Stills from Eisenstein' – 'The Third Meaning' (1970) – from which Wahl abstracted it to offer an orientation for reading a 'writing of the visible', not least as it addresses *theatre* with an obtuse (or left-handed) question of – and for – dramaturgy.

*

With respect then to performance, dramaturgy and even poetics, what 'meaning' might be supposed to be either obvious and/or obtuse in Barthes's reading of theatre, taking into account the 'double movement' (Wahl) of the 'change in the object itself'? What might be supposed of and by the oblique allusion to these practices by way of another, that of painting, or, more specifically, by way of reading (or writing with) the gesture and hand, the art and wisdom, of Cy Twombly? What difference is engaged by 'the discrete rejection of any desire to capture' such practices – distinct from the metalinguistic claims of aesthetics and criticism (Barthes 1991: 152) – in terms of the 'communication' or 'signification' from which Barthes distinguishes such a 'third' (or 'obtuse') meaning? Indeed, as Barthes notes, one can '[r]emove it [the obtuse] and communication and signification remain, circulate, pass. Without it I can still speak and read' (54). The enigmatic is not necessary for communication, for a 'standard' (of) legibility and yet is the latter what one would have the sense of dramaturgy reduced to (as if to eschew what may be baffling in its staged reading)?

How might the 'erotics of the Tao' open up a question of and for dramaturgy, distinct from reference to 'gestus' (in place of 'subject' or 'topic'), for instance, with Brecht and Diderot (Barthes 1991: 95)? How does the question of 'what is happening here?' or of the 'event' (177) change when posed by Twombly (rather than by Brecht) in Barthes's reading – with reference to its continued framing by 'the Italian curtain-stage' (91) or the 'theatre *à l'Italienne*' (177)? There is, perhaps, an 'obvious' contrast to be made here with the dramaturgy of Michel Foucault's reading of *Las Meninas*, which sets the scene for his genealogy of those modes of knowledge called 'human sciences' (1970 [1966]: 1–16). Although Foucault's analysis addresses the question of light, the conditionality of the visible is primarily oriented in his example by the social hierarchy of art and patronage, of painter and sovereign, and with the power of viewpoint encoded in that 'drama'.[5] In

---

5. Appropriately enough in this context, Michael Jacobs, in his sceptical reading of discussions of *Las Meninas* that prove to be, rather, 'philosophical

Barthes's reading of Twombly, by contrast, between the obvious and the obtuse (where the latter is a mode of the oblique), how are questions of – and for – theatre 'staged', as it were, without representative actors or performers? This returns us to the question of translation – of an impersonal (or neutral) dramaturgy – of 'it' rather than 'he' concerning the subject of such theatre. As we shall see, this appears to displace a 'dramatic' concern with recognition (*anagnorisis*) and reversal (*peripeteia*) in favour of a 'post-dramatic' concern with matter (*pragma*) and surprise (*apodeston*).

For, in the context of theatre studies, we might obviously think of Aristotle, whose *Poetics* remains a 'founding' text for dramaturgy, part of the 'adult code' of what Barthes (1991: 64) calls 'the myth of C5 BC Athens'. In his essay on 'Greek Theatre' (1965), for example, which is also included in Wahl's collection, Barthes observed that

> what Aristotle contributed to the modern theatre was less a tragic philosophy than a compositional technique (this is the meaning of the various *ars poetica* of the period): a kind of tragic *praxis* was released by Aristotelean poetics, accrediting the notion of a dramatic craftsmanship: Greek tragedy became the model, the exercise and the *askesis*, one might say, for all poetic creation. (1991: 86–7)

By contrast, in 'The Wisdom of Art' (1979), a change in the notion of poetics is proposed – not the prescriptive 'compositional technique' of Aristotle (or even the 'model' example of Brecht), but the suggestion of 'another logic, a kind of challenge offered by the poet [Paul Valéry] (and the painter [Twombly]) to the Aristotelean rules of structure' (185).

At the risk, then, of reducing the Taoist 'wisdom' of art to the obvious sense of a non- or even anti-Aristotelean poetics or dramaturgy, what are the terms of this 'other logic' in Barthes's oblique account of theatre, discussed through the analogy of Twombly's painting? Although one of those terms is, indeed, 'drama', this new poetics expresses a shift from the traditional concerns of dramaturgy toward what Barthes calls (in another Greek term) an 'ergography' (1991: 152; 'ergographie', 1982 [1969]: 141) – that is, a dramaturgy that reads the writing of the 'work' as a process (or 'task') rather than a product, a verb rather than a noun. The subject of the analysis – as of (its) 'drama' – is here part of a set of

responses to *The Order of Things*, uses precisely the term 'obtuse' to characterize them (2015: 49).

relations (including 'ergon') which would resist its simple recuperation by dramaturgy as, for example, being inscribed in 'the [tragic] code of grown-ups'. In the five categories of 'The Wisdom of Art', the sense of 'drama' is displaced by its relation to and within a new constellation of terms (distinct from Aristotle's) exploring the structure of an 'event'. Here drama is one term within the set, rather than that which defines the set in terms of a generic name of and for its composition.

In this oblique account of theatre (with Twombly), Barthes's 'other logic' offers these five terms, with each given (perhaps ironically, in honour of a 'discipline') a Greek name: *pragma* (fact), *tyché* (accident), *telos* (outcome), *apodeston* (surprise) and *drama* (action). The terms of this 'challenge ... to Aristotelean rules' are disguised, then, in the very language (or 'semiotropy') of the knowledge being challenged. Even if ironic, the use of Greek terms conforms to the value given to the classical as addressed not only to, but also by, Twombly. For the haunting intertext here (at least, in Barthes's reading) is given by Paul Valéry and Nicolas Poussin, that is by the espousal of the classical as modern, rather than (for example) by John Cage and Robert Rauschenberg, ostensibly espousing an aesthetic that might be 'postmodern'. Here we might compare Barthes's 'wisdom' with an earlier essay by Allan Kaprow, that also draws performance out of the frame of composition (as that of painting, with reference to Jackson Pollock) into an event (or 'happening') with his own set of categories: act, form, frame, scale and space (2003 [1958]: 4–6).[6]

While Barthes's dramaturgy of art bears upon the specific qualities of painting – the uses of colour, for instance – the 'wisdom' of the essay is fundamentally concerned with what he identifies in the introduction (or prologue) as its 'event' (1991: 177). The principle of temporality in and of both the work (its 'gesture' or, we might say, 'performance') and its reading is key to the analogy that is founded in a neutrality, rather than a hierarchy, between interpretative disciplines (or faculties) and artistic practices (as, here, between art history and theatre studies).

Comparing the construction of the visible between painting and theatre, Barthes's essay begins with an analogy between the frames of the pictorial support and the proscenium stage: 'What happens on the stage proposed by Twombly (canvas or paper) is something which

---

6. One might further compare Barthes's private reading of art catalogues to Kaprow's appeal to public participation. The erotics of a 'change in the object' are, after all, particular, not necessarily universal. (An intriguing instance of this can, perhaps, be glimpsed in Barthes's 'acting' appearance in André Téchiné's film, *The Bronte Sisters* (1979), playing the part of William Thackeray.)

participates in several types of event' (1991: 177). But it becomes immediately clear that the new poetics (as equally its politics) has little to do with such framing directly (the condition of its fetishization), in contrast to Barthes's earlier work on what is 'well-composed' (91) with Diderot and Brecht. Indeed, as Barthes had already observed in 1973, anticipating this change:

> It would probably not be difficult to collect, in the post-Brechtian theatre and in the post-Einsteinian cinema, certain productions and performances marked by the dispersion of the tableau, the disintegration of the 'composition', the exhibition of 'partial organs' of the figure, in short, the jamming of the work's metaphysical meaning, but also of its political meaning – or at least the transfer of this meaning toward a *different* politics. (92, emphasis in the original)

Each of Barthes's five (Greek) terms itself evokes an 'obtuse' attention to a detail of (and as) the 'jamming of the work', running counter to anything synoptic (*pace* Aristotle). While not really generalizable, nor necessarily 'applicable' in other cases, these terms nonetheless work to open up a question of dramaturgy (or staging), refracting a sense of theatre through an analogy with painting.

Concerning relations between the reading and the writing of such a dramaturgy, towards the end of 'The Wisdom of Art' Barthes notes that

> there is in French [and in English – Trans.] a useful lexical ambiguity: the 'subject' of a work is sometimes its 'object' (what it talks about, what it offers to reflection, the *quaestio* of the old rhetoric), sometimes the human being who thereby represents himself, who figures there as the implicit author of what is said (or painted). In Twombly, the 'subject' is, of course, what the canvas is talking about; but since this subject-object is only a (written) allusion, the whole burden of the *drama* shifts to the one who produces it: the subject is Twombly himself. (1991: 190, emphasis in the original)

Despite the earlier question of translation concerning the person of a 'third meaning' – venturing into a neutrality of the verb, rather than the hermeneutics of a personal pronoun – this 'lexical ambiguity' (and the subject of its drama) concerns not only Twombly but Barthes 'himself', whose own question, or staging, of the 'subject-object' – of its dramaturgy even – we are, after all, reading here.

*

To return to the opening instances of this essay – with the thought-figure of what might (or might not) be thought childish, or even gauche, in the knowledge or practice of writing (at least, when thinking of and with Twombly) – it is notable that Barthes was himself left-handed (1977b: 42). With the everyday drama of this embodied 'formation' (with its mystification of cultural practice in terms of 'nature') – reflected on, for instance, in *Roland Barthes by Roland Barthes* (a text that concludes with three facsimiles of Barthes's own graphism [187–8]) – there reappears here, paradoxically (if not so bafflingly), a staging of anagnorisis. What is affirmed in the very appearance of this recognition is that it does not reinstate dramaturgy as a meta-language (1979 [1977]: 13) but remains continuous with a play in and of its own practice of reading-writing, as 'the labour of displacement' (6).

In a paragraph that shares essentially the same title with another one in the essay addressing Twombly's works on paper ('Gauche', 1982: 150; 1991: 163), Barthes writes of that novel 'character' who is 'himself' (1977b: 1):

> *Gaucher* – left-handed: To be left-handed – what does it mean? You eat contrary to the place assigned to the table setting; you find the grip of the telephone on the wrong side, when someone right-handed has used it before you; the scissors are not made for your thumb. In school, years ago, you had to struggle to be like the others, you had to normalize your body, sacrifice your good hand to the little society of the *lycée* (I was constrained to draw with my right hand, but I put in the colours with my left: the revenge of impulse); a modest, inconsequential exclusion, socially tolerated, marked adolescent life with a tenuous and persistent crease: you got used to it, adapted to it, and went on. (98)

What, indeed, does it mean 'to be left-handed'? Between the 'code of the grown-ups' and 'the revenge of impulse' is this not another way to be obtuse? (The obtuse is both a quality of someone who apparently makes no effort to understand and an angle, opposed to the acute, that is greater than 90 degrees – that is, an angle that exceeds the standard of the perpendicular and, as it were, offers a parody of the correct.) What might be the dramaturgy, then, of (and perhaps for) the left-handed, especially if – as Barthes says of 'the French language' (1991: 163) – that of Aristotle is right-handed? Is this, perhaps, a clue to the baffling subject in and of Barthes's dramaturgy?

Here the appeal to drama turns in the direction of what one might call a 'post-dramaturgical' poetics where what is symbolic ('obvious') also falls out of this coding, being in excess of it ('obtuse'), displacing the 'tragic' work of defining character by means of recognition and reversal. With respect to Twombly, Barthes reflects, for example, that

> by producing a writing which seems *gauche* (or left-handed), [Twombly] disturbs the body's morality: a morality of the most archaic kind, since it identifies 'anomaly' with deficiency, and deficiency with error. The fact that his 'graphisms', his compositions, are 'gauche' refers [Twombly] to the circle of the excluded, the marginal – where he finds himself, of course, with the children. (1991: 163)

Although this sounds a little disconcertingly like an evocation of Jesus' recognition of children before the corruption of adults (Mark, 10.13-16), Barthes continues by giving specific attention to the 'controlling' or 'repressive rationality' of the eye within the European history of painting, concluding that 'in a certain sense, [Twombly] liberates painting from seeing; for the "gauche" (the "lefty") undoes the link between hand and eye: he draws without light (as [Twombly] actually did, in the army)' (1991: 163). This 'gauche' sense of drawing (between the poetic and the political) suggests what we might call an 'unwriting of the visible', an inscription of *tyché* within *telos* and of *apodeston* within *pragma*, which opens up possibilities for thinking (or reading) questions of *drama* in and as theatre (without having to accede to the all-too-familiar exclusions supposed, for instance, by discourses of performance art). The oblique sense of theatre as a 'subject' of and for staged reading ('dramaturgy') does not mean a return to the literary in preference to the theatrical (let alone art), but an 'ergography' of metaphor that oscillates (in its 'wisdom') *between* the obvious and the obtuse. It also offers a palimpsest of the proper name Roland Barthes in dramaturgy, not least through the staging, or performance, of writing between the childish and the enigmatic, the theoretical and the practical.

References

Barthes, Roland (1973), *Mythologies*, ed. and trans. Annette Lavers, London: Paladin.
Barthes, Roland (1977a), *Image Music Text*, ed. and trans. Stephen Heath, London: Fontana.
Barthes, Roland (1977b), *Roland Barthes by Roland Barthes*, trans. Richard Howard, New York: Farrar, Strauss and Giroux.

Barthes, Roland (1979 [1977]), 'Lecture in Inauguration of the Chair of Literary Semiology', trans. Richard Howard, *October* 8: 3–16. https://doi.org/10.2307/778222 (accessed 29 October 2022).
Barthes, Roland (1982), *L'obvie et l'obtus*, Paris: Éditions du Seuil.
Barthes, Roland (1986), *The Rustle of Language*, trans. Richard Howard, Oxford: Blackwell.
Barthes, Roland (1991), *The Responsibility of Forms*, trans. Richard Howard, Berkeley: University of California Press.
Barthes, Roland (2005), *The Neutral*, trans. Rosalind Krauss and Denis Hollier, New York: Columbia University Press.
Chuang Tzu (2006), *The Book of Chuang Tzu*, trans. Martin Palmer, London: Penguin.
Foucault, Michel (1970 [1966]), *The Order of Things*, trans. Alan Sheridan, London: Tavistock Publications.
Hermanis, Alvis (2014), 'Hello Darkness, My Old Friend' (interview with Alan Read), in Margherita Laera (ed.), *Theatre and Adaptation: Return, Rewrite, Repeat*, 181–95, London: Bloomsbury.
Jacobs, Michael (2015), *Everything Is Happening: Journey into a Painting*, London: Granta.
Kaprow, Allan (2003), *Essays on the Blurring of Art and Life*, Berkeley: University of California Press.
Schefer, Jean Louis (1995), *The Enigmatic Body*, ed. and trans. Paul Smith, Cambridge: University of Cambridge Press.
Shakespeare, William (2016), *Hamlet*, eds. Ann Thompson and Neil Taylor, Revised ed., London: Bloomsbury Arden Shakespeare.
Tzu, Lao (1963), *Tao Te Ching*, trans. D. C. Lau, London: Penguin.
Tzu, Lao (2019), *Tao Te Ching*, trans. Ursula Le Guin, Boulder: Shambala.
Ubersfeld, Anne (1999 [1976]), *Reading Theatre*, trans. Frank Collins, Toronto: University of Toronto Press.

Chapter 12

CHOREOGRAPHY, CAPTURING AND BARTHES'S NOTION OF THE PUNCTUM

Sandra Parker

Choreography, or the practice of devising movement as repeatable actions or sequences, can be defined as a process of 'capturing' movement in known forms – wherein it is understood that movement patterns or actions are 'set' and can be returned to, to be performed again and again on subsequent performances. 'Capturing' connotes deliberate fixation, a term used in photography to describe the arrest of a moment in time within the photographic frame. The desire to 'capture' movement through the mechanism of choreography answers to the perceived problem of dance's ephemerality and loss – its 'evolutions in time' (Lepecki 2007: 120). André Lepecki, in 'Choreography as an Apparatus of Capture', describes choreographic capturing as a delimiting 'mechanism that simultaneously distributes and organizes dance's relationship to perception and signification', and he cites Martha Graham and Isadora Duncan as examples of choreographers who 'extracated dance from its participation within the choreographic apparatus of capture' (ibid.). Liberating dance through practices of 'becoming', Lepecki talks to 'the strata of the choreographic' opening within these choreographers' practices, with Graham and Duncan exemplifying 'redoing the choreographic itself' (123).

In my choreographic practice, I recognize the limitations of setting choreography, or what Lepecki terms 'capturing'. When I work, after generating movement through improvisation or other means, eeking out and testing movement, I undertake a process to define *what* it is, *how* it is performed and *where* it originates and resides within the body. Through this process, I detail each movement using verbal description, visual images, physical directions, anatomical information and other metaphors to identify and affirm what is understood as *the* choreography. This leads to the creation of each choreographed movement or series of movements. For example,

> I am focusing on my elbow, the tip of the ulna, rotating inwards while thinking of the image of 'corkscrewing' that part of the body in space, as I do this, I drop the arm from the shoulder socket and step forward with the left foot.

Like a score or script (as understood in musical or theatrical terms), the body parts, qualities or metaphors that make up the choreography are defined to the point where it can be remembered and performed again. However demarcated the movement becomes, there is, as Lepecki notes in critiquing the choreographic, the need to resist the apparatus of capture, and a responsibility, on the part of the choreographer, to address this imperative in order to open up the possibilities for choreography, and invite its further 'becomings'.

On reading Roland Barthes's seminal 1980 work *Camera Lucida* (1988), my exploration and understanding of the process of choreography expanded. I'm not a philosopher, or a photographer; I'm a choreographer, and I come to Barthes from this perspective. In *Camera Lucida*, Barthes locates and puts to work the relationship between the captured photograph and what can be felt beyond the photograph through the resistance of the *punctum*. Applied to dance, this offers a conceptual and poetic framework for thinking of choreography beyond the act of simply devising movement patterns (i.e. the setting down of movement into ordered and defined movement), and considering the encounter between the choreography as a 'known' captured image and its performance through the dancers interpretation. This has implications for several aspects of dance making and performance, feeding into questions of what choreography might be, the process of making dance and the performance of choreography. These realizations extend not only to the making of choreography in its initial conception, but also to its performance, where the dancer simulates a similar encounter between choreography and performance as the relationship formulated by Barthes in the encounter between photograph and viewer. This problematization of choreography through Barthes's framework pushes beyond the 'majoritarian origins and imperatives' of choreography, as Lepecki reminds us (Lepecki 2007: 123).

In this chapter I discuss aspects of Barthes's well-known notions of *studium* and punctum in relation to my choreographic practice, along with Barthes's notion of the *noeme*, borrowing aspects of Barthes's triangulated framework that encompasses 'all of us who glance' at an image ('The *Spectator*'), the subject of the photograph ('target') and the photographer ('The *Operator*') (1988: 9). As a choreographer, I create and devise in collaboration with the dancers, fluidly watching and making, making and watching – maker and viewer at once – bridging between '*Operator*' and '*Spectator*' in Barthes's terms, with the objective of creating movement that has evocative potential on subsequent performances. In this writing, I move across what Barthes refers to as the 'object of three practices – (or of three emotions, three intentions): to do, to undergo, to look', bringing Barthes into the dance-making process to potentialize Barthes's thinking in and for dance practice, as a provocation to evoke new 'becomings' rather than 'apply' the framework per se (ibid.).

To make it clear, it is not possible to delimit the positions of 'subject', 'operator' and 'spectator' in relation to my practice. In the studio, I work in and through the evolving movement, in the body, rather than 'on' the body of the dancers. The process works through bodies in response to other bodies, using a circuitous process of kinaesthetic sensing and organization to evolve the choreography. This process of sensing and responding to the evolving movement, selecting movement and editing movement is not easily delineated because often these processes are happening simultaneously. Movement is not 'on the surface'. Similarly, 'dancers' are not mute 'objects' of the choreography, that is, 'subjects', but activate the 'doing', 'undergoing' and 'looking' intentionally, as Barthes notes, in relation to the evolving choreography.

To expand on this, I draw on an example from my choreographic practice *The View from Here*, a full-length choreography for five dancers, that was inspired by the vast difference in the geographic location of the collaborating artists involved, who lived and worked across Melbourne, Australia and Berlin, Germany, and related themes of travel, disconnection, estrangement, proximity and distance. In this project, I was interested in how I could conceive of, and develop, a choreographic process that would hold images of people and places in our consciousness, memory and physical body, and how our search for people and place through the efforts of our imagination, as well as our physical movement, could be defined. The project was created some years ago, and presented in Australia, Germany and New York spanning the period 2005–7. It represents a singular turning point in my thinking about choreography and performance that still remains a haunting influence in my work.

Early in *Camera Lucida*, Barthes speaks to the principle of the studium, writing that, on looking at an array of photographs, images hold a certain 'average affect' (26). This affect is akin to what he terms an 'application to a thing, taste for someone, a kind of general enthusiastic commitment, of course, but without special acuity' (ibid.). Herein, he writes, in this response to looking, the viewer engages with the photograph through a 'very wide field of unconcerned desire, of various interest', but doesn't necessarily feel a deep 'poignancy' in relation to each image; it is an order of 'liking' not 'loving' (27). The studium, for Barthes, 'mobilizes a half desire, a demi-volition' (ibid.) in relation to the photograph.

On making choreography, devising sequences movement by movement, I'm exercising my sense of the studium of each movement choice as Barthes describes. It is a general sense of 'liking' and of 'various interests' made in response to the practicalities of devising movement; where movements are strung together in sequences and composed as choreography, because there is a possible physical, actionable progression. Particular movements might be selected, that is, 'liked', because the organization of the body, governed by weight distribution, dexterity of limbs, timing and the practicalities of shifting from one movement to another without being thrown off balance, might dictate the best possible choice of movement in that instance to preserve the overarching sequential flow. These considerations often override a purely aesthetic choice, because the dancer cannot move from A to B if the preceding position prohibits that shift. The work of formulating linear sequences of movement (i.e. moving from movement one, to two, to three, to four and so on) is partially based on an 'order of *liking*' but is often constrained by physical capability. Under this conception, separate movements one after another, action after action, are conceived of as a certain set of 'functions'. To Barthes, functions are aimed at mythologizing the photograph through a process of 'reconciling the photograph with society', wherein there is a 'contract arrived at between creators and consumers' (1988: 28). I recognize that choreography can be created to the same intent, where the choreographer's role is to form movement with certain flows and effects that meet the demands of the audience's expectations through known tropes which are reconciled in the moment of performance. At play are known methods and processes, along with the physical possibilities and probabilities of movement derivation that guide the creation of choreography but limit its potentials.

However, a moment in the creation of *The View from Here* opened up new thinking as to the relationship between choreography, as set organized sequences, and affective potential, or new 'becomings' as Lepecki argues for.

Choreography and repetition

At first glance, Barthes's explanation of the studium as an order of liking, when applied to the practice of devising and ordering movement, conceived of as an intentional setting down of movement actions (as choreography is traditionally understood), aligns with my practice. However, this practice can also be understood as 'recapturing', as Andre Lepecki observes, rather than 'capturing', a term which describes an 'endless striving to *recapture* a perfect moment, a perfect pose, spin, intention, that we believe can be realized again from its own disappearance' (Lepecki 1996: 73, emphasis added). In these terms, movement that has already been felt to have the potential to be defined or 'captured' is then formulated as such, but on repetition is rarely found to be the same.

From the beginning of my creative process, when movement is conceived and initially developed, differences between repetitions of movement are experienced as detail is added, subtracted or redefined. Often, these differences are noticed consciously as changes are made, or triggered through human error, technical difficulty or simply through that awareness of the physical body's shifting sensations from one day to the next. Even when movement has been captured to the point of definition so that it can be repeated, difference pervades – it takes over, permeating a movement with a slight change and knocking it off course, or causing a vibration which affects other movements in a sequence, despite the dancer's best effort to always perform movement the same way. A sudden twinge, an itch, a headache appearing with no apparent cause, this is the way the body operates: asynchronous to consciousness.

Letting go of the endless reach for the 'perfect moment' is essential to recognizing how repetition disrupts sameness (Lepecki 1996: 73). A preconceived movement cannot be expected to perform a particular 'function' the same way each time, despite the artist's intention – to do so would be to create a type of 'artifice', as Harry Wilson observes, noting that Barthes treats this type of 'setting' up of an image or theatricality 'with suspicion' (Wilson 2017: 270). In movement performance, noted difference is less of an overt or graphic annunciation in a gestural sense, and more of an experiential difference that may be subtlety felt or perceived and disrupts the expected sense of the movement. To expect 'sameness' would discount these important enactive and affective potentials of the movement that can be found outside of, or under the surface of, the constructed choreographic pattern.

For Barthes, there is more beyond the constructed image of a photograph, what Barthes names the punctum, described as 'detail' that enables a 'co-presence' (1988: 55). Barthes notes that 'it is not possible to posit a rule of connection between the *studium* and the *punctum* (when it happens to be there)' (42). An opening for a 'supplement', perhaps 'brief' and 'active', Barthes asserts that the punctum 'is an addition' (55). Barthes notes, 'It is what I *add* to the photograph' (55, emphasis added) that enables a certain apprehension of the image, completed through personal supplementation. In relation to choreographed movement, additions would be possible through activation if the dancer engaged with the potential of the movement of what is 'triggered' or 'sensed' in relation to the choreography, activating co-present details. The dancer, in a sense, could go 'off script' to bring in additional movement attributes, sensed through their engagement in the performance of the choreography. Further to this, Barthes goes on to write that the punctum holds the possibility for development beyond its surface appearance, explaining that 'the *punctum* has, more or less potentially, a power of expansion' (45). In conceptualizing a choreographic movement as being able to extend beyond its defined boundaries, this power is significant. For in practice, a prescribed movement might only be defined to the point that supplements can be brought about by the dancer through improvisation or derivation in performance, with the guidelines for such deviations part of the choreographic instruction.

Beyond choreographic deviation, the notion of 'expansion' offers the possibility to explore the affective as felt by the dancer – an opening up of each movement to felt difference. As Barthes asserts, this affect is 'nameless', or unarticulated, noting, 'The incapacity to name is a good symptom of disturbance' (1988: 51). Here, what can be affectively felt is beyond language, rendering the 'naming' of movement by the choreographer or dancer during the conception and capturing process as insufficient. A dancer could make use of or enact affective disturbances in the momentary act of performance to expand the movement, digressing, even slightly, through the felt sense of the body, addressing the aforementioned problems of repetition and felt bodily difference, changes that are felt on any given day. If felt differences arise unexpectedly on subsequent performances, are there not opportunities for the dancer to activate these differences, rather than disguising them in order to adhere to the dictates of the choreographic studium? While this may or may not be discernable to the viewer in performance, given that affect is felt, the potential for agency and activation – to recast that which is beyond what is seemingly held or 'captured' – becomes possible. The problems of 'capturing' can then be mitigated, engendering the 'becomings', proposed by Lepecki, and implicating the performer.

Under these terms, despite the work of carving out and defining movement wherein choreography claims repeatable movements, each choreographed moment is enduringly unstable. This radically shifts thinking around the process of defining set movement and the repetitious work to develop choreography. The intention to secure the detail of each movement and the process of capturing detailed forms also involves an escape, where some aspects of the movements evade capture through repetition. In addition, the choreographer's and dancer's perspectives on, or relationships to, the choreography as they are enacted and viewed, are not necessarily aligned or agreed upon, which complicates the process further. I watch and sense a dancer's realization of the choreography from inside the work, that is, the internal bodily sensations of remembered actions I have performed myself, but also feel it differently from a perspective external to the dancer. Barthes notes that when the punctum is felt, it 'animates me, and I animate it' (1988: 20), yet many photographs are 'inert under my gaze' (27). What is felt by the dancer is not necessarily felt by the choreographer or viewer, opening up a chasm between them. 'Inert' also speaks to a stilling, a lack of movement possibility or, more importantly, affective potential. There is a paradox here, a desire for affect, yet an inability to force that affect. Barthes writes that the punctum cannot be 'intentional, and probably must not be so' (47), nor forced into a movement form only to revert to the studium. Through awareness and attention to the body's sensorial feedback mechanism, generative differential affects can be found in repetition. In these terms, the 'power of expansion' of the punctum does not overtake the image entirely or replace the captured movement and erase its previous form, but imbues and informs, where the relationship between studium and punctum remains.

With these understandings of the punctum, the choreographer's role can be understood as one that invites sensorial affect to pervade the instant of the passing flow of the movement, rather than one that focuses on the finite detail of a gesture in each choreographed movement. Aiming to capture and describe that which is expanded within a movement image as it occurs on each subsequent repetition (i.e. to successively make changes and redefine each movement) is a circuitous process of adjustment and readjustment. To continue to focus on retaining precise movement detail over and again only reiterates the instability of choreography on subsequent performances, as each movement is exposed to the play of the punctum or 'the subtle beyond' each time (1988: 59). Barthes reminds the reader that the punctum is only made possible by stepping away from the form of the photograph itself to 'allow the detail to rise of its own accord into affective consciousness' (55). In these terms, the choreographer creates changeable and moveable outlines subject to affective change, as opposed to a fixed form, where compositional strategies relinquish precise detail in favour of flexible choreographic referents that potentialize its affective enactments – movement pathways that can shift and change beyond what is pre-prescribed. Barthes furthers the evocation of the punctum to speak about time within the image, where evocations of temporal affect are uncovered. In the next section, I discuss an example from my practice as it relates to Barthes's theory, opening up the punctum further into choreographic practice.

Time

The process to create *The View from Here* moved through two stages: first, inventing movement, then fragmenting and recomposing this movement though a series of manipulations. This method was heavily influenced by my study with American postmodern choreographer Sara Rudner who is renowned for her approach to training dancers, where she optimizes an individual's performance capabilities through rigorous processes of movement deconstruction and reconstruction (Dempster 1992; see Figure 12.1). As a dancer learning from Rudner, I was drawn to the way in which her approach to movement education – to interrupt the comfortable and known neuromuscular pathways of the body in movement by imposing restrictions, additions or subtractions to movement phrases – caused unexpected physical and emotional responses.

In her class, Rudner would teach a phrase of movement which would then be 'deconstructed', that is, taken apart through tasks such as *perform only the co-ordination of the movement of the left leg with the movement of the right arm*. In these tasks, movement gestures and pathways through the body are re-combined in a new way and the dancer must find an alternate way to coordinate the action. This is often uncomfortable and difficult, yet by deconstructing movement and only performing parts of the phrase different emphases can emerge,

12. Barthes's Notion of the Punctum 179

Figure 12.1 *The View from Here*, 2005–7.
Source: Copyright Sandra Parker.

and aspects of the movement pathway that were less consciously felt or present to attention can come into focus. At the conclusion of the deconstruction process, the dancer returns to the original movement phrase, having experienced different versions of the phrase, and re-integrates what was learnt into the performance of the material. For me, this often resulted in the movement feeling fuller, or, within the body, producing greater knowledge of the pathways, connections, regions or parts of the body engaged in movement. While Rudner's process developed my understanding of performance, I was also struck by the potential of her process to prise open movement structures and to elicit new sensations and responses. Rudner's method of deconstructing movement presented a way to feel the absence of movement as present, as still current and felt internally within my body, shifting my attention beyond the obvious 'steps'. The moment of deconstruction, or the loss of movement, offered a new way of experiencing choreography.

Inspired by these experiences of Rudner's processes, *The View from Here* involved extensive composition, fragmentation and re-composition of movement in a similar vein. When I watched the dancers undertake the process, I perceived tangible traces of choreographic patterns left in the body after movement was broken down. The imprint or the impression of the pattern remained. If a dancer learnt a whole-body sequence, but then only performed that sequence in their arms, it seemed, to me, that the dancer was still embodying the whole pattern of the choreography without actually performing it – that is, still 'feeling' the movement. 'Traces' of the absent choreographic movement resonated in their legs or torso, the body vibrating in response to the felt sensation of the movement. It seemed that the movement actions that were made absent were still present, although they were not being demonstrated literally. What was left at the end of the process was residual or fragmented movement that referenced other points in time, movement that always referred to something other, to a movement pattern that was not being performed per se but had left a felt sense within the body of the dancer. The movement material that made up the final choreography was a version of something other; it had a history of a series of workings and re-workings.

During rehearsals, one particular moment illustrated how this method held potential for further investigation. The dancers undertook a series of choreographic explorations combining two phrases together. The first phrase, a fluid, sitting phrase that shifted around on the floor, explored 'disconnection' from another person in the 'here and now' or 'present'; and the second phrase, a series of gestural actions created from the dancer's memory of their duet partner touching, or connecting with their body, investigated a feeling of 'connection'. For the purposes of our experiment, we named the sitting phrase 'present' and the touch gestures 'past', as they were drawn from the dancer's memory. The process then involved switching between phrases. The dancers improvised the switch, performing the sitting phrase (present) and then splicing the action to insert the touch gestures from the second phrase (past) and then back again. This was a complex task because the dancers were required to cut the flow of the movement, perform with clarity the exact sensation of another person's touch gesture on their own body, then seamlessly switch back, embodying in an instant the difference.

In one particular moment, the significance of what we were trialling was overwhelmingly potent. As I watched, I noticed that one of the dancers, Deanne Butterworth, created this exchange with all the fullness of the time 'present' and time 'past'. It was as if, magically, it was not her hand but the hand of another. Time had become fractured, and Deanne remained within the present moment in her own body but also combined a previous moment into her performance at the same time. I could sense two moments in time at once. The transformation of her hand, disconnected from her body, was entirely 'other-worldly'; she had, for that instance, embodied the action of her duet partner on herself. It seemed that Deanne had successfully enacted a layering of time in movement – a moment from the past – preserving the precise quality of the touch and fullness of the gesture within a complex choreographic construction.

When I remember this moment, it is almost like a photographic still, rather than as a series of movements flowing together as is traditional in dance. I don't recall the movements that led up to this moment, or after it. I was struck by the clarity and intensity of Deanne's performance to evoke multiple choreographic moments at once: the moment from the past in the present moment of performance, in the here-and-now of performance. The possibilities of embodying and re-performing evocations of time within choreographic forms can be found in this moment too. More than illustrating how a complex compositional movement form might be created, there was a type of layering of time physically held within that one moment. Time had seemingly 'broken through' Deanne's performance, sharing Barthes's element of surprise in relation to the punctum. It is not just 'detail' (i.e. the insertion of a gesture within the ongoing movement phrase) that was noticeably different but what he names the '*noeme* (that-has-been), its pure presentation' of another moment in time (1988: 96).

Barthes's writing on the noeme in his discussion of the punctum, and his example of a photograph of a boy to be hanged, is useful in formulating the potential to understand time beyond the surface movement image. When looking at the image, for Barthes, the boy holds '*[t]his will be and this has been*', together and at once, and he 'observe[s] with horror an anterior future of which death is the stake' (1988: 96; emphasis in the original). The still image allows this type of scrutiny, a way to 'know' the image and uncover more. He references Marey and Muybridge, and early chronophotography's ability to hold the moment, noting that he too wishes to be able to 'decompose', 'enlarge' or 'retard' the image, to hold it still in a sense, 'in order to *know*' (99).

At play here is the following: a relationship between the stilling or retarding of the image and what this lends to temporal and experiential understandings of movement and choreography; the potential for opening up affective consciousness and the problem of 'photology', as discussed by André Lepecki; and the issue of relegating dance to appearances, which discounts its affective, felt and experiential attributes (Lepecki 2004: 130). In the essay 'Inscribing Dance', Lepecki speaks about the pervasive attitude in dance studies towards dance's ephemeral nature as a 'loss'. Dance's inability to be captured within the boundaries of forms of inscription (such as writing, or filming/photography) produces a type of mourning for that which has disappeared, which is countered by a focus on the visual appearance of 'what "happened on stage"' as a way to hold on to the form (133). For Lepecki, drawing on Derrida, concentrating on appearances to apprehend and preserve dance is a metaphysical approach, a form of 'photology' which is defined as 'the illumination and arrest of presence for the sake of History' (130), where Metaphysics is concerned with 'an undivided point of origin, the *logos*' where 'logos can mean logic, reason, the word, God' (Collins 2005: 47).

In metaphysics, to locate the 'origin' or the 'centre' and bring it to full 'presence' to determine the nature of being, opposing terms are used, one of which is privileged and carries the weight of full 'presence', and the other 'subordinate ... the term of absence or of mediated, attenuated presence' (49). Photology, therefore, is concerned with the 'illumination' of one of the two terms. This is considered to be the metaphysical origin of the phenomena in question. Lepecki asserts that in adopting photology to document dance, a metaphysical approach is taken where dance's ontological status is relegated to visible appearances, to what is most obviously brought to light under the gaze of the viewer, prioritized and privileged to counter the disappearance of dance.

However much retarding images might enable the decomposition that Barthes speaks of at the risk of 'photology', stillness is not a purely fixed entity but contains, rather, vibrations and microscopic movements, as is well argued in relation to dance in another of Lepecki's writings (Lepecki 2000). Rather than a reduction to stilled detail in this manner, evocations of time become possible through Barthes's offer of the noeme that can activate temporality within the image, creating a sense of temporal movement. Applied to movement practice, a singular movement can 'move' in several temporal directions at once, if the affective potential of the movement is considered and given an opening within the form. Under this pretext, *The View from Here* is a challenge to Barthes's conception of the noeme in relation to the moving image. He writes that the noeme is 'swept away and denied' (1988: 78) by movement in the example of cinema and the moving image, yet in the example of *The View from Here*, the layering or intersecting of time within the flow of the movement was felt. Deanne retained and combined multiple experiences of time together at once, and although I felt it as a still instant, what had been, together with where she was in the present moment, occurred within the flow of the choreography.

Conclusion

Through Barthes's discussion of the noeme in relation to the photograph and an analysis of the potential implications, there are now complex evocations of the punctum possible in relation to choreography. The forces of repetition and the felt-sense of the body, and the layering of time and the experiential in performance brought about through the dancer's affective consciousness, are at play. While the receptiveness or otherwise for 'the viewer', or indeed the dancer, in relation to the play of the noeme in the rehearsal and performance of choreography is not 'known' in an epistemic sense, the 'affective' is key here, in that, despite conceptions and formulations, the experience of dance may carry its own phenomenological power (as Barthes notes in relation to the moving images of cinema). Choreography as a practice of formulating that movement has a part to play in activating that potential.

But even further to this, dance feeds the noeme of the form; it is, in a sense, noeme itself. Dance folds in temporal dimensions that are rich with the experiences of rehearsal and re-rehearsal, where the formation of movement at another point in time is re-experienced over and again in performance. In this process, experiences are accumulated, layered, and immersed within the performer's body, and consequentially, the performance itself, in both the present performance and in those yet to come. Even if the choreographic construction is not as complex as was shown in the example of *The View from Here*, the potential remains for choreographic 'capturing' to be dismantled through the potential for a 'blind field' (1988: 57) in relation to the image, as Barthes puts it – a 'subtle *beyond*' of the image to emerge (59; emphasis in the original). As a paradigm for thinking, practising and moving towards the affective within choreography, making present the 'beyond' of the image, Barthes's notion of the punctum broadens understandings of choreographic potential, leaving the choreographer with the challenge of how to formulate its activation.

References

Barthes, Roland (1988), *Camera Lucida*, trans. Richard Howard, London: Fontana Paperbacks.
Collins, Jeff (2005), *Introducing Derrida*, London: Icon Books.
Dempster, Elizabeth (1992), 'Sara Rudner Dances: A Conversation', *Writings on Dance*, 1: 35–41.
Lepecki, André (1996), 'As If Dance Was Visible', *Performance Research*, 1 (3): 71–6.

Lepecki, André (2000), 'Still: On the Vibratile Microscopy of Dance', in G. Brandsetter, H. Völckers, B. Mau, and A. Lepecki (eds), *ReMembering the Body*, 334–66, Ostifilturn-Ruit: Hatje Cantz Publishers.

Lepecki, André (2004), 'Inscribing Dance', in Andre Lepecki (ed.), *Of the Presence of the Body*, 124–39, Middletown, CT: Wesleyan University Press.

Lepecki, André (2007), 'Choreography as Apparatus of Capture', *TDR: The Drama Review*, 51(2): 119–23.

Wilson, Harry (2017), 'The Theatricality of the Punctum: Re-viewing Roland Barthes' *Camera Lucida*', *Performance Philosophy*, 3: 226–85.

Chapter 13

BODY AND MASK: DRAMATURGIES OF THE FACE IN ROLAND BARTHES

Michael Bachmann

From the pained face of the wrestler, exhibiting 'human suffering with all the amplification of the tragic masks', to the showgirl who 'manifests the human face ... as a product that can be bought', many of Roland Barthes's early writings share an attentiveness to the face in performance (Barthes 2002, vol. 1: 235 and 239; Barthes 2012: 8).[1] This interest is not restricted to cinema and dramatic theatre. It cuts across various media and art forms and extends to performances of the everyday. In a loose cluster of essays published between 1952 and 1957, Barthes writes about the face in publicity photographs of stage actors, in theatre, film and popular modes of performance. He also describes or imagines the faces of unwitting performers in mundane encounters: a waiter at Parisian café Les Deux Magots, a clerk at the post office, an old woman on the train.

The most famous of these early texts is the mythology on Swedish American actor Greta Garbo. 'Garbo's Face' (1955) analyses her screen image as a transitional moment in the history of cinema that at the same time indicates a wider cultural shift regarding Western concepts of the face. The other articles are less well-known and often overlooked. Only a few were reprinted, like the Garbo text, in the seminal 1957 book edition of the *Mythologies* (or other Barthes collections); most remain untranslated.[2] As a consequence, Barthes's 'attention to the human face

---

1. Where no English translation is available, I am quoting from the revised French edition of Barthes's complete works (Barthes 2002). In these cases, the translation is mine.

2. The most relevant articles are 'Le Monde où l'on catche' (1952), 'Visages et figures' (1953), 'Folies-Bergère' (1953), 'Une tragédienne sans public' (1954)

as paradigmatic figure ... in his early thought has not been recognized' (Steimatsky 2017: 81). When dealt with at all, this happens in relation to the face on film, not the face in performance.³

In contrast, this chapter analyses Barthes's contributions to a thinking of the face from the vantage point of theatre and performance studies. Without a doubt, his writing on the face is heavily invested in questions of cinematic and photographic representation. For instance, the 1953 essay 'Visages et figures [Faces and Figures]' asserts that 'it is only the cinema that will constitute the historical era of a sociology of the face' (Barthes 2002, vol. 1: 269).⁴ Later, post-structuralist publications like *Empire of Signs* (1970) and *Camera Lucida* (1980) refer to the face in photography and make their points not only in writing, but also through reprinted photographs of faces.⁵ Nevertheless, Barthes's interest in the face is firmly rooted in his thinking about theatre and performance. When writing about the face, he continuously draws on theatrical figures even where his main interest is mediated images. Garbo's face is likened to 'the mask of antiquity' (Barthes 2012: 73), *Empire of Signs* devotes a chapter to the 'theatrical face' (Barthes 1982: 88–94) and *Camera Lucida* famously describes photography as 'a kind of primitive theatre ..., a figuration of the motionless and made-up face beneath which we see the dead' (Barthes 1981: 32).

Typically, these theatrical figures are seen as mere points of reference to support an argument about the face as mediated image: they are not linked back to questions about the face in performance. This is indicative of a wider rift within contemporary critical thinking that

---

and 'Le Visage de Garbo' (1955). 'Le Monde-objet' (1953), while on Dutch painting rather than performance, is another important early essay on the face. All can be found in Barthes (2002), vol. 1.

3. See Steimatsky (2017) and ffrench (2020). Both acknowledge Barthes's writings on the face in theatre and performance 'only' as a means to an end, namely to discuss his contributions to analysing the face on film. Conversely, and again keeping with their disciplinary background, contributions on Barthes and theatre prioritize the figure of the mask over the face (e.g., Scheie 2006).

4. The title 'Visages et figures' is difficult to translate: In French, 'figure' can mean a rhetorical figure, body or image yet is also synonymous with 'face' (*visage*).

5. See Kawashima (2006) on the 'photographed face' in *Empire of Signs* and Arribert-Narce (2009) on the role of the face in what he calls 'Barthes's photobiographical project' (245).

aligns the face with film, and the body with theatre. With some notable exceptions, theatre is rarely discussed as a practice of the face, despite the frequent insistence on live performance as a face-to-face encounter, and despite theatre historiographical narratives invested in a teleological sequence from the masks of antiquity to the 'facial presence' of modern theatre.[6]

As I will argue, Barthes allows us to rethink the value of the face for theatre and performance. His contributions on the face traverse different media, art forms and types of performance (wrestling, erotic cabaret, bourgeois theatre, mundane encounters). This complicates the reduction of the face to an image, a reduction that many of Barthes's essays seem to support, for instance when 'Visages et Figures' proposes as 'a kind of law of the face' that it 'only exists at a distance, as a mask' (2002, vol. 1: 270). While the mask may be understood as mere theatrical metaphor in a text on film ('Garbo's Face'), it is something else with regard to live performance, for example, when the wrestler's or the showgirl's face becomes a mask. This points to a second complication, namely that the face in Barthes is poised between mask (image) and body (corporeality). However, the face is not a discrete entity, on top of the body and behind a mask. Rather, the face itself oscillates between being mask and being body, thus undoing the all-too-easy alignment of face/film and theatre/body.

To make this argument, I will first outline the constellation of face-body-mask in Barthes and relate it to the genealogical operations that have, in the early twentieth century, aligned the face with film in opposition to the body of theatre. I will then analyse the different ways in which Barthes approaches the face-as-mask, on the one hand, and the face-as-body, on the other. I propose that Barthes's thinking of the face can be related to two models of theatre/performance: first, theatre as a 'frame' that spectacularizes the face-as-mask and makes it legible (*a semiotic model*) and, second, performance as 'affect' that returns the corporeality of the face through absenting it in representation (*a post-structuralist model*). I understand these approaches as 'dramaturgies of the face' in the sense that they point to different ways in which the face may appear and mean – or resist meaning – in performance.

---

6. See, for instance, the theatre chapter in Hans Belting's cultural history of facial representation, *Face and Mask* (Belting 2017: 48–63).

The face of Maria Casarès

In May 1954, Barthes dedicates an entire article, 'Une tragédienne sans public [A tragedienne without an audience]', to the Franco-Spanish actor Maria Casarès. At the heart of this still untranslated text is a long passage on the face in theatre. The 'lesson' to be drawn from Casarès's acting style, or so Barthes claims, is that 'the face, the whole face, needs to be involved in the adventure of theatre; one needs to turn upside down its deep tissues [*il faut bouleverser ses tissus profonds*] ... in order to regain, as Casarès does, the beauty of a total movement' (2002, vol. 1: 494).[7] For the purposes of this chapter I am interested in the close alignment of theatre and face that this sentence suggests. What does it mean to understand the 'adventure of theatre' as engaging 'the whole face'? How is this different from the more common proposition, in contemporary theatre and performance studies, to see live performance as a privileged site for the ethical 'face-to-face' encounter? And how does the fleshy corporeality of this facial adventure, the 'upheaval' of deep tissues, compare to the mask-like character of the face on screen?

A closer look at the passage reveals that Casarès's face, as described by Barthes, is entangled in a series of binaries that evolve around the relationship between mask and body, between commodified beauty and the 'beauty of a total movement', between signification and materiality and – last but not least – between theatre and mediated image. Barthes favourably compares Casarès's upheaval of deep tissues with the publicity shots of actors: her acting style 'renounce[s] on stage the pasty or ethereal beauty of the [photo] studios Harcourt', itself the subject of one of Barthes's mythologies (2002, vol. 1: 494). Furthermore, Barthes writes:

> The face is usually the property of an actress (some have nothing else), and thus well-guarded; the means of saving [*moyens d'épargne*] are varied: to vanish behind a mask of eternal make-up, or else to put up the idea, in [the mind of] the public, of a fairly conventional face-about-town to give the expectation of a different face-on-the-stage, or else to subtilize the expressions, to replace the marks of passion

---

7. I am following Barthes's French spelling of Casarès's surname. In Spanish, the name is Casares (without the accent). As Maria Delgado has argued, the 'dual spellings of [the] name' embody the Franco-Spanish actor's identity as exilic performer between two theatre cultures (Delgado 2003: 92–3).

with the nuances of psychology. Maria Casarès never protects herself when her face transforms itself, distorts itself, unreservedly returns to the folds of ancestral masks that signify pain, panic or joy. (ibid.)

It is notable that the binaries in this passage are on the verge of collapsing. The mask refers to the artificial beauty of the made-up or carefully staged face as commodity within the economic matrix of spectacle: here, the face *disappears* behind the mask. In the next sentence, however, the mask refers to signification, with Casarès's face *becoming* a mask precisely because she does not 'protect herself' against the distortions of (commodified) beauty.

As in much of Barthes's semiotic writing, this latter type of face/mask relationship refers to an ideal of pure exteriority and signification: like the 'folds' of the ancient mask, the 'distortions' on Casarès's face signify, seemingly without any ambivalence, 'pain, panic [and] joy' (2002, vol. 1: 494). A 1953 essay on the 'force' of Greek tragedy, 'Pouvoirs de la tragédie antique', exemplifies this by comparing 'the ancient mask' with 'the suffering face of the pinned wrestler, beaten and presenting … the allegorical head of ravaged humiliation' (263). Rather than emotion itself, the wrestler presents 'the *signs* of emotion … The fighters display their state of mind [*état d'ame*] (pain, joy, rage, revenge, regularity), all of their expressions are chosen to present … an immediate and as if exhaustive reading of their motives' (ibid.). The physical spectacle of wrestling – while still bearing traces of corporeality in the language of its description (beaten, ravaged, rage, etc.) – is read for its production of images, the coagulation of a face into an allegorical mask.

Importantly, the relationship between corporeality and face/mask is different in the Casarès text. Like the wrestlers and Greek theatre, her acting style is rooted in 'the obviousness of passion' and 'flooded with clarity' (Barthes 2002, vol. 1: 493). However, this 'exposure of the sign until its very end' implicates a corporeality of the face that does not limit itself to the mask of signification. As Patrick ffrench notes, Casarès's 'use of the face', as described by Barthes, is 'exhaustive', her 'acting style … pushes sense to its limit and beyond, deep into the physicality of the performer' (2020: 21 and 250). Involving 'the whole face' in the 'adventure of theatre' activates 'the deep tissues' of the face in a language that is already reminiscent of what Barthes will later call 'the grain of the voice' (see Barthes 1977a: 179–89). What Casarès does with her face, according to Barthes, is quite different from the wrestler's display of emotions:

If she cries, it is not enough to understand that she suffers, you also need to feel the materiality of her tears, [you need] to endure this suffering long after you have understood it. If she waits, you also need to wait, not with thoughts [*non de la pensée*], which is easy for you in your seat, but with eyes, muscles, nerves, to suffer the horrible torture of an empty stage where no one speaks and where one watches a door that will open. (Barthes 2002, vol. 1: 493)

There is a movement here from the face-as-mask to the face-as-body that does not replace the one with the other. Both exist simultaneously – the clarity of meaning and understanding (mask) as well as a materiality and corporeality of the face and its parts (the eyes) that affects even the audience in a bodily way.

This entanglement is at the core of my reading of Barthes. Two distinct dramaturgies of the face can be inferred from his writing: the first one privileges the face-as-mask and understands theatre as a frame that spectacularizes the face even in mundane encounters, for example, when observing a waiter at Les Deux Magots. The second one has the face-as-body at its centre, yet acknowledges that the face's corporeality can ultimately not be grasped in representation. In late Barthes, this leads to an affective, bodily relationship with the other's face. Paradigmatically, *Camera Lucida* withholds the photograph of Barthes's mother in which he sees not a 'mask' but 'the truth of the face I had loved' (Barthes 1981: 67). The Casarès article draws our attention to the entanglement of body, face and mask that remains operational across both dramaturgies and prevents any clear-cut separation between the two.

Barthes criticizes any representation that attempts to sever the face (as mask) from the body, for example, in the mythology of the Harcourt photo studios. Writing about the publicity shots of French theatre actors, he distinguishes between the 'pure countenance [*pur visage*]' of their photographed faces and the messiness of their stage faces (Barthes 2012: 19). The photographs represent 'the actor's face' as 'an ascension [to heaven] without haste and without muscles, quite contrary to the onlooking humanity which ... must return to its apartment on foot' (20). It is relevant that Barthes analyses the photographed faces of *stage* actors, even though the rest of 'Visages et figures' – from which the mythology was excerpted – is about film stars.[8] The publicity photograph,

---

8. 'The Harcourt actor' is the middle section of 'Visages et Figures', and the only part of the essay that was reprinted in *Mythologies*. As Steimatsky

as mediated image of the actor's face, betrays the corporeality of theatre and the relationship between performer and audience.

In the Casarès article, the physicality of her acting style becomes an affective bridge to the audience. The Harcourt actors, by removing the face from the body, remove themselves from those in the audience who are 'capable of movement only by the legs (and not by the face)' (Barthes 2012: 20). Importantly, this is not a clear-cut distinction between theatre as site of corporeality and film/photography as site of its suppression. The publicity shots are shown in theatre foyers and their function is to impress upon the audience the idea that the actors are of 'a different zoological class' (ibid.). In this sense, the alignment of face/film and theatre/body is at work in Barthes as well, though with a difference. I will now outline some of the genealogical operations that have led to this alignment before returning to the two dramaturgies of the face in Barthes.

Face/film and body/theatre

Faces, or a generalised notion of the face, do appear in writings about theatre and performance. These include the ethics of the 'face-to-face' encounter, the relationship between face and mask, the physiognomy of the humanist actor and the question of painted or made-up faces (including blackface). However, with some rare exceptions, contemporary theatre and performance studies rarely put the face centre stage, as it were.

In contrast, film and media studies knows no shortage of monographs on 'the face'.[9] These books can be said to take up a thread from early film theory that emphasized ' "concepts of the face" ... as the cinema's generative-creative principle' (Steimatsky 2017: 34), maybe most influentially in the writings of Jewish Hungarian film critic Béla Balázs. The discursive operations that differentiate between film as an art of the face and theatre as a practice of the body are particularly explicit in his works. Writing in 1924, Balázs offers a succinct comparison of the

---

notes, 'standing on its own, [the mythology] offers a sharp and unambiguous debunking of the visual rhetoric of glamour when compared to the corporeal presence of the stage actor' (2017: 102).

9. See, for instance, Aumont (1992), Coates (2012), Davis (2004), Schmidt (2003) and Steimatsky (2017).

face in film and in theatre: it would be wrong, he admits, to speak 'of physiognomy and the play of facial expression as if they were a speciality and even a monopoly of film' (2011: 37). Faces appear on the stage as well, but – in a way – we do not see them, or so Balázs claims: 'Firstly, because we listen to the words and so ... notice only the crudest, most schematic expressions'; secondly, because actors distort their faces in order to 'speak clearly for our ears'; and, thirdly, because the stage lacks proximity: 'We can never observe a face for so long, in such detail and as intensively as in a film close-up' (ibid.). Ultimately, '[in] the theatre, even the most important face is never more than one element in the play. In film, however, when a face spreads over the entire screen in a close-up, this face becomes "the whole thing" that contains the entire drama' (ibid.).

It might be tempting to dismiss Balázs's media comparison on account of his narrow understanding of theatre (and of film, for that matter). However, the evidence – on the basis of book titles alone – seems overwhelming that there is some truth to Balázs's distinction between film as the art of the face and theatre as a space where the face gets lost amongst the elements. At first glance, such a distinction, and the marginalisation of the face that it implies for theatre and performance (studies), is at odds with a basic – albeit not uncontested – tenet of these disciplines: of theatre as privileged site for a face-to-face encounter.

According to Peggy Phelan, amongst others, if 'the face-to-face encounter is the most crucial arena in which the ethical bond we share becomes manifest, then live theatre and performance might speak to philosophy with renewed vigor' (2004: 577). The reorientation of theatre and performance studies, from the late 1980s onwards, away from semiotic towards performative models of analysis (of course I am generalising here), brought with it an investment in the ephemerality and liveness of performance.[10] Theatre's political potential – its continuing relevance amidst a mediatized 'society of the spectacle' – was located in performance's ability to disrupt, via ephemerality, corporeality and bodily co-presence, the commodified exchange of images and representation in late global capitalism. In works such as Hans-Thies Lehmann's seminal *Postdramatic Theatre* (1999), theatre becomes the site of the 'face,' as opposed to the 'interface' of media. He explicitly frames the logic of disruption with reference to 'the intensity of a "face

---

10. See Jackson (2004) for a genealogical study of 'Theatre in the Academy from Philology to Performativity'.

13. Dramaturgies of the Face in Roland Barthes 193

to face" communication' in performance that 'cannot be replaced by even the most advanced interface mediated communication processes' (2006 [1999]: 135). While some contemporary theatre practices, for example, one-to-one performance, can indeed be said to focus on an encounter of faces, it is important to note that the face itself is not relevant to Lehmann's conceptualization of theatre at all. The face is just a trope, or at best an instance of post-dramatic theatre as a site of the 'real'.

In theatre and performance studies more widely, this post-1980s investment in the face-to-face, and with it a reading of the face as figure of liveness and/or ethicality, is one of the reasons why our disciplines rarely engage with the face as more than 'just' a site of ethics. In recent years, the notion of live performance as face-to-face encounter has increasingly been questioned. As Nicholas Ridout notes, 'The appeal of Levinas' ethics' in the work of Phelan, for instance, 'seems to derive ... from the centrality of the encounter with the "face"' (Ridout 2009: 53). Emmanuel Levinas's ethics of alterity conceptualizes the face of the Other (*le visage d'Autrui*) as the intersubjective basis for responsible living. The face of the Other is understood as a 'naked face ... beneath all particular expressions', that is, it is not the individual faces that others may put on in our interactions with them, but 'the nakedness and destitution of the expression as such, that is to say extreme exposure, defencelessness, vulnerability itself' (Levinas 1989: 82-3). In this sense, the 'naked face' is what Michael Taussig calls 'the figure of figurations ..., a contingency at the magical crossroads of mask and window to the soul' (1999: 4). If the face were to become completely legible or a complete mask (in the sense of concealment), it would lose its status of the face. Ridout seeks to propose a different framework for discussing theatre as an art of the face-to-face encounter. Rather than in the 'abstracted', transhistorical face of the Other, Ridout is interested in 'actual or potentially real faces, worn by historical actors, with genders, class positions and so forth' (2006: 35). Nevertheless, these 'realities' of the face remain, to a certain extent, marginalised. The 'different instances of the face to face' that Ridout analyses all converge in the idea of theatrical failure: 'The face to face is both offered ... and withheld, made available and turned down, an opportunity and a threat. ...That there is something wrong with theatre is the sign that it is theatre' (33).

Thus, the criticism or reconfiguration of the face-to-face has not usually led to an understanding of theatre as a practice of the face – the 'lesson' that Barthes proposes in his text on Casarès. When Alan Read revises his earlier investment in theatre as a site of the face-to-face encounter, he does so by insisting on 'performance's inherent facial banality', bluntly stating that 'one thing that is obvious from any witness of [theatrical] performance … is the lack of anything that could be described as "face engagement"' (2008: 36).[11] The displacement of the face in theatre remains operational in the turn-away from the face-to-face (as one of the sites of this displacement).

In a rare chapter devoted explicitly to faces in, rather than the face-to-face of, live performance, William Worthen asserts that the primary object of his analysis – Thomas Ostermeier's *Hamlet* production (Schaubühne Berlin, 2008) with Lars Eidinger in the main role – operates, at least partly, via 'the disjunction between the theatrically mediated body and the cinematically mediated face. … *Theatrical acting is sustained by the body; film acting is the art of the face*' (2020: 54; emphasis added). Worthen analyses how 'the "face" in the theatre always emerges from disciplined regimes of enactment', which, in Ostermeier's case, includes the representation of a character (Hamlet), the actor (Eidinger)'s physical work and a large movie screen onto which Eidinger/Hamlet's face – or, rather, a *representation* of this dual face – is projected in close-up (41). Worthen undoes the binary between film/face and body/theatre when he concludes that rather than creating a distinction between the false (screen) and the real (body), Ostermeier's production positions theatre as 'the space for a certain kind of meditation on the ethical dimension of the different forms of mediated proximity theatrical performance enables' (65). Nevertheless, in order to make this point, both the production and Worthen must operate on the basis of that very binary (body/theatre, film/face). While also drawing on this alignment, Barthes's dramaturgies of the face do not remain caught up in the binary of film/face and body/theatre. Rather, both the face-as-mask and the face-as-body operate across different media, with theatre and performance at their centre.

The face-as-mask

Barthes's writing is deeply invested in what art historian Hans Belting calls 'the indistinct boundary between face and mask' (2017: 18). As an instance of the shifting boundary between the two, Belting refers to the emergence of veristic acting and physiognomic paradigms in the

---

11. He is revising his position as outlined in Read (1993).

eighteenth century: 'Instead of being a separate attribute, the mask was now internalized in the face where it could be changed according to desire or necessity. ... This transformation into a mask forced the actor to gain control over the mimic expressivity of his own face. Expression now *is* the mask, which is why the face can produce it' (55).

Another instance is the difference in face-mask relationships between ancient Greek and Roman culture that links theatre to questions of identity. Fifth-century BCE Greek only knows one word, *prosōpon*, which can roughly be translated as 'before the gaze', for both face and mask. As David Wiles puts it, 'In the age of Sophocles, ... donning a face was no negative act of concealment' – *masking* in the modern sense – 'but a positive act of becoming' (2007: 1).[12] Latin, in contrast, distinguishes between the face (*vultus*) and the theatre mask (*persona*), though it is the latter term that gives rise to the modern idea of personhood – of an individual identity that is distinguishable from social masks (Weihe 2004). Both notions of the mask appear in Barthes. The idea of the mask as *persona* is used to 'unmask' as ideological fiction, as it were, the psychologically coherent and unified *person*, whose acts and words allegedly express a pre-existing interior substance.[13] In *Roland Barthes by Roland Barthes*, for instance, the author-position is understood as the succession and simultaneity of 'several masks (*personae*), distributed according to the depth of the stage (and yet *no one – personne* ... is behind them)' (Barthes 1977b: 120).

More relevant to the question of the face is the notion of the face-becoming-mask, not as an 'act of concealment', but as that which makes the face legible as a privileged site of signification. As quoted above, this idea of the face-as-mask is at work in the texts on Greek tragedy, on the tragic acting style of Maria Casarès and on the spectacle of wrestling where the signs refer to the passions and 'states of the soul'. Another version of this face/mask relationship appears in *Camera Lucida*. Writing about photographer Richard Avedon's portrait, 'William Casby, Born a Slave' (1963), Barthes asserts that in this image 'the essence of slavery is ... laid bare' (1981: 34). The face of one individual human being becomes, in Avedon's photograph and Barthes's reading of it, a clear sign for socio-historical forces: 'Photography cannot signify (aim

---

12. See Frontisi-Ducroux (1995) for a detailed discussion of the mask-face relationship in ancient Greece.

13. See Bachmann (2021: 176–9) on interiority as a cultural formation of modernity.

at a generality) except by assuming a mask…: the mask is the meaning insofar as it is absolutely pure (as it was in the ancient theater)' (ibid.). Even in this late text, his final book, the face-as-mask in the sense of pure semantic meaning still retains something positive. Barthes acknowledges the subversive political force that such photographs may assume, for example, in August Sander's *Faces of the Time* (1934). However, there is a clear unease with the move from the particularity of an individual face to the 'generality' of the mask. The erasure of the face for meaning is always a possibility in this semiotic approach to the face-as-mask. In what is the most complete suppression of the face-as-body in Barthes, 'The Diseases of Costume' (1955, reprinted in 1964s *Critical Essays*) asks of the 'healthy' costume – the costume that is in the service of meaning – that it 'must be able to *absorb* the face' (Barthes 1972: 49).

In the later Barthes, the unease with such an approach seems to point to the question of concealment (where the face vanishes behind the mask) but is more accurately described as an issue of misrecognition inherent in the face-as-mask. *Roland Barthes par Roland Barthes* imagines a dialogue, printed alongside two photographs of Barthes that both focus in on the face (one from 1942, one from 1970): ' "But I never looked like that!" – How do you know? What is the "you" you might or might not look like?' (Barthes 1977b: 36–7). One can misrecognize or not identify with oneself without assuming to know (or even possess) a true self or face. A variation of this is the photograph of Barthes that appears in *Empire of Signs*, again a picture of his face surrounded by Japanese text: 'This Western lecturer, as soon as he is "cited" by the *Kobe Shinbun*, finds himself "Japanned," eyes elongated, pupils blackened by Nipponese typography. …What then is our face, if not a "citation"?' (Barthes 1982: 90). In the first instance, misrecognition is related to the image one has of oneself at a given moment in time; the second misrecognition is where (the image of) the face changes according to context, impacting the face itself: the face, not its reproduction, becomes a citation of 'Japan'. The third instance is the difficulty of recognizing the 'essence' of a loved one in the image of their face. Famously, *Camera Lucida* withholds the Winter Garden photograph of Barthes's mother in which he sees 'the truth of the face I had loved' (Barthes 1981: 67). This 'true' face stands opposed to – but also has the power to transform – the other photographs of the mother that 'were a little like so many masks; at the last, suddenly the mask vanished: … [this] was the person I used to see, consubstantial with her face, each day of her long life' (109–10).

While the face-as-mask may entail a misrecognition, the discovery of the 'true' face of the mother is not a question of 'likeness', as Barthes makes clear. He uses the word 'air' to describe the 'expression of truth' in her face/photograph. As an 'intractable supplement of identity', this face is the opposite of the stillness of the mask that freezes the face in Barthes's description of photography as primitive theatre of the dead. (1981: 32 and 109–10). In the 1950s texts, the stillness of the face-as-mask is mostly seen as positive. It is that which makes the face visible at all. In the 'Folies-Bergère' mythology, the link between face, mask and death that reappears in *Camera Lucida* has a different valence. The 'showgirls' of the erotic cabaret appear to the spectator in Barthes's text as lifeless masks, face-objects (*visages-objets*) that 'only death can produce ... to this degree' (2002, vol. 1: 238). At first glance, this objectification of the female face through the male spectator – whom Barthes imagines to be a horse dealer, a hat merchant or a tradesman from Brussels – their reduction to commodities in an economic exchange, would appear as negative.

However, in early Barthes, the erotic cabaret becomes a 'theatre of Money [*théâtre de l'argent*]' held in higher regard than bourgeois dramatic theatre. Here, the entrance fee does not buy the illusion of emotion (by which the spectator may or may not be affected). Rather, money is openly exchanged for money, in the form of the beautiful face as product (Barthes 2002, vol. 1: 234). In contrast, bourgeois dramatic theatre is also determined by money, as Barthes writes in a January 1954 editorial for *Théâtre Populaire*: 'The conceited luxury of sets and costumes ... postulates a whole sordid economy of false gold [and] visual lies, minted against the thousand franc note of a place in the stalls' (459). The difference between the economic exchange in so-called high art as opposed to the popular bourgeois theatre of the Folies-Bergère is one of visibility: the latter one is, in Barthes's reading, open about its structures of commodification whereas the former presents sets and costumes not in the name of money. It 'hypocritically' frames them 'in the name of "French good taste"' (ibid.).

Within the obvious and superficial commodification of the Folies-Bergère, the objectification and stillness of the face offers a positive visibility that is usually withheld in the mobility of life: 'Here, this human Face [*Visage humain*] that is usually nothing but a presence, finally manifests itself to me as a product' (Barthes 2002, vol. 1: 239). Stillness (and the economical matrix of spectacle) becomes a problem, however, when the product is deceitful. The publicity shots of the Harcourt actors show them always already 'in repose', thus suppressing the work of acting as well as the careful staging that produces this face (Barthes 2012: 19). In the Folies-Bergère, in contrast, the money is shown at work; the transformation of ephemeral face into buyable product happens in front of the spectators' eyes. The face-as-mask is positive if it is open about its mask-like quality and if it points to its own artificiality.

In the essay on Garbo and in 'Visages et Figures' the mask-like face refers to the face as concept for all humanity. Barthes describes the actor's face as an object (again the *visage-objet*) with 'the snowy density of a mask; it is not a painted face but a face in plaster' (2012: 73). Garbo's face is mask insofar as it becomes 'an archetype of the human face ... a sort of Platonic idea of the human creature' (73–4). In Barthes, this is not an ahistorical claim, as if any face at any time could represent humanity. Rather, Garbo becomes a transitional 'moment' in the history of cinema, bringing to a close the period when 'people literally lost themselves in the human image as if in a philter, when the face constituted a sort of absolute state of the flesh which one could neither attain nor abandon' (73). In contrast to Rudolf Valentino's 'ultra-face' which still completely belongs to that period, Garbo points towards a 'humanification' that Barthes sees epitomized in Audrey Hepburn. Hepburn's face is no longer a 'concept', a Platonic idea, but it is an 'event' (75). This is not only the move from one concept of the face to another, but rather from a face that stands in for a concept (i.e. humanity) to a face that is no longer conceptual in the same sense, but 'an infinite complexity of morphological functions' (ibid.).

The face-as-body

In Barthes, the face-as-mask can refer to a hollowing out of interiority, to pure semantic meaning and legibility, to misrecognition and disidentification, to stillness, commodification and artificiality, and to a conceptual order of the image.

Roughly speaking, in all of these instances, the mask becomes problematic when it is concealed. Hence, Barthes's preference for the object-faces of the Folies-Bergère and of Garbo as opposed to the myth of interiority that he sees epitomized in the faces of French post-1945 cinema. In 'Visages et Figures', these faces are described as 'authoritarian face-types' that relieves ordinary people from thinking. The 'sociology of the face' that Barthes proposes at the beginning of that mythology relates to 'a sort of dialectic through which the individuum chooses his or her face [*sa tête*]' (2002, vol. 1: 269). The problem with the faces-as-masks of cinema that are, in contrast to Valentino and Garbo, no longer divine, but seem attainable, is that 'real' human beings no longer 'think' their faces: 'Because the cinema offers excellent ones, [they] run quickly to shelter the uncertainty of their [physical] person' behind the masks of cinema (ibid.). The essay ends with Barthes's description of an old woman on a commuter train. She is reading a movie magazine, opposing 'without revolt her poor face to the icy iconography of the Masters' (278). Barthes perceives a 'truth' in her 'earthly face' that is

> beyond expression, in the skin, in the very density of this face tired for life, brought about by the long sedimentation of pains, to the state of a stubborn substance [*substance têtue*], unalterable if not by death. No effect of pity came from this all-too human face [*figure trop humain*], but it was enough to confront it with its luxurious double [in the magazine], to understand that humanity [*l'homme*] has been robbed of its own face [*visage*]. (278–9)

This passage brings the body into play through a series of binaries: the woman's earthly face (*visage terrestre*) opposes the faces of the Harcourt actors that appeared earlier in the essay as ascending, without a muscle, to heaven (of which the movie magazine's 'iconography of the Masters' is an echo). The 'stubborn substance' belongs to the face-as-body if the face-as-mask is understood as that which can be staged. The woman's face is too 'stubborn' to be the mask of pure legibility or the commodified product of popular spectacle, that is, it is an effect of 'long sedimentation' rather than of an intentional mise-en-scène. The all-too human face or figure (*figure trop humain*) seems to stand in contrast to the 'archetype' (Platonic idea) of humanity presented by Garbo. Whereas the Garbo text is positive towards the face-as-mask standing in for all humankind, the woman on the train belongs to a different historical period. The mediated face is of the 'authoritarian' type mentioned towards the beginning of the article, or so we are led to assume. Humanity has its face stolen because the face of the woman cannot be represented and/or because the ordinary person, in Barthes's words, no longer 'thinks' their face, instead choosing from the 'wrong' representations on screen.

In the middle section of the essay, the resistance of the face-as-body that the woman on the train could be said to point towards is closely related to theatre.[14] The publicity shots of the Harcourt actors remove them from the stage, as it were. They are shown 'in town, reduced to a

---

14. Steimatsky (2017: 102) wonders why the middle section of 'Visages et Figures' turns to *stage* actors rather than exercising its criticism of publicity

face purged of all movement. Further, this pure countenance [*pur visage*] is rendered utterly useless – i.e., luxurious – by the aberrant angle from which it is shot … as if this countenance [*ce visage*] [is] floating between the theater's crude earth [*sol grossier*] and "town"'s radiant sky' (in English, Barthes 2012: 20; in French, 2002, vol. 1: 689). The 'crude earth' of theatre and the 'earthly face' of the woman on the train relate to one another, in particular because they share the 'luxurious' as their other. The stillness of the Harcourt actors ('purged of all movement') is the opposite of the face-as-body in Casarès: a body that becomes visible in the distortions of the face – distortions that are both the 'folds' of the mask *and* the upheaval of deep tissues. The Harcourt actors withdraw their faces from their profession: whereas on stage, the actor needs 'to mime on occasion old age, ugliness, in any case the dispassion of himself, he now recovers an ideal visage [*visage ideal*]' (2012: 19; 2002, vol. 1: 688).

Frame and affect: Dramaturgies of the face

The movement between face-as-mask and face-as-body can be related to two different models of the relationship between theatre/performance and the face. The 'semiotic' model freezes the face-as-mask to make it visible, with theatre becoming a frame that can be applied to bring about the face across a variety of situations. The 'post-structuralist' model affects the viewer through the face-as-body, though the body is no longer in the face itself but rather in the performative relationship between face and spectator – a relationship that ultimately erases the face. These models of theatre and performance imply different dramaturgies of the face that are distinct yet relate back to one another. The remainder of this chapter briefly maps the two models, drawing on and expanding the previous discussion of face-as-mask and face-as-body.

The dramaturgy of the face that uses theatre as a frame becomes most apparent outside the theatre space. When Barthes writes about dramatic theatre in the narrow sense, for instance in the Casarès text, the theatrical frame is almost invisible. Following the semiotic model, the actor's performance, like that of the wrestler and the showgirl, produces a face that is fully legible. However, Casarès's face is not fully framed or contained in this semiotic legibility; rather, Barthes's description focuses on the physicality of acting and its visibility in

shots with regard to Hollywood stars. Theatre lets the corporeality of the face, as opposed to its image, appear more clearly.

13. Dramaturgies of the Face in Roland Barthes   201

the face. Yet, this is no disruption of meaning through the flesh, but a simultaneous presence of mask, body and face. Such simultaneity is made possible only through the – in this case, implied or invisible – theatrical frame: that Casarès's face is given to someone at a distance, as an object to be gazed at despite its fleshiness.

The continuum between dramatic theatre, popular modes of performance, film, photography and painting that traverses Barthes's contributions to a thinking of the face expands to performances of the everyday. Here, the relationship between theatrical frame and face-as-mask is more pronounced than in the theatre itself. 'Visages et Figures' features a series of mundane encounters like the one with the woman on the train. The others are mentioned only in passing, as examples of face-objects (*visage-objet*). While Barthes 'pursue[s] in vain the face that is closest to me', for example, of a loved one, he has no trouble to see and remember the face of a waiter at Les Deux Magots and of the post-office clerk. This corresponds to the 'law of the face' that Barthes introduces at this point of the essay, that it 'only exists at a distance, as a mask' (Barthes 2002, vol. 1: 270). The theatrical metaphor is important as it points to the fact that this is more than just a question of proximity and distance. The faces become visible, as it were, only via an act of theatrical distancing and the separation of spectator (Barthes) and performer (waiter, *demoiselle des postes*). Here, Barthes explicitly introduces what I call the theatrical frame. He writes that he can grasp the faces of others if they are exhibited behind 'the shop window of a show [*le guichet d'un spectacle*]' (269–70). This implies an objectification of the performer, in the case of the waiter and post-office clerk *unwitting* performer, without which the face cannot be had. The 'guichet' is reminiscent of the way in which Barthes describes the Folies-Bergère as a 'display-theatre [*théâtre-vitrine*]', the only difference being that the former is movable (post office, café) whereas the latter is a fixed display (at the cabaret theatre). Their effect, however, is the same. As Barthes writes in 'Folies-Bergère',

> Life routinely provides me with faces composed through unsteady movements[.] I can never grasp a face, it slips away, it vanishes ... I can never keep it unchanged under my gaze, I can never give it its quality as an object because it is also looking at me. Here, this theatre face is a miracle of immobility: it is available because it is fixed, it gives me its permanence and I can finally possess it. (238)

The construction of the face is dependent on the withdrawal of (inter-)subjectivity: no longer the face that I watch and that watches me, but instead an objectified face. Barthes writes about the 'continuous death [*mort incessante*]' in the 'permanent face[s] ... of those we love the most' (Barthes 2002, vol. 1: 269.). The objectification is thus not only inherent in the spectatorial power relation of this type of theatre (precisely not a *face-to-face* encounter), but also because it is no longer about emotional investment. The difference between the frame of theatre and the frame of cinema/photography, however, is that the body may return at any moment; the face as a product can be lost and – as such – retains an instability and connection to what Barthes calls the 'terrestrial' that some mediated framings of the face (the Harcourt actors) seek to sever. The dramaturgy of the face that operates via theatrical framing, objectification and distance entails ethical problems, as Barthes's theatre of the everyday encounters make abundantly clear. However, the theatre frame always allows for the return of the body, and for the other to look back.

This is where the post-structuralist model emerges, a dramaturgy of the face that invests in affectivity and aligns with performance rather than theatre. Such an approach entails ethical complications as well. Gayatri Spivak criticizes *Empire of Signs* for placing 'the face "under erasure," keeping it abundantly visible though crossed out by a draining of affect,' so that no 'form of assigned subjectivity' may emerge (1999: 346). The Japanese faces that populate that book are, for Barthes, an instance of the neutral, an 'exemption of' and '*from* meaning': The Bunraku master's face, 'apparent, smooth, bright, impassive, cold as "a white onion that has just been washed" ... is offered to the spectators to read; but what is carefully, preciously given to be read is that there is nothing there to read' (Barthes 1982: 48 and 62). If faces are usually thought of as that which conceals and reveals,[15] Barthes's 'Japanese' face does neither. As Spivak points out, this presupposes an appropriation. The face can only be neutral, a positive erasure of meaning, because of its difference to the Western (concept of the) face. As a neutral face, however, it is at the same time particular – it needs to signify Japan as a fiction of difference – and not: it cannot signify Japan if it is an absence of meaning, thus placing the Japanese face under a negative erasure with '[t]he clear-headed innocent arrogance of [the] assumption of a subject-position that claims the other as grounds for difference' (Spivak 1999: 345).[16]

15. See, for instance, Belting (2017: 17).

16. Here, Spivak is referring to Barthes's assertion, in *Empire of Signs*, that 'Orient and Occident cannot be taken ... as "realities"' in his text: 'What can be

The Japanese face in *Empire of Signs* creates a relationship to the viewer by withdrawing from legibility yet firmly remaining within a semiotic register (*to read: nothing*). The insistence in Barthes's text that the face does not *represent* meaninglessness but *performs* it (as an exemption of and from meaning) remains, as Spivak's criticism shows, caught up in a paradox. However, it points towards an affective relationship that exceeds representation. *Camera Lucida* introduces a different politics of erasure. The 'true face' is to be had only in the absence of representation. In contrast to the Japanese faces of *Empire of Signs*, the Winter Garden photograph of the mother is absent from the book. It is also the face of a little girl – his mother as a child – in which Barthes finds her 'intractable' essence. If the face is in itself an image that moves (it ages, it changes countenance etc.), then the 'true face' of the mother is not only absent as photograph, but is also beyond its changes in time.

In both models, the face remains displaced: in the semiotic model through theatrical distancing (framing the face as mask); in the post-structuralist model through the singularity of the affective, performative relationship that cannot be generalized. Yet, the dramaturgies of the face inferred from Barthes allow us to think the face in performance as something else than what it usually stands in for: a sign for psychological interiority, a trope for the liveness of theatre (face-to-face encounter) and a figure of ethicality. Maybe the face comes into being in the movement between framing and exhibiting the face, on the one hand, and building an affective relationship through its elusiveness, on the other.

References

Arribert-Narce, Fabien (2009), 'Roland Barthes's Photobiographies: Towards an 'Exemption from Meaning', *Colloquy: Text Theory Critique*, 18: 238–53.
Aumont, Jacques (1992), *Du Visage Au Cinéma*, Paris: Ed. de l'Etoile.
Bachmann, Michael (2021), 'German Radio Drama and the "Cultural Formation" of Interiority', in Tracy C. Davis and Peter W. Marx (eds), *The Routledge Companion to Theatre and Performance Historiography*, 167–85, London: Routledge.

addressed, in the consideration of the Orient … is the possibility of a difference, of a mutation, of a revolution in the propriety of symbolic systems' (Barthes 1982: 3-4). Kawashima (2006), in contrast, reads the photographs of *Empire of Signs* as a parody of ethnographic photography.

Balázs, Bela (2011), *Early Film Theory: 'Visible Man' and 'The Spirit of Film'*, ed. Erica Carter, trans. Rodney Livingstone, New York: Berghahn Books.
Barthes, Roland (1972), *Critical Essays*, trans. Richard Howard, Evanston: Northwestern University Press.
Barthes, Roland (1977a), *Image Music Text*, trans. Stephen Heath, London: Fontana Press.
Barthes, Roland (1977b), *Roland Barthes by Roland Barthes*, trans. Richard Howard, Berkeley: University of California Press.
Barthes, Roland (1981), *Camera Lucida: Reflections on Photography*, trans. Richard Howard, New York: Hill and Wang.
Barthes, Roland (1982), *Empire of Signs*, trans. Richard Howard, New York: Hill and Wang.
Barthes, Roland (2002), *Œuvres complètes: Nouvelle edition*, ed. Éric Marty, 5 vols., Paris: Ed. du Seuil.
Barthes, Roland (2012), *Mythologies: Complete Edition*, trans. Richard Howard and Annette Lavers, New York: Hill and Wang.
Belting, Hans (2017), *Face and Mask: A Double History*, trans. Thomas S Hansen and Abby J. Hansen, Princeton: Princeton University Press.
Coates, Paul (2012), *Screening the Face*, Basingstoke: Palgrave Macmillan.
Davis, Therese (2004), *The Face on the Screen: Death, Recognition and Spectatorship*, Bristol: Intellect.
Delgado, Maria (2003), *'Other' Spanish Theatres: Erasure and Inscription on the Twentieth-Century Spanish Stage*, Manchester: Manchester University Press.
ffrench, Patrick (2020), *Roland Barthes and Film: Myth, Eroticism and Poetics*, London: Bloomsbury.
Frontisi-Ducroux, Françoise (1995), *Du masque au visage: Aspects de l'identité en Grèce ancienne*, Paris: Flammarion.
Jackson, Shannon (2004), *Professing Performance: Theatre in the Academy from Philology to Performativity*, Cambridge: Cambridge University Press.
Kawashima, Kentaro (2006), '…dem Lächeln nah: Das photographierte Gesicht in Roland Barthes', *Das Reich der Zeichen. Parapluie*, 23: 1–8.
Lehmann, Hans-Thies (2006 [1999]), *Postdramatic Theatre*, trans. Karen Jurs-Münby, London: Routledge.
Levinas, Emmanuel (1989), *The Levinas Reader*, ed. Seán Hand, Oxford: Basil Blackwell.
Phelan, Peggy (2004), 'Marina Abramović: Witnessing Shadows', *Theatre Journal*, 56 (4): 569–77.
Read, Alan (1993), *Theatre and Everyday Life: An Ethics of Performance*, London: Routledge.
Read, Alan (2008), *Theatre, Intimacy & Engagement: The Last Human Venue*, Basingstoke: Palgrave Macmillan.
Ridout, Nicholas (2006), *Stage Fright, Animals, and Other Theatrical Problems*, Cambridge: Cambridge University Press.

Ridout, Nicholas (2009), *Theatre & Ethics*, Basingstoke: Palgrave Macmillan.
Scheie, Timothy (2006), *Performance Degree Zero: Roland Barthes and Theatre*, Toronto: University of Toronto Press.
Schmidt, Gunnar (2003), *Das Gesicht: Eine Mediengeschichte*, München: Fink.
Spivak, Gayatri Chakravorty (1999), *A Critique of Postcolonial Reason: Toward a History of the Vanishing Present*, Cambridge, MA: Harvard University Press.
Steimatsky, Noa (2017), *The Face on Film*, Oxford: Oxford University Press.
Taussig, Michael T. (1999), *Defacement: Public Secrecy and the Labor of the Negative*, Stanford: Stanford University Press.
Weihe, Richard (2004), *Die Paradoxie der Maske: Geschichte einer Form*, München: Fink.
Wiles, David (2007), *Mask and Performance in Greek Tragedy: From Ancient Festival to Modern Experimentation*, Cambridge: Cambridge University Press.
Worthen, William (2020), *Shakespeare, Technicity, Theatre*, Cambridge: Cambridge University Press.

Chapter 14

TRACING BARTHES'S EASTERN THEATRES: *EMPIRE OF SIGNS* AND THE STAGING OF INDIVIDUAL CULTURAL INTERPRETATION

Pamela Genova

Since the advent of *Japonisme*[1] in the second half of the nineteenth century, French aesthetes and intellectuals have often displayed a prolific interest in Japan's rich cultural forms (as well as those of other Asian nations). Roland Barthes is no exception, and his engagement with Eastern aesthetics unfolds vividly in *Empire of Signs* (1982). This book, as Jonathan Culler reminds us, ranked highly among Barthes's own favourite writings (1983: 20). Through an expansive approach that both recalls and rethinks, formally and thematically, his 1957 *Mythologies*, in *Empire*, Barthes addresses a diversity of social, historical and artistic forms of expression in interpreting the Japanese iconographical landscape as a markedly performative space. In this 'gem of an essay', as Hwai Yol Jung phrases it (1987: 144), he presents an acutely personal appreciation of the spectacle of Japan from an outsider's equivocal perspective (given that Barthes did not speak Japanese, his photographic *punctum*-laden impressions of visual and linguistic phenomena – of signs and movements – in a word, of expressions related to performance – significantly influence his reactions). Barthes even states that it is not the authentic country of Japan that interests him, but rather, he explores a kind of 'utopia' (a term

---

1. The term *Japonisme* has been traditionally used to describe the cultural phenomenon of the impact of the techniques, compositional styles, theoretical foundations and popular motifs of Japanese visual arts on European artists of the late 1880s, especially with regard to French Impressionist painters.

he employs frequently in *Empire*), fashioned from his own imaginative art, in a move indicative of an engaged interdisciplinary construction, as with writing, directing or interpreting a play or an actor's role.²

Empire proposes numerous hypothetical observations of Japanese cultural expression, and an examination of explicitly performance-based sections proves critical to Barthes's assessment of Western theatre, as compared to Eastern modes. Nevertheless, beyond those specific sections, exploring the interpretations presented elsewhere in the book also adds significantly to the appreciation of Barthes within a framework of performance studies.³ For example, Patrice Pavis states that 'moving from the semiology of the 1960s towards the "situation of writing", Barthes anticipates the performance studies of the 1980s. He abandons a system of objects or relevant characteristics of a semiological whole, leaning towards a place in the "situation of writing", a dynamics of writing that is now called performative writing' (2012: 8–9). From this wider stance, we discover Barthes's disappointment with Western misinterpretations of Eastern theatre's questioning of mimesis and its relationship to the real; his dissatisfaction with the West for often overlooking theatre as a valuable space for the sacred, against that which Antonin Artaud had extoled; and his admiration of Japanese puppet theatre (*Bunraku*), indicating comparisons with his earliest writings on Bertolt Brecht's reflections on 'theatricality'.⁴ In *Empire*,

---

2. Among many sources, see Darko Suvin, who explores Barthes's 'escape into a signic utopia' (1991: 501). See also Diana Knight (1988) and Bernard Comment; the latter depicts Barthes's 'fantastic elsewhere' as part of Barthes's plan not so much to discover new symbols, but to 'work in his own symbolic system through a *fiction of a Neutral*' (1991: 68). Obviously, for Barthes, the term 'neutral' is one charged with complexity, and much critical work has addressed it, especially given Barthes's treatment of it in his penultimate lecture course at the Collège de France. One pertinent definition of the term is offered by Alice Lagaay as the 'poetics of negative performance' (2016: 37). See also the 2020 special issue of *Theory, Culture & Society*, entitled *Neutral Life/Late Barthes*, edited by Sunil Manghani.

3. An excellent example of the metaphor of theatrical performance in Barthes's work, as well as of the relationship of drama on stage or film and photos of it, with a focus on 'scenic writing' and on the ways in which Barthes explores the 'still' in filming, can be found in Jim Carmody (1990). See also De Vos (2004) on the relationship between *Empire* and the notion of theatrical spectacle.

4. For more on Barthes's reading of Brecht's theatrical practice and theory, particularly with regard to Japanese theatre, see his 1977 *Image Music Text*.

14. Tracing Barthes's Eastern Theatres   209

many of Barthes's sections formulated in his exceptional spin on an encyclopedic prototype propose at once extraordinarily personal and evidently objective universal considerations, thus contributing a valuable outlook on his overall experience as a thinker and an observer of theatre in a country of which he will never become a 'native'. These are elements that reflect the paradoxical nature of the double intellectual and instinctive experience of Barthes as a spectator in and of Japan and show how *Empire* illuminates new angles on performance theory and praxis and on Eastern and Western aesthetics.

It is noteworthy that the book contains as much visual material as it does text, and we find, in epigraphic form, Barthes's statement regarding his book's delicate balancing of interdisciplinary elements:

> The text does not 'gloss' the images, which do not 'illustrate' the text. For me, each has been no more than the onset of a kind of visual uncertainty, analogous perhaps to that *loss of meaning* Zen calls a *satori*. Text and image, interlacing, seek to ensure the circulation and exchange of these signifiers: body, face, writing; and in them to read the retreat of signs. (1982: n.p.: emphasis in the original)

In fact, the final sentence of this citation could be interpreted as a description of the elemental dynamics at the core of theatre, in the sense that the aspects involved already invoke the factors at play at the most basic and purest levels. Thus, even before the reader enters the actual text per se, Barthes introduces a protean description of the methods by which he perceives what one says or writes and what one sees, a dialectic linked to the key Zen notion of *satori* (understood as an incredibly striking incidence of epiphany not without parallels to the ancient Greek theatrical aims of evoking pathos and catharsis among the spectators – although in the case of catharsis, we generally expect to see some form of resolution with regard to a specific conflict, while in speaking of Japanese *satori*, that sense of resolution is in fact suspended, as meaning itself is emptied out), but consequently, the dialectic evokes unequivocally strong links to theatrical art. Even a quick scan through Barthes's book accents an inventive presentation of the blending of word and image, as drawings and photographs are interspersed with textual

---

On Barthes's collaboration in the journal *Théâtre Populaire* (1953–1964), see Bernard Dort (1995), as well as Louis-Jean Calvet, who examines Barthes's 'sociologie du spectacle' (1990: 145).

musings; at times, the author includes remarks in his own handwriting on, under or above the images, implicating that while word and image carry on a complicated, ever-changing semiotic relationship, they also conjure, as I am suggesting here, a parallel akin to the variations that a play produced on a stage, night after night (and from the perspective of different directorial interpretations and productions) might evoke: unique for every actor and for every director, as well as for every spectator.

In an examination of the relationship of Barthes to theatrical modalities (literal and methodological) in *Empire*, the author refers indirectly to the vital *punctum/studium* distinction that he details in his 1980 *Camera Lucida* (1993).[5] In *Empire*, Barthes reflects on the intricate relationship between photography and lived experience, between viewing and engaging in an artistic and emotive gesture:

> The author has never, in any sense, photographed Japan. Rather, he has done the opposite: Japan has starred him with any number of 'flashes'; or, better still, Japan has afforded him a situation of writing. This situation is the very one in which a certain disturbance of the person occurs, a subversion of earlier readings, a shock of meaning lacerated, extenuated to the point of its irreplaceable void, without the object's ever ceasing to be significant, desirable. Writing is after all, in its way, a *satori*: *satori* (the Zen occurrence) is a more or less powerful (though in no way formal) seism which causes knowledge, or the subject, to vacillate: it creates *an emptiness of language*. And it is also an emptiness of language which constitutes writing; it is from this emptiness that derive the features with which Zen, in the exemption from all meaning, writes gardens, gestures, houses, flower arrangements, faces, violence. (1982: 4)

This 'writing' of physical objects and actions alludes to the unusual displays of human life via its mores and traditions, a performance of the

---

5. It is important to note that the photos Barthes includes in *Empire* are hardly 'innocent' (Shawcross 1996); many are more than fifty years old at the time of publication, a choice on the part of the author that may belie the representation of a Japan that no longer existed when Barthes's nostalgic-tinged text appeared (the same has been written about his remarks on Japanese literature, which omit the work of more modern genres and forms, to concentrate extensively on *haiku*).

relationship of the self to the other observed by the writer who typifies the foreign presence in this circumstance. The 'theatre' of life takes place every day, on every street, and can propose powerful connotations in situations that might appear at first as mundane.

In the section 'Faraway', Barthes impresses again upon the reader his personal, often unabashedly biased interpretations of the 'spectacle' of a culture unlike his own (and engages us as participants, however vicariously, in his experience as a stranger in a new land – a notion that can be extended to that of a spectator confronting a novel form of theatrical performance):

> If I want to imagine a fictive nation, I can give it an invented name, treat it declaratively as a novelistic object ... I can also – though in no way claiming to represent or to analyze reality itself (these being the major gestures of Western discourse) – isolate somewhere in the world (*faraway*) a certain number of features ..., and out of these features deliberately form a system. It is this system that I shall call: Japan. (3)

Here, the onlooker Barthes takes the assertive step to possess the experience, declaring that he reformulates the very meaning of the name of a nation, presenting a definition he deems most suited to the phenomenon observed. He continues daringly:

> Hence Orient and Occident cannot be taken here as 'realities' to be compared and contrasted historically, philosophically, culturally, politically. I am not lovingly gazing toward an Oriental essence – *to me the Orient is a matter of indifference*, merely providing a reserve of features whose manipulation – whose invented interplay – allows me to 'entertain' the idea of an unheard-of symbolic system, one altogether detached from our own. What can be addressed, in the consideration of the Orient, are not other symbols, another metaphysics, another wisdom (though the latter might appear thoroughly desirable); it is the possibility of a difference, of a mutation, of a revolution in the propriety of symbolic systems. (3–4)[6]

6. Regarding the provocative phrase I italicize here, I have explored elsewhere (Genova 2017) the problematic question of Orientalism in Barthes's reading of the East. For more on this rich topic, see Scott Malcomson (1985), Tom Beebee (1980), Lisa Lowe (1991), Diana Knight (1993), Marie-Paule Ha

This idea of writing Japan, of being provoked (by the lack of meaning) into the very real act of writing, represents a key element for the critic, who also, for all intents and purposes, actually visits the country foremost as a tourist, not as an individual engaged directly in an anthropological or linguistic scholarly project. His goal is not to present an analytical study of the country; rather Barthes deliberately reads Japan as a text (Allen 2003: 72–3). Obviously, one need not necessarily be a foreigner in Japan to read the country as 'a text', and within this framework, the eccentric life of the celebrated writer Yukio Mishima comes to mind, but clearly the notion of the touristic stance of Barthes poses many ethical questions, a problem tackled by other critics over time. As an example, Lynn A. Higgins suggests:

> Barthes called *L'Empire des signes* a book of 'happy mythologies' because, as an outsider, he was able to put out of his field of vision the bourgeois preoccupations of both France and Japan. Industrial Japan, postwar Japan, capitalist Japan are conspicuously absent from this characterization. What he chooses to dwell on are facets of the host culture that give him pleasure, an attitude that makes him more willing to redefine himself than to take an Orientalizing posture. (1981: 166)

It seems clear that, particularly in the post-colonial era, one must face the thorny question of how to read Barthes today. Linked to the early Orientalist critiques that appeared in the critical press from the time of the publication of the book, issues of cultural appropriation have come to the forefront of much scholarly analysis (and pragmatic creation) of all spheres of art, particularly in an era of the often forced displacement of peoples across the globe. Doubtless, Barthes is quite

---

(2000) and Elisabeth Birk (2003). See also Dalia Kandiyoti: 'In his fiction of Japan, there is a quasi-erasure of the contemporary in favor of an Ur-Japan as it can be imagined before foreign contamination (and the subsequent collapse of difference)' (1997: 234–5). However, other critics, such as Célestin (1996) and Roger Laporte (1972), suggest that Barthes's book succeeds at surpassing in profound ways the image of a narcissistic, ethnocentric Orientalism, an awareness evident early in the book, where Barthes addresses directly his approach in aiming to avoid Orientalist temptations (Barthes 1982: 4). Finally, as analysed by Emily Apter (1994), there are many fascinating connections between Orientalism, sexuality and theatre in Barthes's work.

aware of his own difference in Japan in comparison to those around him, to their mores and their traditions, and he makes repeated allusions to the imaginary nature of the 'Japan' he has created, which is exactly what makes it a daunting task to declare definitively how deep his awareness of difference may actually go. As I mention in the previous footnote, there has been much division among critics as to whether Barthes can see how problematic his plan to reformulate another nation's sense of self, especially within an ideological framework that includes identity politics and the freedom of other cultures as perceived from the eyes of a white, male, European intellectual.

Further, in a related vein, Dennis Porter stresses the unusual tone this book sounds within traditional interpretations of the generic form of 'travel writing', by accentuating the ways in which Barthes avoids the conventional pitfalls of the genre; describing Barthes's idea of travel as a 'mode of displacement that allowed him to explore the nature of his own desire by means of a detour through otherness' (1991: 288), it also gave him the opportunity to rethink the very nature of representation (in the mind, in the world, on the stage, etc.).[7] It is the very opacity, the blankness, the sheer neutrality of simply being alien to the culture at hand and faced with the daunting endeavour to interpret other lifestyles that proves gratifying to him as an outsider (as an actor, perhaps, on an unfamiliar stage, confronted with an unknown role? Or as an author faced with an unfamiliar world?). Barthes exclaims with delight in the section entitled 'Without Words':

> In foreign countries, what a respite! Here I am protected against stupidity, vulgarity, vanity, worldliness, nationality, normality. The unknown language, of which I nonetheless grasp the respiration, the emotive aeration, in a word the pure significance, forms around me, as I move, a faint vertigo, sweeping me into its artificial emptiness, which is consummated only for me: I live in the interstice, delivered from any fulfilled meaning. (1982: 9)

It could be argued that what we see at work in *Empire* is a series of 'writerly' acts on the part of the French author, who, as a veritable interloper in the Japanese context, creates meanings, crafts bonds and renders 'readerly' that which he cannot grasp as would a local

---

7. On Barthes's unique perspective on the genre of the travelogue, see also Rolf J. Goebel (1993) and David Scott (2004).

inhabitant of the country.⁸ I use these distinctive terms *à la Barthes* carefully, for if some have argued that Barthes imposes meaning on Japanese culture (in our interest here, specifically on Japanese theatrical forms and dramatic theory), it is also conceivable that he is encouraging innovative meanings by other readers/spectators, much like a writer of a literary myth might breathe new life into the myth of Sisyphus or the parable of the Prodigal Son.⁹

It is also intriguing that a unique example of the notion of theatrical performance at work in this text arises in the section entitled 'The Interstice', which emphasizes the delicate yet substantial work of a tempura chef.¹⁰ Barthes is fascinated with the undeniably aesthetic

8. Barthes's 2002 *SZ* (originally published in French in 1973, just two years after the appearance of *Empire*) is an engaging re-reading of Honoré de Balzac's 1830 short story, *Sarrasine*, offering different codes by which to interpret a canonical text (as with 'hermenudic' and 'proairecic'). This approach explains the distinctions Barthes establishes between 'readerly' and 'writerly' texts. For him, the former term describes a passive acceptance by the reader of a conventional fictional work (particularly discernable with French Realist literature), while the latter descriptor presents a more engaged, more inventive stance (works of the New Novelists are exemplary), one that invites the active participation of the reader to create a multifaceted signification of the work at hand. What is important to us here is the possibility of Barthes's reading of Japan – or at least certain elements of it – can be read as more 'readerly' than 'writerly'.

9. I think here of the popularity of Greco-Roman mythological figures who revived French theatre in the first half of the twentieth century, as with Jean-Paul Sartre's *The Flies*, Albert Camus's *Caligula*, Jean Cocteau's *The Infernal Machine* and Jean Anouilh's *Antigone*, among others. I believe that these plays prefigure some of Barthes's critical thoughts about the longstanding, foreign forms of Japanese theatre, as he presents them in *Empire*.

10. The motif of food and its relationship to the individual who prepares it and/or consumes it is essential here; Barthes also writes that 'the elementary characters of the writing [are] established upon a kind of vacillation of language, and indeed this is what Japanese food appears to be: a written food, tributary to the gestures of divisions which inscribe the food stuff, not on the meal tray … but in a profound space which hierarchizes man, table, and universe' (1982: 14). For parallels aligning food with avant-garde theatre, see Hill: 'Barthes echoes Brecht's attack on so-called "culinary" theatre and generalizes his condemnation of the hypnotic or hysterical effects of the naturalistic stage' (1988: 116).

expertise of this unexpected creative artist; he writes that 'the foodstuff joins the dream of a paradox: that of a purely interstitial object, all the more provocative in that this emptiness is produced in order to provide nourishment (occasionally the foodstuff is constructed in a ball, like a wad of air). *Tempura* is stripped of the meaning we traditionally attach to fried food, which is heaviness' (1982: 24). Unmistakably, for Barthes, tempura is 'on the side of the light, the aerial, of the instantaneous, the fragile, the transparent, the crisp, the trifling, but whose real name would be *the interstice* without specific edges, or again: the empty sign' (26). Particularly germane to the subject of performance studies, Barthes also makes direct allusions to theatre in this section, while he refers as well to the art forms of writing and the work of a calligrapher, identifying in the manifestation created, produced, and acted out just for him and his guest(s) an event of deep beauty and valuable meaning; after a brief first sentence to begin his final paragraph of the section, Barthes presents a long, subtle, and evocative single sentence that forms the rest of the paragraph, leaving one breathless (and perhaps hungry – for food, for meaning, for another semiotic and/or three-dimensional performative enactment?):

> If he prepares our food *in front of us*, conducting, from gesture to gesture, from place to place, the eel from the breeding pond to the white paper which, in conclusion, will receive it entirely perforated, it is not (only) in order to make us witnesses to the extreme precision and purity of his cuisine; it is because his activity is literally graphic: he inscribes the foodstuff in the substance; his stall is arranged like a calligrapher's table; he touches the substances like a graphic artist (especially if he is Japanese) who alternates pots, brushes, inkstone, water, paper; he thereby accomplishes, in the racket of the restaurant and the chaos of shouted orders, a hierarchized arrangement, not of time but of tenses (those of a grammar of *tempura*), makes visible the entire gamut of practices, recites the foodstuff not as a finished merchandise, whose perfection alone would have value (as is the case with our dishes), but as a product whose meaning is not final but progressive, exhausted, so to speak, when its production has ended: it is you who eat, but it is he who has played, who has written, who has produced. (1982: 26; emphasis in the original)[11]

11. In passing, it is worth recalling Ridha Boulaâbi on the frequent use of parentheses (evident in the passage quoted); interestingly, the critic evokes

In his references to both the art of the calligrapher and that of the graphic artist, Barthes's depictions entail a truly interdisciplinary performative level of aesthetic activity, as well as of the clearly essential nature of the artistic gestures of the chef that are carried out with an ever-changing audience facing him directly, very close to him physically. While, as Barthes points out, it is the audience who eats the final product (members of a public who serve in the end as 'witnesses' and consumers), it is evident that the chef himself holds simultaneously the complex creative power of dramaturg, producer and actor. As the theatrical action unfolds, the 'progressive' nature of the performance of the chef is only fully realized once 'its production has ended', a moment only he himself can decide, a moment when his 'grammar' reaches a syntactical culmination. This focus on the preparation and ritualized manners in which to prepare a meal (not unlike Barthes's musings in *The Neutral* (2005) on the detailed complexities of tea ceremonies) brings to mind a comment by Vincent Leitch, who accents the importance in Japan of the wrapping that envelops a gift, highlighting the idea that the preparation and presentation of the gift – its staging – are highly valued by the recipient (1983: 204); indeed, as Jung imaginatively suggests of *Empire* (which includes a section related to this issue, entitled 'Packages'),

> The title of Barthes's work is, as it were, the wrapper of the content of Japanese culture as a system of signs. To decipher or zero in on the content, we must unwrap the wrapper. The content is packaged with a decorous plethora of cultural *bonsai* cultivated as miniaturized texts. If however, the wrapper were the gift itself, the title would be the content: there would be no inner soul separate from the textual flesh. (1987: 148–9)

Now, significantly, in some sections of *Empire*, Barthes ponders specifically certain quintessential differences he identifies in the evaluation of Eastern and Western dramatic genres. In 'The Three Writings', 'Animate/Inanimate' and 'Inside/Outside', he focuses primarily on *Bunraku* puppet theatre, which emerges for him as a beguilingly emblematic form. He groups the sections closely, with the first of the three listed above presenting Barthes's explanation of what

parallels between Barthes's use of this form of punctuation and the common Japanese discursive trait to turn to detailed contextualization in the decoding of meaning in language (2011: 315).

the art of *Bunraku* actually entails, that is, an extraordinary mélange of levels of action, figures, images and sound. He describes the puppets as ranging from three to five feet high and, using a quotation from the most celebrated poet in the history of Japanese *haiku*, he explains to his readers that:

> Each doll is moved by three quite visible men who surround it, support it, accompany it; the leader works the upper part of the doll and its right arm; his face is apparent, smooth, bright, impassive, cold as 'a white onion that has just been washed' (Basho); the two helpers wear black, a piece of cloth conceals their faces; one, in gloves but with the thumb showing, holds a huge pair of shears with which he moves the doll's left arm and hand; the other, crawling, supports the body, and is responsible for the doll's walking. These men proceed along a shallow trench which leaves their bodies visible. (1982: 48)

To a Westerner unaccustomed to this Eastern art, such variations on the choice of visible prominence conjure curiosity, as with the various roles of the men who work so closely with the puppets. The interconnected relationship of the humans' garments and their actions, with an emphasis on the rather strange details of their bodies, such as showing only the thumb on the hand of one of the helpers or holding suggestively menacing shears to move the puppets (openly viewed by the audience), creates a metaphysical dramatic space that poses significant questions, such as which figures should or should not represent fundamental sites for the viewer's attention. Plainly, the action of the storyline embodied by the puppets' movements is essential to the production, but equally necessary is the presence of these men, whose black and white shapes cannot help but draw the eye, especially one unfamiliar with the practice of exposure to the bare bones of theatrical performance. The accent on artificiality, on the very aspects kept behind the scene in more conventional forms, recalls of course Brechtian theory while it emphasizes the notion of difference for a culturally limited Western spectator as Barthes represents himself.

Additionally, as he continues his highly visual depiction of *Bunraku*, we learn that there is a dais to one side with musicians and speakers whose role is 'to *express* the text (as one might squeeze a fruit)' (1982: 48). The text is 'half spoken, half sung, punctuated with loud plectrum strokes by the samisen players, so that it is both measured and impassioned, with violence and artifice' (ibid.). We see that this inclusion of the art of sound adds to the corporeality and to the symbolic power of the human face (the vehicle for the voice) in a larger drama:

> Sweating and motionless, the speakers are seated behind little lecterns on which is set the huge script which they vocalize and whose vertical characters you can glimpse from a distance, when they turn a page of their libretto; a triangle of stiff canvas, attached to their shoulders like a bat's wing, frames their face, which is subject to all the throes of the voice. (48–9)

The complex imagery of this passage, expressed directly in the second person, takes on power even over the soundwaves, through the music and voices that complement the visual elements of the production. The very humanity of those situated on a secondary kind of stage, underscored by their noticeable perspiration, blends with their more figurative, symbolic dramatic presence. The fact that the script is 'huge' and allows spectators glimpses of the concrete linguistic characters, permitting them access to the writing that serves as the origin of the performance, is undoubtedly remarkable, but perhaps the most striking element to retain from this passage is the description of the triangular canvases bordering the speakers' faces, poised as a mysterious symbolic vehicle for the voice and the words they pronounce. Again, the apparent strangeness of these triangular shapes attracts and puzzles the Western eye. What indeed is the Occidental spectator to make of this complicated and foreign ritualistic spectacle, either in Barthes's time or today? How does our own humanity enter into the complex machinations of the artistic happening? Are we to compare ourselves to the seemingly emotionless puppets and/or the men who manipulate them? Barthes leaves these questions open, accenting again his role as a witness, not as a participant, to the artistic performance he has the unique opportunity to experience.

Despite the fact that *Bunraku* begins in the seventeenth century, and is still practiced as a popular theatrical form in Japan, its presence in *Empire* feels strangely familiar, almost like an event staged by the European avant-garde (such as the pioneering Western interdisciplinary piece *Parade* (1916–17) which involved influential figures such as Jean Cocteau, Erik Satie and Pablo Picasso). Barthes clearly senses the layers of meaning at play, through the precise resonance of the intensity of the voice, a component still controlled by the parameters of the genre: '*Bunraku* thus practices three separate writings, which it offers to be read simultaneously in three sites of the spectacle: the puppet, the manipulator, the vociferant: the effected gesture, the effective gesture, and the vocal gesture' (1982: 49). At this point, involved chiefly with the affective impact of sound, he elucidates the intricate symmetry between restriction and unfettered fervor, expressed by the human voice, comprising 'exaggerated declamation, tremolos, a falsetto tonality, broken intonations, tears, paroxysms of rage, of supplication, of astonishment, indecent pathos, the whole cuisine of emotion, openly elaborated on the level of that internal, visceral body of which the larynx is the mediating muscle' (ibid.). Yet Barthes insists that the excess of the vocal remains in the realm of the written, in the veiled linguistic realm, an element subject to an irony absolutely necessary to the form (ibid.). Because the voice is literally moved aside from the puppets' action, but is not entirely erased – which is an interesting observation on Barthes's part, since in his text he seems both to move away from 'emotion' and, at the same time, to include this element through the presence of the vocal dynamic, Barthes identifies in this art form a way to align sound with its counterpart: action, often accompanying periods of silence (49, 54), creating an equilibrium that reminds him of Brecht's work (54) and he shows how the most pioneering forms of Western art have learned much from the experimentations of Eastern drama over time.

In 'Inside/Outside', we encounter another tactic for interpreting the art of *Bunraku* opposed to a Western sense of spiritual morality. Barthes contends that over the past few centuries, the goal of Occidental theatre has been to make visible gradually that which is normally hidden, such as ambiguous feelings and subconscious struggles; this 'space of Sin', 'the space of this lie' is evaluated by Barthes as theological (1982: 61), while with the Eastern dramatic form, 'the sources of the theater are exposed in their emptiness. What is expelled from the stage is hysteria, i.e., theatre itself; and what is put in its place is the action necessary to the production of the spectacle: work is substituted for inwardness' (62). The 'hysteria' with which Barthes identifies the very art of Western theatre recalls of course certain foundational forms of antique dramatic expression, such as Greek Dionysia and Roman Bacchanalia, the wildly frenzied festivals, the legendary erotic displays of what one might argue represent a truly unique kind of theatrical spectacle, an unsuspected blending of religious and earthly desires, oddly prescient when one thinks of the much later theories (in very different disciplines) of Sigmund Freud and Artaud. Further, in Barthes's claim that *Bunraku* expels hysteria from the theatre, he overlooks a kind of oblique yet powerful form of outwardly expressed, primal conflict inherent to the nature of the human psyche. Yet, as Hill argues, this Japanese form of dramatic art represents for Barthes an example of how theatrical expression fits into a much larger human framework: 'And theatre in Barthes's texts is often used as a means of contrasting different values, different ethical systems and different types of culture' (1988: 117). For Barthes, *Bunraku* also recalls Brecht's admiration for the notion of code; he declares in *Empire*: 'As in the modern text, the interweaving of codes, references, discrete assertions, anthological gestures multiplies the written line, not by virtue of some metaphysical appeal, but by the interaction of a *combinatoire* which opens out into the entire space of the theater: what is begun by one is continued by the next, without interval' (55; emphasis in the original). Yet while Barthes's vision of *Bunraku* may return to Brecht's appreciation of 'code', there are also significant differences between Brecht's and Barthes's views on the nature and function of theatre generally. Certainly, it is well known that for Brecht, the aim to unveil the illusions associated with Occidental theatrical prejudices, particularly with regard to the underlying forces of political thought, is undeniable in his evaluation of Western drama; for the Barthes of *Empire*, the focus and value of the art lie elsewhere. Specifically, as we have seen, Barthes does not seek out a political platform in his analysis of *Bunraku*'s theatrical dynamics and seems to have little interest in a possible ideological aspect to the form. Given that Barthes's original French version of *Empire* was published in 1970, he had already explored Brecht's multifaceted appreciation of the art of theatre for many years, and by the time he writes *Empire*, we see that the world of semiotics, comprising the dynamics of the systems of signs – in language, in culture, in theatre – has become for him integrated into a larger viewpoint in his commentary on cultures. We can understand how he moves to consider more closely the subtleties of Eastern theatrical spectacles, reflecting as he does on the at-times conflictual relationship between the theatrical aesthetic realm and the 'real' aspects of performative spectacles.

Ultimately, then, we unearth in *Empire of Signs* abundant and impactful theoretical and metaphorical foundations of theatrical art that will resurface – honed, rendered more specific and more refined – in his later lectures at the Collège de France. The profoundly interdisciplinary stance of *Empire* therefore reflects a prefiguration of essential elements of later performance studies, such as necessarily interdisciplinary methodological approaches, an accent on the truly 'artificial' aspects of the theatre, the relationship of spectacle and practice to the quotidian world of the public and the importance of oral traditions, as well as physical gesture and ethnical custom. Likewise, the reflections on linguistics and on narrative discourse, present within and complementary to direct commentary on theatre, come across as revelatory, as Barthes also proposes in *Empire* a radical rethinking of the potential of our identity as global citizens, in a way, as actors on a global scale. We also realize that the field of performance studies turns often to a mix of methods in the elaboration of its work, both theoretical and in praxis, and we can see that *Empire* participates as well in the author's inventive exploration of a world that he knows (as with France) and that which is originally utterly remote from him, as with Japan (and other nations, such as China and Morocco).[12] We discover in Barthes an elaborately ambivalent figure, one who succeeds in some ways of overcoming the confines of his Western European background, but who also displays certain beliefs and methodologies (even indoctrinations?) that he cannot escape, elements of which he may very well not have realized had influenced his work (this idea is ironic, given Barthes's critique of Balzac in *SZ*). What we can acquire from these textual investigations is finally a fascinating new look, not only at Barthes, irrefutably one of the most influential cultural figures of the European twentieth century, but also at the ever-changing, incredibly productive discipline of theatrical art and theory.

References

Allen, Graham, ed. (2003), *Roland Barthes*, New York: Routledge.
Apter, Emily (1994), 'Acting Out Orientalism: Sapphic Theatricality in Turn-of-the-Century Paris', *L'Esprit Créateur*, 34(2): 102–16.
Barthes, Roland (1972), *Critical Essays*, trans. Richard Howard, Evanston: Northwestern University Press.
Barthes, Roland (1977), *Image Music Text*, trans. Stephen Heath, London: Fontana Press.
Barthes, Roland (1982), *Empire of Signs*, trans. Richard Howard, New York: Hill and Wang.
Barthes, Roland (1992), *Incidents*, trans. Richard Howard, Berkeley: University of California Press.
Barthes, Roland (1993), *Camera Lucida: Reflections on Photography*, trans. Richard Howard, London: Vintage.
Barthes, Roland (2002), *S/Z*, trans. Richard Miller, London: Blackwell.

---

12. See for example, Barthes's 2012 *Travels in China*. As for Morocco, his original collection of essays, *Incidents*, appeared in English in 1992.

Barthes, Roland (2005), *The Neutral: Lecture Course at the Collège de France, 1977–1978*, trans. Rosalind Kraus and Denis Hollier, New York: Columbia University Press.
Barthes, Roland (2012), *Travels in China*, ed. Anne Herschberg Pierrot, trans. Andrew Brown, Cambridge: Polity Press.
Beebee, Thomas (1980), 'Orientalism, Absence and the *poème en prose*', *The Rackham Journal of the Arts and Humanities*, 2(1): 48–71.
Birk, Elizabeth (2003), '"L'Orient m'est indifférent": Roland Barthes' Japan', in Jane Conroy (ed.), *Cross-Cultural Travel*, 407–16, New York: Peter Lang.
Boulaâbi, Ridha (2011), *L'Orient des langues au XXème siècle*, Paris: Geuthner.
Calvet, Louis-Jean (1990), *Roland Barthes, 1915–1990*, Paris: Flammarion.
Carmody, Jim (1990), 'Reading Scenic Writing: Barthes, Brecht and Theatre Photography', *The Journal of Dramatic Theory and Criticism*, 5(1): 25–38.
Célestin, Roger (1996), *From Cannibals to Radicals: Figures and Limits of Exoticism*, Minneapolis: University of Minnesota Press.
Comment, Bernard (1991), *Roland Barthes: Vers le neutre*, Paris: Christian Bourgois.
Culler, Jonathan (1983), *Roland Barthes*, New York: Oxford University Press.
De Vos, Patrick (2004), 'Le spectacle du théâtre dans *L'empire des signes*', *University of Tokyo Center for Philosophy Bulletin*, 2: 142–50.
Dort, Bernard (1995), 'Barthes: le corps du théâtre', in *Le Spectateur en dialogue*, 135–46, Paris: P.O.L.
Genova, Pamela (2017), 'Beyond Orientalism? Roland Barthes' Imagistic Structures of Japan', *Romance Studies*, 34(3–4): 152–62.
Goebel, Rolf J. (1993) 'Japan as Western Text: Roland Barthes, Richard Gordon Smith, and Lafcadio Hern', *Comparative Literature Studies*, 30(2): 188–205.
Ha, Marie-Paule (2000), 'Another Barthes', in *Figuring the East*, 95–117, New York: State University of New York Press.
Higgins, Lynne A. (1981), 'Barthes' Imaginary Voyages', *Studies in Twentieth-Century Literature*, 5(2): 161–66.
Hill, Leslie (1988), 'Barthes's Body', *Paragraph*, 11(2): 107–26.
Jung, Hwal Yol (1987), 'The Joy of Textualizing Japan: A Metacommentary on Roland Barthes's *Empire of Signs*', *The Bucknell Review*, 30(2): 144–67.
Kandiyoti, Dalia (1997), 'Roland Barthes Abroad', in J.-M. Rabaté (ed.), *Writing the Image After Roland Barthes*, 228–42, Philadelphia: University of Pennsylvania Press.
Knight, Diana (1988), 'Roland Barthes in Harmony: The Writing of Utopia', *Paragraph*, 11(2): 127–42.
Knight, Diana (1993), 'Barthes and Orientalism', *New Literary History*, 24(3): 617–33.
Lagaay, Alice (2016), 'Sleepwalking Through the Neutral (with Roland Barthes and Maurice Blanchot)', *Performance Research*, 21(1): 37–41.
Laporte, Roger (1972), 'L'Empire des signifiants', *Critique*, 302: 583–94.

Leitch, Vincent (1983), *Deconstructive Criticism*, New York: Columbia University Press.
Lowe, Lisa (1991), *Critical Terrains: French and British Orientalisms*, Ithaca, New York: Cornell University Press.
Malcomson, Scott (1985), 'The Pure Land Beyond the Seas: Barthes, Burch and the Uses of Japan', *Screen*, 26(3–4): 23–33.
Manghani, Sunil, ed. (2020), 'Neutral Life: Roland Barthes' Late Work', Special issue of *Theory, Culture & Society*, 37(4): 3–34.
Pavis, Patrice (2012), 'Empire of Signs: From Japan towards Korea?', trans. Joel Anderson, *Forum Moderns Theater*, 27(1–2): 7–15.
Porter, Dennis (1991), *Haunted Journeys: Desire and Transgression in European Travel Writing*, Princeton, NJ: Princeton University Press.
Scott, David (2004), *Semiologies of Travel*, Cambridge: Cambridge University Press.
Shawcross, Nancy (1996), *Roland Barthes on Photography*, Gainesville: University Press of Florida.
Suvin, Darko (1991), 'The Soul and the Sense: Meditations on Roland Barthes on Japan', *The Canadian Review of Comparative Literature*, 18(4): 499–531.

Chapter 15

UNRAVELLING TEXTUAL SOUNDSCAPES: READING BARTHES'S 'THE GRAIN OF THE VOICE' THROUGH SÖDERBERG'S *ENTANGLED PHRASES* AND LINEHAN'S *BODY OF WORK*

Rosa Lambert

Introduction

There currently seems to be a heightened interest in the role of sound and voice in theatre and performance studies (cf. Brooks 2010; Collins 2018; Curtin 2014; Home-Cook 2015; Kendrick 2017; McGrath et al. 2021; Ovadija 2013). This renewed scholarly interest is particularly timely considering the rise of choreographic performances in which spoken words are used together with corporeal movement, or in which language is introduced as a medium to evoke movement. In these performances, words often give rise to physical choreographies, and vice versa, while the words themselves function as a medium that can itself be choreographed: through inner rhymes, rhythm and other poetic strategies, choreographers seek to establish movement *within* a text. By unmuting dance, these artists demonstrate that choreography can become both an auditory as well as visual art form. It is therefore crucial to attend meticulously to the sonorous dimension of speech when considering text in its relation to physical movement and as a choreographic medium in its own right. In an attempt to delineate such an analytical approach, this chapter will focus on the use of voiced language in terms of its sonorous specificity and its choreographic character in *Body of Work* (Linehan 2019) and *Entangled Phrases* (Söderberg 2019). By analysing these performances, I aim to shed new light on the current tendency to employ spoken text in the context of dance.

To do so, I turn to Roland Barthes's essay 'Le grain de la voix' (1972).[1] His study of the art of opera singers developed in the essay focusses on the interaction between a performer's body and language's sonorous and material aspects. Before summarizing the main arguments of Barthes's essay, I will first briefly introduce Linehan and Söderberg's performances. Throughout the course of this chapter, these two performances will reveal that Barthes's essay on opera performers can be highly useful in the context of contemporary dance experiments with spoken text. This is because his essay draws attention to the interaction between sound, voice and language – precisely the interaction that I believe uncovers the choreographic force behind recent deployments of spoken language in dance performances. Moreover, as embodied manifestations of the interaction between language, body and sound that is the focus of Barthes's essay, the performances themselves will also be helpful to navigate through Barthes's hermetically constructed argumentation and highly specific terminology. Consequently, together with Barthes's insights, they profoundly contribute to and set the parameters for an understanding of voiced language as a means to create sonorous choreographies.

Moving words

The first performance that will contribute to the development of such an understanding is Daniel Linehan's *Body of Work* (2019). In deSingel's Theaterstudio (in Antwerp),[2] the usual audience tribune has been removed and a rectangle of chairs, which almost covers the entire room, establishes the minimalistic performance space set-up. Consequently, each spectator, positioned quite close to the performance, takes up an individual perspective on the piece and looks at another row of spectators in front of them. Apart from the chairs for the audience and six surround speakers, there are no other objects in the space.

1. Throughout this chapter, I will refer to the translated essay 'The Grain of the Voice', as it is included in *Image Music Text* (1977), translated and edited by Stephen Heath. The original essay 'Le grain de la voix' was first published in 1972.

2. The performance has also toured throughout Belgium, The Netherlands and France. I attended the premiere in deSingel, in Antwerp in March 2019 and in this chapter, I am relying on the video documentation of the performance in that location.

Body of Work is Linehan's attempt to relocate and re-perform the choreographic traces from his career as a dancer and choreographer. While the audience enters to take their seats at one of the rectangle's four sides, Linehan is already using his body to measure various distances in the room. For instance, he places one foot behind the other to measure the distance between two chairs, walks to the other side of the rectangle, where a microphone is placed, and announces through the microphone 'take seven of my feet'.[3] He then steps out of the rectangle to measure a part of the wall in between black theatre cloths. To do so, he places his leg horizontally alongside the wall, walks back to the microphone and announces, 'Take three quarters of my leg'. He measures the distance between two other chairs: 'Take three of my lower legs and one of my hands'. He estimates the distance between two walls, which 'take eleven of [his] feet'. These sentences not only refer to the measurements of the room; these imperative phrases also seem to function as commands that Linehan addresses to himself, to remember and keep track of the movement sequence he is performing. In previous performances, Linehan frequently explored the interrelationship between voice and physicality. As such, in the journey through his choreographic archive, spoken words and bodily movements are central protagonists; in *Body of Work*, verbal language figures as an indispensable element within the crux of bodily memory and bodily movement.

In *Entangled Phrases* (2019), Alma Söderberg stages a poem that she has written herself. In this performance, spoken language functions differently than it does in Linehan's piece. Of importance in the context of this chapter is Söderberg's background in flamenco – which is by its very nature about the dialogue between sound and movement – insofar as that aesthetic strongly determines her oeuvre as a dancer and choreographer. This consists of several pieces in which the conversational exchange between sound and physical movement is being explored. During the first thirty minutes of *Entangled Phrases*,[4] performers Anja Müller, Angela Peris Alcantud and Alma Söderberg are seated next to each other on three chairs that are positioned alongside the *côté cour* wall. The rest of the stage is empty, and the performers are gazing towards the *côté jardin*. Söderberg, who is sitting in the middle, initiates the soundscape: she places

---

3. Unspecified quotes refer to text from the performances.
4. I am relying on the video documentation of the performance as it took place in beurrschouwburg in November 2019.

her two arms in front of her, moves them as if she is pulling a rope and pronounces 'the time that, the time that, the time that, the time that…'. Müller copies the movement and joins the sentence with something that sounds like: 'needs that, needs that, needs that…'. When Alcantud joins them, it has become almost impossible to discern what she and the other two performers are saying. The rhythm of the performers' speech and the occasional overlap of their sentences sometimes produce specific words such as, 'institution', 'problem' or 'solution'. What emerges is a hypnotic, rhythmic and dynamic soundscape, in which the three separate voices collide into a heterogeneous, yet consistent sound. As the performers nearly never simultaneously change their repeated sequence – and when one performer does break the repetition of her phrase and switches to different words it almost goes unnoticed – modifications within this soundscape occur very subtly. This gives the impression that, as the title suggest, the phrases are glued together and are pronounced by one single body.

To some extent, *Body of Work* and *Entangled Phrases* can be assembled under what dance and performance scholar Leonie Persyn has called (after Benjamin Vandewalle and Yoann Durant) 'auditory choreography', performances in which sound no longer functions as 'a small building block in the actualization of a choreography' (2019: 200) but becomes the locus where choreography takes place. These choreographic works, that play on both the visual and the auditory realms, participate in a broader and more expanded development within Western-based contemporary dance, that is, the experimentation with media other than the human body to enact choreographies. For example, in her chapter 'Protocols of Encounter: On Dance Dramaturgy', dance scholar Sandra Noeth considers dance performances that 'have formulated a new understanding of choreography that exceeds the organization of movement in time and space' (2011: 247). She characterizes these experiments by a tendency towards conceptualism, where the (privileged) presence of the human body is critically questioned and where a medial hybridity emerges through the exchange with genres such as theatre, music or sculpture (247–8). Importantly, as Noeth observes, in some of these pieces, the human body appears to be vividly present in its seeming absence (247). Another insightful angle on this contemporary development is dance scholar Rudi Laermans's notion of 'dance in general', which refers to contemporary dance experiments that withdraw from portraying bodily movement. He explains, 'besides physical movements also lighting, sounds, props, text fragments or video images are all deliberately deployed as active agents, as components that do something and therefore co-define the overall performativity of a dance piece' (2008: 11).

Common to both Noeth and Laermans's view is the idea that contemporary dance is not necessarily enacted within or by means of human bodies, but that its creators seek other loci to create, express or perform movement. These formal experiments can therefore be interpreted as attempts to 'redefine the ontological ground of dance' (Protopapa 2013: 275), so that 'any choreographed piece that presents itself as dance potentially proposes a concept of dance by its very nature (of being dance)' (277). *Body of Work* and *Entangled Phrases* expose some affinities with this tendency because both performances reshuffle the strict and exclusive connection between dance and bodily movement. In these pieces, *voiced language* is enmeshed within the choreographic structure. Speech not only actively contributes to the creation of the dance piece, but also becomes its very medium, so the pieces 'situate the place of choreography in the materiality of language' (Noeth 2011: 248). As already mentioned in the introduction, these performances therefore necessitate a reorientation of the understanding of dance and movement as something primarily bodily and visual, towards something that can also be expressed through language and through sound. To avoid misunderstandings, these textual and auditory choreographies are not working towards an uncomplicated erasure of corporeality within choreography; choreographing language does not imply that the body disappears altogether. On the contrary, I would rather argue that the particular use of text in these performances confronts us with the fact that language is always already an embodied thing and that, in Linehan and Söderberg's pieces, corporeality manifests itself in the language. To put it differently, the dancing body, besides being physically present on stage, also becomes an auditory presence, evoked through the speaking voice delivering the choreographed text.

In what follows, I will illuminate how Barthes's 'The Grain of the Voice' offers useful parameters to unravel these textual soundscapes of *Body of Work* and *Entangled Phrases*. To do so, I will first offer a close analysis of the argument that Barthes develops in his essay, and I will emphasize how the performances also offer opportunities to expand Barthes's thought, which is primarily centred around the analysis of an individual human voice. The two performances I analyse illuminate how the interaction between language and technology (*Body of Work*) and the interaction between multiple voices (*Entangled Phrases*) influence the dynamics between voice, language and body. The second part of the chapter is then devoted to uncovering the common ground between speech and dance. There, I will highlight the crux between writing and speaking on which the notion of the grain is conceived by Barthes, which, furthermore, provides a suitable avenue to discern the impetus of using words as a locus for (choreographed) movement. I will at this point, however, briefly return to one of Barthes's earlier writings, *Writing Degree Zero* ([1953] 1970). This short detour will allow me to more profoundly grasp the interplay between writing and speaking as it figures in 'The Grain of the Voice'. In all upcoming sections, I will treat Barthes's writings as he himself tended to treat works of art: 'Not by asking what they are trying to do, but by prolonging their obsessions into his own writing' (Brown 1992: 8).

'The Grain of the Voice'

'The Grain of the Voice' was written during the last part of Barthes's career, which has often been characterized as a period in which 'his writing moves away from the theoretical and towards the literary' (Moriarty 1991: 157). In this essay, Barthes looks closely into the art of opera singers from the perspective of the intersection between language and music. His prime locus of interest is 'a part of vocal music (*lied* or *mélodie*): the very precise space (genre) of *the encounter between a language and a voice*' (Barthes 1977: 181, emphasis in the original). In this encounter, he writes, the voice's 'grain' can materialize. Importantly, the grain emerges when the voice is simultaneously producing sound and language: when words are set to music and are produced through a singer's voice. However, not all vocal performances produce a grain: its emergence also depends on the specific way in which the singer performs the music. Throughout his essay, the grain is used to appraise the performances of (a certain type of) opera singers. It offers Barthes an alternative to what he considers as a major flaw of music criticism, namely, its tendency to translate musical experience into 'the poorest of linguistic categories: the adjective' (179).

To further conceptualize this 'grain', Barthes draws a comparative analysis between two singers: the opera singer Charles Panzéra, a singer whose voice produces a grain and who Barthes prefers over the voice of the more famous singer, Dietrich Fischer-Dieskau, whose approach towards the art of singing Barthes dislikes because the grain remains absent in his performances. Barthes then draws a second comparison, one between two aspects of a song, the 'pheno-song' and the 'geno-song', neologisms which are derived from Julia Kristeva's distinction between pheno-text and geno-text. With the term 'pheno-song', Barthes aims to capture the qualities that belong to the structure of language and its signifying and expressive function. The pheno-song has primarily to do with the content of the song and the language, with 'everything in the performance which is in the service of communication, representation, expression' (1977: 182). The 'geno-song', on the other hand, refers to the sounds of the music and the materiality of the language being sung. The 'geno-song' denotes the 'volume of the singing and speaking voice, the space where significations germinate "from within language and in its very materiality"' (ibid.). As this quoted definition of the geno-song already reveals, Barthes resists a facile dichotomy between text (or, in this case, the text set to the music score) and performance. The geno-song, namely, is something that is manifested both in the performance of a song (it denotes the volume of the voice) and, meanwhile, is described as something that is part of the text itself (it appears 'from within language and in its very materiality'). For that reason, the geno-song can function as a helpful notion to conceptualize the interaction between body, voice the materiality of the text and sound, since it assembles both the textual and performative dimension of spoken language.

At first sight, the grain is mainly used to describe the presence of a body in the act of singing. Describing the grain of a Russian bass singer, Barthes clarifies that it is

> something which is directly the cantor's body, brought to your ears in one and the same movement from deep down in the cavities, the muscles, the membranes, the cartilages and from deep down in the ... language, as though a single skin lined the inner flesh of the performer and the music he sings. (1977: 181)

However, as Barthes explains later in the essay, the appearance of the 'grain' is not only dependent on whether or not the body manifests itself in the act of singing (by emphasizing the sounds of 'the cavities, the muscles, the membranes, the cartilages'); it also depends on whether the song's 'geno-song', rather than its 'pheno-song', is emphasized in performance. Although it feels risky to distil an unequivocal answer from Barthes's (later) writings, he seems to suggest that the grain appears when the song's geno-song – the materiality and the sonority of the language being sung – is amplified. The grain of the voice, Barthes elucidates, 'is not – or is not merely – its timbre; the *significance* it opens cannot better be defined, indeed, than by the very friction between the music and something else, which something else is the particular language' (1977: 185, emphasis in the original). The 'particular' language here refers to the prosodic characteristics of a language; the difference, for instance between French – where hard consonants are only rarely pronounced at the ends of words creating a sense of on-goingness – and English – where the second syllable of words is generally accented preventing a sonorous continuity (Gardner 2010: 362). To conclude, the grain refers to the efforts of the body that are audible in an act of singing, provided that the specific materiality and musicality (rhythm and music) of the language being sung are emphasized.

Words as body-sounds in *Body of Work* and *Entangled Phrases*

Now that I have set out the central lines of thought of Barthes's essay, I will focus on how the dynamic between the pheno-song, geno-song and grain is staged within *Body of Work* and *Entangled Phrases*, as a way to discern the sonorous qualities of the performances' textual soundscapes. The soundscape that Söderberg, Müller and Alcantud's words create in *Entangled Phrases* sometimes sounds as if a technological or computer-based intervention is modifying the sound, even though the soundscape in the beginning of the piece is exclusively produced by human bodies. For instance, when certain consonants of words are emphasized, it seems as if a beat is added to the text. Or when one performer, throughout the incessant repetition of one phrase, gradually moves towards a higher pitch, she gives the impression that not she but instead a technological sound effect is modifying her words. These effects spring from the performers' incessant experiment with the words' musical and material qualities (their geno-song), such as its pitch, tempo, intonation and volume, as well as the careful and intensified pronunciation of certain letters or syllables. These prosodic experiments all result in the feeling that the words themselves are dancing.

    Barthes explains how Panzéra – the singer who produces a grain and whose 'art … was in the letters' (Barthes 1977: 183) – shows that 'an extreme rigour of thought regulated the prosody of the enunciation' (ibid.). Similarly, the performers in *Entangled Phrases* use language not as a medium to convey a content, but, rather, by placing the phrases in a strict choreography of repetition, variation and moments of unison and disharmony, as a way to draw attention to the phrases' musicality and materiality. In other words, by experimenting primarily on the level of the geno-song, the semantic aspect of the words more often than not remains inaccessible. In a way, the performers' mode of speaking reduces (or maybe even eliminates) the pheno-song of the phrases. Compared with our everyday use of language, this feels quite unusual, and for that reason, we sometimes get the impression that the performers are merely producing sounds instead of words. However, as also mentioned above, we sometimes do catch a glimpse of the pheno-song, and during these moments, it does become possible to distinguish actual words or phrases within the dense soundscape. In this performance, the voice is not used for its 'service role' (Cavarero 2005: 35). Rather, resulting from the performers' experiment on the level of the geno-song, the voice's role in producing language is more explicitly accentuated. As is the case in Panzéra's performance, in the performance of Müller, Alcantud and Söderberg the grain of their voices emerges as a result of their emphasis on the geno-song. Because we are not distracted by the semantic meaning of the words that are being uttered, we become more fully aware of the phrases' musicality and materiality and of the bodies' efforts producing them.

As sound scholar Adriana Cavarero outlines, a central characteristic of voice and sound is their capacity to create a relational space. Drawing on Jean-Luc Nancy, she argues that the 'most naked function' of language is 'the maintenance of a relation that communicates no other meaning than the relation itself' (Cavarero 2005: 194–5). As mentioned above, it is virtually impossible to discern the different individual voices within the soundscape in *Entangled Phrases*. The unique materiality of the individual voices becomes fully incorporated into this relational space which creates a specific (collective) sound and timbre. As a result, the grain in *Entangled Phrases* materializes through the interplay of *three* voices.

This adds a new dimension to Barthes's argument that is primarily focused on the voice of one singer. The performance allows us to recognize that the grain can also be produced by a collective voice. Through formal strategies (by amplifying the voiced and sounded quality of language, and by foregrounding the text's geno-song), Söderberg, Müller and Alcantud draw attention to the ambiguous difference between collective and individual bodies. The composed grain of the three voices that emerges in this performance exposes, in a highly formal way, how language primarily functions a medium to reveal the fundamental entanglement between individual bodies. Moreover, Barthes frequently refers to the engagement with the grain of the voice as a pleasurable experience. In *Entangled Phrases* as well, the sonic experiments explicitly generate a relation of pleasure, both between the audience and the performers and also amongst the performers themselves. In order to create the soundscape, Söderberg, Müller and Alcantud have to simultaneously act as performers and attentive listeners. This somewhat dissolves the boundary between performer and audience, thereby creating a kind of pleasure that emanates from blending those two roles. Quite often, the performers' body language and facial expressions reveal the enjoyment they are experiencing while composing this collective soundscape together.[5]

The largest part of the text in *Body of Work*, on the other hand, primarily functions to communicate content and meaning. As mentioned, during this performance, Linehan reactivates bodily memories to introduce several movement sequences from previous performances into *Body of Work*. For example, when he drops his head down to the ground and slaps his thighs several times, he references the performance *dbddbb* (2016). The sequence where he crawls to an audience member and kisses their feet is a movement from *Making It*, a short solo that he made in New York in 2006.[6] Throughout some of the physical movements that he makes, Linehan counts steps out loud, talks about personal memories from his childhood or traces his family lineage back to the Irish potato famine in 1848. These linguistic interventions mainly emphasize the text's pheno-song (its content and expressive function). Similar to the movement sequences that echo previous performances, these sentences evoke the past in the present through memory.

There are, however, certain movement sequences in which Linehan uses language differently, and where it, such as in Söderberg's performance, turns into a medium that is being choreographed. In the rectangular performance space of *Body of Work*, six surround speakers are positioned behind the audience to produce a rotating sound effect and to let the sound literally move from one speaker to the other. For instance, Linehan pronounces the sentence 'I have a question, it is about

---

5. Instead of the more general term 'pleasure' that appears several times in the essay, Barthes also uses his more specific notion 'jouissance'. For instance, when he describes Fischer-Dieskau's performances and mentions that 'from the point of view of the pheno-song', he is 'an artist beyond reproach: everything in the (semantic and lyrical) structure is respected and yet nothing seduces, nothing sways us to jouissance' (Barthes 1977: 183). It would probably require another chapter to elaborate on the connection between the grain of the voice and jouissance; for more on this, see: Barthes, Roland ([1973] 1975), *The Pleasure of the Text*: 66–7.

6. Email correspondence with the artist.

your plans, I want to ask you, what happens after', and while doing so, he records it by means of a loop station. Afterwards, this phrase is transmitted through the surround speakers. By dividing the text into separate units that are then each played through a different speaker, Linehan creates the impression that his voice circulates through space and that it moves from one speaker to the next. Moreover, because we hear the exact same enunciations of the same sentence several times, our attention gradually moves towards the words' materiality and musicality (their geno-song) and less towards their pheno-song, since, after hearing the sentence several times, we already know the content of the words. As a result, the grain of Linehan's technologically mediated voice becomes gradually more audible.

Interestingly, in this performance, a non-linguistic grain emerges as well. Toward the end of his essay, Barthes mentions that the grain does not only emerge in vocal music but that it can be perceived in instrumental music as well: 'Leaving aside the voice, the 'grain' – or the lack of it – persists in instrumental music' (1977: 188). During the first part of the performance, Linehan brushes a microphone against his sweater, his chest, his jeans, his beard, his ears and his hair and records these (indeed, grainy) sounds through a loop station. Afterwards, these sounds are played on repeat while he dances. This strategy can be read as an attempt to capture the grain of *the dancing body*, or to capture the sounds of the body's materiality. While he dances on the soundtrack of his own body-sounds, the sounds of the microphone brushing against Linehan's body come across as the sounds of his muscles, hamstrings and bones that he uses while dancing and their 'grain' reminds us of the very materiality of Linehan's dancing body.

This brings us to an important footnote to Barthes's conception of the grain. At the outset of his essay, Barthes emphasizes that the grain produces the efforts of the singing body, but always *in the encounter between language, music and voice*. Towards the end of his text, however, he suggests that the grain can emerge through instrumental music as well, in which language is usually absent. By including an instrumental grain into his essay, Barthes (indirectly) suggests that nonverbal music (or in Linehan's case, the sounds recorded on the loop station) also consists of a language component, of a *text*. This would imply that it also consists of a pheno-song and a geno-song. In other words, his suggestion that the grain can emerge in instrumental music does not necessarily introduce a paradox in relation to his conception of the grain in the beginning of the essay. Instead, it might rather reveal something about instrumental music's ontology as a text.

Speech as dance

Until now, I have primarily interpreted Barthes's essay as a way to scrutinize the vocal and sonorous aspect of voiced language. The second question that this chapter seeks to address, however, still remains unanswered. More specifically, in order to consider speech not as an additional element that is subordinate to the dance performance, but that rather functions as a medium in which dance expresses itself, I still need to examine how (or why) speech can function as a medium of dance. Surprisingly, Barthes's notion of the grain also (albeit again indirectly and cryptically) offers a starting point. Although his own writings 'do not consider the implications of this promising theoretical opening for theatre' (Scheie 1992: 107), the grain of the voice can function as an indicator that the performer uttering the words is 'a choreographer whose expression happens to be literature' (Spångberg 2017: 363). In the previous section, I highlighted how through the entire textual soundscape of Söderberg's performance a *collective* grain emerges, and how in some sequences of *Body of Work* the grain is evoked with the help of technology.[7] Simultaneously, I have suggested that, in both cases, a sense of movement emerged *within* the words, as if the words are choreographed and become the very medium of dance. I did not, however, make a similar point about the textual elements in *Body of Work* that tended more towards the pheno-song, where the grain remained absent. In already making this distinction while developing the first part of my argument (how can Barthes's terminology function as a way to discern the sonorous dimension of voiced language?), the second part of my argument has already become apparent (how can that same terminology help to expose the affinity between speech and dance?).

Towards the end of my analyses of these performances, the grain gradually turned into an evaluative category that enabled me to distinguish between speech in dance (such as is the case with the verbal memory sequences in *Body of Work*) and speech *as* dance (such as is the case in the rest of the phrases in *Body of Work* and in the largest part of the language that is produced in *Entangled Phrases*). The reason why the grain can operate here in this double manner is that Barthes equates the

---

7. In this section, I will temporarily bracket the non-instrumental grain as a form of dance in *Body of Work*, because it does not relate to the question on the common ground between speech and dance that I am addressing in this part of the chapter.

geno-song with *writing* towards the end of his essay. After he claims that 'the song must speak, must *write*', Barthes mentions, almost in passing, 'for what is produced at the level of the geno-song is finally writing' (Barthes 1977: 185; emphasis in the original). This rather confusing suggestion – that when the text's geno-song (its materiality and musicality) is amplified, speech can function as writing – in actuality offers a valuable insight to further pursue the question on the affinity between speech and dance. So let us expatiate on it for a bit longer. To disentangle the meaning of this phrase, I will first focus on how Barthes conceptualizes the relation between speech and writing and then consider how the notion of 'writing' should be interpreted in (late) Barthes's thinking.

In Barthesian terms, speech does not so much refer to the product of the act of speaking, nor is writing necessarily the result of the act of writing. Instead, speech and writing function as *qualities* of a text, regardless of the medium – either the voice or the paper – that stores them. As such, the voice can operate as an instrument that produces writing or an '*écriture vocale*' (Brown 1992: 215). In 'The Grain of the Voice', as the passage I am currently interpreting demonstrates, he equates the capacity to portray writing in speech with an emphasis on the geno-song, and thus with the emergence of the grain. A similar point on the simultaneous emergence of the grain and an *écriture vocale* is made in *The Pleasure of Text*. When he talks about 'writing aloud' (or writing produced through speech), he mentions that it 'belongs to the geno-text; … it is carried … by the *grain* of the voice (Barthes 1975: 66; emphasis in the original). In other words, speech can be considered as writing when the grain of the voice emerges and when the geno-song of the text is emphasized in performance.

Writing itself, then, has another specific connotation in Barthes's discourse that needs to be taken into account here as well. To fully grasp the meaning of 'writing' in the current essay, it is useful to first return to Barthes's *Writing Degree Zero* ([1953] 1970), where the seeds of an intimate relation between body and language were planted and where we also find the first mention of this 'writing' in his oeuvre. In this work, he tries to capture the various mechanisms of language(s) at work in the creation of literature by means of another conceptual triad. Barthes explains here that the first component of Literature is the 'language' in which the piece is written, the linguistic horizon of possibilities or 'a corpus of prescriptions and habits common to all the writers of a period' (15). Language interacts with the 'style' of a writer, which has nothing to do with the writer's intention, but rather with the characteristic facets of the writer, which 'spring from the body and the past of the writer and gradually become the very reflexes of his art' (16). On the terrain of 'writing', then, Barthes locates the freedom of the individual writer, where artistic choices can be made. In Literature, Barthes explains, an artistic choice ('writing') is always restrained by the language in which one writes and by the writer's corporeality. Literature thus consists of an interplay between the specific language, the writer's corporeality and artistic choice.

Although *Writing Degree Zero* can be considered as a first step in his development of semiology, Barthes would lose sight of the body's materiality in his successive writings. Because of semiology's insistence on the dynamic of the sign, these writings focussed less on the interaction between language and body. *Sur Racine* (1963), for instance, neglects the corporeality of the individual performer (Scheie 1992: 73), and his writings collected in *Mythologies* (1957) primarily stage a body that is incorporated into the logic of the sign. In sharp contrast, his later writings, as theatre and Barthes scholar Timothy Scheie highlights, are characterized by 'a preoccupation with corporeality in representation, and more specifically the voice's "grain," … signalling one of the main breaks with structuralism' (ibid.). In other words, during the second half of his career, Barthes's later reflections resume where *Writing Degree Zero* left off: they continue to explore an interactive view between language and body.

Barthes scholar and translator Annette Lavers aptly explains that in Barthes's work, we often 'find the ambivalence between authenticity and spontaneity and the belief that the world is entirely coded. It is in trying to bridge these terms that Barthes evolved some of his most original theories' (1982: 50). 'The Grain of the Voice' was written precisely in the vein of this ambivalence. Crucially, this writing aloud that the grain produces is essentially a kind of writing in which the effort of the body is audible. As mentioned above when discussing *Writing Degree Zero*, 'writing', in early Barthesian terms, refers to a segment of Literature in which the writer's individual freedom is expressed. In the later Barthes, the Barthes from, amongst others, 'The Grain of the Voice', this understanding of writing slightly changes. As convincingly argued by Scheie, 'writing re-thought by poststructuralism synthesizes its previous definition with the notion of *style*, the mark of the author's corporeality' (1992: 91–2, emphasis in the original). As such, Barthes's notion of writing in 'The Grain of the Voice' harbours the interaction between language and body, so when Barthes writes in his essay that 'for what is produced at the level of the geno-song is finally writing'

(1977: 185), 'writing' refers to the writer's freedom of artistic choice *and* their corporeality. To summarize this brief detour, Barthes's notion of the grain allows us to think of speech as a form of writing aloud, provided that the geno-song of the text is amplified and that the grain emerges in diction. Crucial for our argument here is the fact that this form of writing is essentially a *corporeal* form of writing since it harbours the co-constitutive interaction between body and language that characterizes Barthes's later writings.

Now that I have established that the grain emerges in a type of speech that is essentially a form of bodily writing, it indeed becomes possible to consider the grain as a signalling category to differentiate between speech as such and speech as dance. At this point, I would like to remind the reader of the etymological roots of the notion of choreography (choreo/graphein). The term 'choreography' literally refers to 'the writing of movement' and thus suggests that dance is, not unlike Barthes's grain, a form of bodily writing. In fact, since the grain emerges when the efforts of the body uttering the words becomes audible, it is also possible to think of the grain as a phenomenon that demonstrates how a dance emerges from the movement of the speech muscles: a choreography of the movement of the larynx, the vocal cords and the throat. Placing the notion of choreography in tandem with Barthes's understanding of bodily writing in speech (generated by the grain) helps to see how language itself can function as the materiality of the dance. One could argue that more conventional dance forms – the ones that are more oriented towards *bodily* movement – embody a form of bodily writing that is expressed visually, while the use of speech where a grain emerges portrays a form of bodily writing that is expressed auditorily. Looking at dance from the perspective of choreography, and looking at speech from the perspective of the grain, makes it possible to notice the affinity between voiced language and dance. In fact, both dance through speech producing a grain and dance with human bodies arise out of a form of bodily writing. As such it becomes evident how some of the spoken language in *Body of Work* and *Entangled Phrases* does not simply function as a soundtrack or a trigger for dance. Considered through Barthes's conception of the grain, speech can also operate as dance's very medium. In this way, the grain transforms from a concept that compensates for the insufficient use of adjectives in the description of music into something that allows us to trace the sonorous dimension that lies at the base of words that 'dance'.

On a final note, I wish to briefly draw attention to an important implication for the analysis of choreographed language when we engage

Barthes's terminology to demarcate the difference between speech as such and speech that produces auditory choreographies. Throughout his essay, Barthes repeatedly makes clear that the grain is something that appears in performance. Nevertheless, by insisting that the geno-song facilitates the emergence of the grain, Barthes also reveals that the appearance of the grain is predicated on the material composition of the text as well – the text's sounds, rhythm and musicality. As mentioned, even though the geno-song needs to be emphasized in performance in order to make the grain appear, the geno-song can already be manifested in how the text is composed prior to the performance: the words' musicality is contingent upon the composition of the text as well. To put it differently, the underlying mechanisms that turn words into a dance are situated at both the level of the enunciation *and* the level of the composition of the words. Text's dancerly quality therefore has to be sought on both the page and the stage.

Concluding thoughts

Barthes's main impetus to write 'The Grain of the Voice' was to introduce a qualitative-evaluative framework to critically analyse different performances of opera singers. Nevertheless, the essay offers helpful tools to analyse the performance of dancers using speech as well. The framework of voiced music – which is always an interplay between the music itself and the musicality of the language being sung – allows us to look at speech from the perspective of an intersection between language, voice and sound. Barthes's terminology helps to stipulate how in *Entangled Phrases* the geno-song (the materiality and musicality of the language) is amplified to conceal the pheno-song (the semantic meaning of the words), which results in an emphasized *collective* grain. In Linehan's performance, the grain resurfaces mainly non-linguistically, and if it does emerge through words it is highly dependent on how the technological interventions mediate the attention of the audience. These two performances furthermore illustrate that spoken words can function as a medium for (choreographed) movement. When a grain emerges in the soundscapes, their speech feels as a dance. It constitutes a movement in itself, and it draws attention to itself as a choreographic medium in its own right. Therefore, as a figure of thought that refers to bodily writing in speech, the grain can function as an analytical tool to pinpoint the difference between mere speech and speech that dances. For that reason, Barthes's terminology of the geno-song, pheno-song and grain also provides a model to dissect the choreographic impetus underlying spoken words as they are staged in contemporary choreographic experiments, such as those from Linehan and Söderberg. Finally, since Barthes's grain is predicated on both the composition of the text and the enunciation of the text in performance, this notion also reveals that dancing words are situated at the intersection between text and performance. Phrased differently, when words start to dance, a sharp distinction between the realm of the text and the realm of the performance dissolves.

In his essay, Barthes complains that 'the French are abandoning their language … as a space of pleasure, of thrill, a site where language works *for nothing*' (1977: 187, emphasis in the original). Both *Body of Work* and *Entangled Phrases* disclose this linguistic space of pleasure – it becomes their locus for choreographic experimentation. Read from the crux between sound, dance and language, Barthes's essay can provide a fruitful ground to analyse the contemporary tendency to use spoken words in and as dance. The essay allows us to see how speech does not necessarily function as an auxiliary companion to dance, but rather as its very medium. Because his essay stands with one foot in the realm of linguistics and with the other in the realm of sound studies, and because it is rooted in a discussion about specific artistic performances, it lends itself to various other uses. Consequently, several threads for further interpretation can be drawn from it. I have thus primarily read Barthes's essay as an invitation to undertake this mode of reading, where insights of various disciplines collide and where, most importantly, actual performances can profoundly contribute to its interpretation. This way of approaching theory and practice was helpful to tackle the ambiguities and uncertainties of Barthes's writing; it prevented me from stumbling over or getting stuck in his sometimes metaphorical and slippery arguments. Apart from analysing the formal strategies underlying words as dance, this chapter was also an exploration of the relation between aesthetic theory and artistic practice, an inquiry which is, I believe, truly Barthesian. This inquiry revealed that a dialogue between 'The Grain of the Voice' and performance and dance studies can guide us towards artistic and theoretical places that stretch far beyond the initial impetus of the essay.

References

Barthes, Roland ([1953] 1970), *Writing Degree Zero*, trans. Annette Lavers and Colin Smith, London: Jonathan Cope.
Barthes, Roland ([1973] 1975), *The Pleasure of the Text*, trans. Richard Miller, New York: Hill and Wang.

Barthes, Roland (1977), 'The Grain of The Voice', in *Image Music Text*, ed. and trans. Stephen Heath, 179–89. London: Fontana Press.
Brooks, Daphne A. (2010), '"This Voice Which Is not One": Amy Winehouse sings the ballad of sonic blue(s)face culture', *Women & Performance: A Journal of Feminist Theory*, 20(1): 37–60.
Brown, Andrew (1992), *Roland Barthes. The Figures of Writing*, New York: Oxford University Press.
Cavarero, Adriana (2005), *For More Than One Voice: Toward a Philosophy of Vocal Expression*, Stanford: Stanford University Press.
Collins, Rebecca (2018), 'Aural Spatiality and Sonic Materiality: Attending to the Space of Sound in Performances by Ivo Dimchev and Alma Söderberg', *Contemporary Theatre Review*, 28(2): 165–78.
Curtin, Adrian (2014), *Avant-Garde Theatre Sound: Staging Sonic Modernity*, New York: Palgrave Macmillan.
Gardner, Sally (2010), 'Translating Laurence Louppe', *Forum for Modern Language Studies*, 46(4): 356–71.
Home-Cook, George (2015), *Theatre and Aural Attention*, London: Palgrave Macmillan.
Kendrick, Lynne (2017), *Theatre Aurality*, London: Palgrave Macmillan.
Laermans, Rudi (2008), '"Dance in General" or Choreographing the Public, Making Assemblages', *Performance Research*, 13(1): 7–14.
Lavers, Annette (1982), *Roland Barthes: Structuralism and After*, London: Methuen.
McGrath, Alice, Marcus Tan, Prarthana Purkayastha, and Tereza Havelková (2021), 'Editorial: Sounding Corporeality', *Theatre Research International*, 46(2): 108–14.
Moriarty, Michael (1991), *Roland Barthes*, Cambridge: Polity Press.
Noeth, Sandra (2011), 'Protocols of Encounter: On Dance Dramatrugy', in Gabriele Klein and Sandra Noeth (eds), *Emerging Bodies: The Performance of Worldmaking in Dance and Choreography*, 247–56, Bielefeld: transcript Verlag.
Ovadija, Mladen (2013), *Dramaturgy of Sound in the Avant-Garde and Postdramatic Theatre*, Montreal: McGill-Queen's University Press.
Persyn, Leonie (2019), 'On Auditory Choreography: How Walking Anticipates Sound and Movement Resonates', *Choreographic Practices*, 10(2): 197–212.
Protopapa, Efrosini (2013), 'Choreography as Philosophy, or Exercising though in Performance', in Jenny Bunker, Anna Pakes, and Bonnie Rowell (eds), *Thinking Through Dance: The Philosophy of Dance Performances and Practices*, 273–90, Hampshire: Dance Book.
Scheie, Timothy (1992), *Body Trouble: Roland Barthes, Theater, and the Corporeal Sign*, Ann Arbor: University Microfilms International.
Spångberg, Marten (2017), 'Post-dance, An Advocacy', in Danjel Andersson, Mette Edvardsen, and Marten Spångberg (eds), *Post-Dance*, 349–93, Stockholm: MDT.

INDEX

action 102–3, 166, 174, 180, 216–17, 219
Alphant, Marianne 1, 25
amateur
 dramaturgy 122–8
 pleasure of adventure 132
 society of 127–8
Aristotle 165, 167, 168
Arratia, Euridice 17
arrogance 103–4
 of theory 119
Artaud, Antonin 208, 219
Aston, Elaine
 Theatre as Sign-System 13, 21
Attridge, Derek 19
Auslander, Philip 4 n.3, 12, 12 n.10
Avedon, Richard 195

Bailes, Sarah Jane 26
Balázs, Béla 191–92
Barthes, Roland
 Camera Lucida: Reflections on Photography 5 n.4, 19, 21, 22, 52, 57, 172, 174, 186, 210
 'The Death of the Author' 14–19, 18 n.18
 Empire of Signs 17, 186, 196, 207–10, 210n.5, 213, 216, 220
 The Fashion System 1
 'The Grain of the Voice' 189, 225–32, 238, 240
 How to Live Together 6
 Image-Music-Text 12 n.11, 13 n.12, 162, 208 n.4
 Incidents 3 n.2
 A Lover's Discourse 137–9, 142, 147
 Mythologies 3, 11–14, 185, 207, 238
 The Neutral 5–8, 10, 25, 27 n.22, 99, 100–2, 105, 119, 120, 139, 147, 149–50, 153–4, 159, 160–1, 216
 The Pleasure of the Text 20, 21
 The Preparation of the Novel 6, 36

 The Responsibility of Forms 162
 Roland Barthes by Roland Barthes 6, 168, 195, 196
 The Rustle of Language 162
 Sur Racine 238
 SZ 214 n.8
 'The Third Meaning' 20, 164
 'The Wisdom of Art' 157–8, 161, 165–7
 Writing Degree Zero 25–8, 230, 237–8
Bataille, Georges 138, 144–5
Battersea Arts Centre 56 n.3
Bausch, Pina 21, 24
Beckett, Samuel 21, 22, 49 n.3
Bel, Jérôme 18, 19, 27
 Jérôme Bel 25–6
 The Last Performance 2 n.1
 Nom donne par l'auteur 25, 26
 Shirtology/Shirtologie 1, 2 n.1, 26
beside-the-point answers 104–5
Blau, Herbert 22
Bleeker, Maaike 23–4
body
 art and 128
 dancing 229
 dramaturgies of 200–3
 emotional 158, 159, 163
 evacuation of 4 n.3
 formal 14
 language and 226–8
 and mask 185–203 (*see also* face)
 visceral 24, 219
Bogart, Anne 47, 49
Bottoms, Stephen 23
Boulaabi, Ridha 215 n.11
Bradshaw, Laura 103, 104
Brecht, Bertolt 13, 208, 220
 Berliner Ensemble 4, 35
 Mother Courage 12, 35
Breuer, Lee 16
Bunraku 120, 208, 216–20
Burroughs, William S. 16, 49 n.3

Cade, Rosana 103
The Making of Pinnochio 106, 107
Cage, John 49 n.3, 101, 150, 166
Camus, Albert 214 n.9
  Outsider 25
capture/capturing 9, 171, 175–7, 181, 183
  choreography 172
  movement 177
  photography 53 n.1, 172
  problems of 177
Casarès, Maria 188–91, 195, 200, 201
Cavarero, Adriana 233
choreography 39, 171–83, 239
  auditory 228
  capturing 171, 175–7, 183
  neutral forms of 27 n.22
  problematization of 172
  repetition and 175–8
  time 178–82
Christopher, Karen 26–7
Cixous, Hélène 16, 20 n.20
Clément, Catherine 139
Clerc, Thomas 153–4
Cocteau, Jean 214 n.9, 218
collective grain 236, 240
Collège de France 2, 3, 5, 7, 25, 36, 120, 121, 127, 159, 162, 208 n.2, 220
Comment, Bernard 208 n.2
corporeality
  bodily co-presence and 192
  disturbing 14
  face/mask and 187–90
  grainy 20
  of individual performer 238
  language 189
  theatre 191
  of writers/authors 238
Corrieri, Augusto 26
culinary theatre 214 n.10
Cull Ó Maoilearca, Laura 5
Cunningham, Merce 18, 49, 49 n.3

dance
  bodily movement and 229
  contemporary 10, 11, 228, 229
  modern 19
  photology and 182
  postmodern 4, 18, 49
  speech and 236–240

Dartington College of Arts 123–6
Davey, Moyra 129–34
de Balzac, Honore 15, 214n.8
de Certeau, Michel 59
Deleuze, Gilles 18, 40
Derrida, Jacques 5, 8, 15 n.16, 119, 121
de Saussure, Ferdinand 12, 59
desire
  bodily 24
  discourse of 138
  for neutral dramaturgies 8, 99, 100
  for neutral forms 25, 26
  to outplay meaning 27
  perpetual 128
  politicized 7
  without mediation 57 n.4
drama 166, 168
  based on conflict 8 n.8
  classical forms of 123
  dramaturgy and 163, 165
  re-examination of the rules of 21
  Western 102, 216, 219, 220
dramaturgy 35–44, 99–107, 157–69
  amateur 122–8
  of face 200–3
  neutral 25–8
Duggan, Patrick 24
Duncan, Isadora 171

Eckhart, Master 150
Eisenstein, Sergei 12 n.11, 20
Elam, Keir 13, 22
ergography 165, 169
Etchells, Tim 2 n.1, 18 n.18, 105
Ezugha, Vivian Chinasa 107

face
  -as-body 198–200
  -as-mask 194–8
  Casarès, Maria 188–91
  concepts of 191
  corporeality and 189
  dramaturgies of 200–3
  engagement 194
  face/film and body/theatre 191–4
ffrench, Patrick 6, 186 n.3, 189
Fischer-Dieskau, Dietrich 230, 234 n.5
Forced Entertainment 123

Foreman, Richard 16
Foster, Hal 23
Foster, Susan Leigh
    Reading Dancing 18
Foucault, Michel 16, 18, 164
Fuchs, Elinor
    The Death of Character 15–16

Gandhi, Leela 43
Garbo, Greta 185, 198, 199
geno-song 20, 231, 235, 237, 240
Glissant, Édouard 38
Goat Island 23, 23 n.21, 24, 26, 27
Goulish, Matthew 2 n.1, 23 n.21, 27
Graham, Martha 18, 171
grain 19–25
Green, Nic
    Cock and Bull 103, 104
Gregg, Melissa 6
Grosz, Elisabeth 137
Guin, Ursula Le 161

Hann, Rachel 106
Hermanis, Alvis 161 n.2
Higgins, Lynn A. 212
Hixson, Lin 23 n.21, 26
Howard, Richard 49 n.3, 162
Howells, Adrian 55

Irigaray, Luce 16, 20 n.20
Iriguchi, Mamoru
    At the Ends of the Day 103

Japan 196, 210–12, 210 n.5, 212
    concept of *ma* 130
    culture 214, 216
    face 202–3
    haiku 217
    Ikebana 134
    puppet theatre 11, 120, 208
    satori 209
Japonisme 207, 207 n.1
jouissance 11, 14, 19–25, 234 n.5
Jung, Hwal Yol 207, 216

Kairos 105–6
Kandiyoti, Dalia 212 n.6
Kaprow, Allan 166, 166 n.6
Kartsaki, Eirini 21

Kermode, Frank
    The Sense of an Ending 61
kinaesthetic sensing 173
Kitson, Daniel 56
Kristeva, Julia 15 n.16, 18, 20 n.20,
    162–3, 230

Lacan, Jacques 15 n.16, 20 n.20
Laermans, Rudi 228–9
Lagaay, Alice 27, 208n.2
Landau, Tina 49
language
    biological ambience of 128
    body and 226, 234, 237, 238, 239
    choreographed 239
    cultural 118
    in dance performances 226
    emptiness of 210
    fascism of 7
    function of 233
    materiality and 20, 231
    musicality of 240
    nonsensical 104–5
    sound and 230
    spoken 227
    staged 159
    technology and 229
    vacillation of 214
    voice/voiced and 226, 229, 236, 239
    written 4
Las Meninas 164, 164 n.5
Lavers, Annette 238
LeCompte, Elizabeth 17
Léger, Nathalie 35–44
    Exposition 36
Lehmann, Hans-Thies 24, 124,
    192–3
    Postdramatic Theatre 4
Leitch, Vincent 216
Lepecki, Andre 26, 171–2, 175,
    177, 181–2
Levinas, Emmanuel 193
lexical ambiguity 167
Linehan, Daniel 241
    Body of Work 225–9, 232–40
    career of 227
    dbddbb 234
    Making It 234
Logie, John 49 n.3

Lübecker, Nikolaj
  Early Barthes, Late Barthes 147, 153
Lyotard, Jean-François
  'The Tooth, the Palm' 24

Mackaskill, Ivor
  The Making of Pinnochio 106, 107
Manghani, Sunil 2, 5, 5 n.5
  Barthes/Bataille: The Writing of Neutral Economy' 138
Marranca, Bonnie 16
materiality 239
  of language 229, 231
  of live bodies 4, 26, 235
  musicality and 232–3, 235, 240
  of performance's thinking 5
  punctum 22
  sensuality of signifiers 13
  signification and 14, 188
  singer's voice 20
Mauss, Marcel 145
  The Gift 144
meaning
  affective 2, 11, 14, 19, 22–4, 175–8, 181–83, 191, 203, 219
  baffling 11, 157–69
  decoding of 11–19, 216 n.11
  disruption of 201
  empty of 104
  excess of 13, 19
  meaning-making 2, 27 n.22, 49, 100
  obtuse 157–69
  open 49, 130
  production of 7, 8, 59, 138
  semantic 196, 198, 233, 240
  suspension of 105
  third 20, 122, 132, 163–4, 167, 196
  thwart 7, 8, 101, 103–4, 122
  violence of 7, 22, 122, 153
memory 51–63, 66
  bodily 227
  collective 128
  cultural 107
  food and 66
  performance 58
  physical body and 173
  punctum 55 n.2
  remembrance and 58
  verbal 236

Michelet, Jules 118
Miller, Arthur
  The Crucible 16–17
Müller, Anja 227–7, 232–3
myth 11–14, 191 n.8
  of interiority 198

neuter 106–7
neutral/neutrality 6, 26–8, 166–7
  dramaturgy 25–8, 99–107
  neutral doer 25
  performance 27, 102
Nietzsche, Friedrich 53
Noeth, Sandra 228–9

obtuse 19–20, 157–69
Occident 211
  spectator 218
Olson, Carl 145
operator 173
Orient 211
Orientalism 212 n.6
Ostermeier, Thomas 194

Panzéra, Charles 230, 232–3
Pasolini, Pier Paolo
  Teorema 142–4
Pavis, Patrice 13, 22, 208
performativity 150, 231
performative models of analysis 192
  performative punctum 24
  performative writing 36, 139, 208
Persyn, Leonie 228
Phelan, Peggy 4 n.3, 192–3
pheno-song 20, 231, 232–3, 235, 236, 240
photography 53
  cinema and 12, 55 n.2
  lived experience and 210
  madness 57 n.4
  painting and 201
  as primitive theatre of dead 197
  punctum 207, 171–83, 210
pleasure 234 n.5
  of amateur's adventure 132
  jouissance 20, 21, 234 n.5
  linguistic space of 241
  radical 20, 20 n.20, 24
  of reading texts 7, 119
  of writerly reading 132

Porter, Dennis 213
post-dance 2, 18
post-dramatic 24, 105, 159, 165, 193
postmodern style 19 n.19
Proust, Marcel 35, 36, 121, 122
punctum 11, 13–14, 19–25, 55 n.2, 171–83, 210
performative 24

queasiness 107

Rabkin, Gerald 15, 16–17
Rainer, Yvonne 21
'No Manifesto' 26, 102
R/B (exhibit) 1–2, 35–6
recipes 65, 67–75
Renoir, Jean
The Rules of the Game 41–2
rhythm 122 n.1
Ridout, Nicholas 193
Roman Bacchanalia 219
Rudner, Sara 178, 179

Sainte-Hilaire-du-Touvet 117–8
Sartre, Jean-Paul 12–13, 162, 214 n.9
satori 209, 210
Savona, George
Theatre as Sign-System 13, 21
Savran, David 17
Schefer, Jean Louis 158, 163 n.4
Scheie, Timothy 5, 13 n.14, 15 n.16, 238
on evacuation of the body 4 n.3
Performance Degree Zero 4
Schneider, Rebecca 23, 107
Schwindt, Grace
Tenant 103
Seguette, Frédéric 26
Seigworth, Gregory 6
semioclasm 163
semiotropy 163
Senkō, Ikenobō
Rikka-no-Shidai Kyūjūsanpeiari (Ikenobō Senkō Rikka-zu) 133
Shakespeare, William 159, 161 n.2
Siegmund, Gerald 14, 26
silent expenditure 145
situation of writing 208, 210
Söderberg, Alma 226, 227, 241
Entangled Phrases 225, 227–9, 232–40

Sontag, Susan 131
Spectator 173, 226
active 27, 49, 210, 214
destabilising interpretation 23
face and 197, 198, 200, 201, 202
of Japan 209, 211
perceptions 13, 22
production of meaning 7, 17, 49
sensations 107
Western 217, 218
speech
as dance 236–40
as writing 239
studium 21–3, 172, 174–7, 210

Taoism 102, 147, 154, 159–60, 164, 165
tempura 215
text(s)
open 15, 19
pleasure of the 20, 21, 132
readerly and writerly 9, 15, 18, 21, 65, 214
textuality 11, 14–19
from work to 14, 18
Théâtre National Populaire 4
theatricality 26, 115, 208
as density of signs 14, 19
of drag performers 13 n.14
of live bodies 13
textuality and 7
time/temporality 41, 107, 129, 130, 166, 178–82
Tomlin, Liz 105
trauma 23–4
travel writing 213
Twombly, Cy 157–69
Tynan, Kenneth 21
Tzu, Lao
Tao Te Ching 159–60

Ubersfeld, Anne 163
unintelligibility 115

Van Kerkhoven, Marianne 125, 130
Vilar, Jean 4
voice/voiced
agency and 154
collective 233

grain of the 20, 189, 230–32
human 219, 229
jouissance and 234
language 225, 226, 229, 236
physicality 227

Wahl, François 3 n.2, 5 n.5, 162, 164
Warhol, Andy 23
Webern, Anton 159
Williams, David 124–5, 134
Wilson, Robert 4, 16, 19, 123
Wou-wei 102–3, 147, 154
wrestling 12, 85–97, 115
  mental 86
  performance 9, 10
  physical 86, 189

writing 131, 168–9, 238–9
  active 132
  bodily 239, 240
  childish 163
  collective 49
  new 159
  performative/performance 5, 12 n.10, 18 n.18, 105, 208
  scenic 208 n.3
  situation of writing 210
  speech as 237, 239
  travel 213
  of the visible 162
  zero degree of 18, 25

Zen 209–10

www.ingramcontent.com/pod-product-compliance
Lightning Source LLC
Chambersburg PA
CBHW070723020526
44116CB00031B/1352